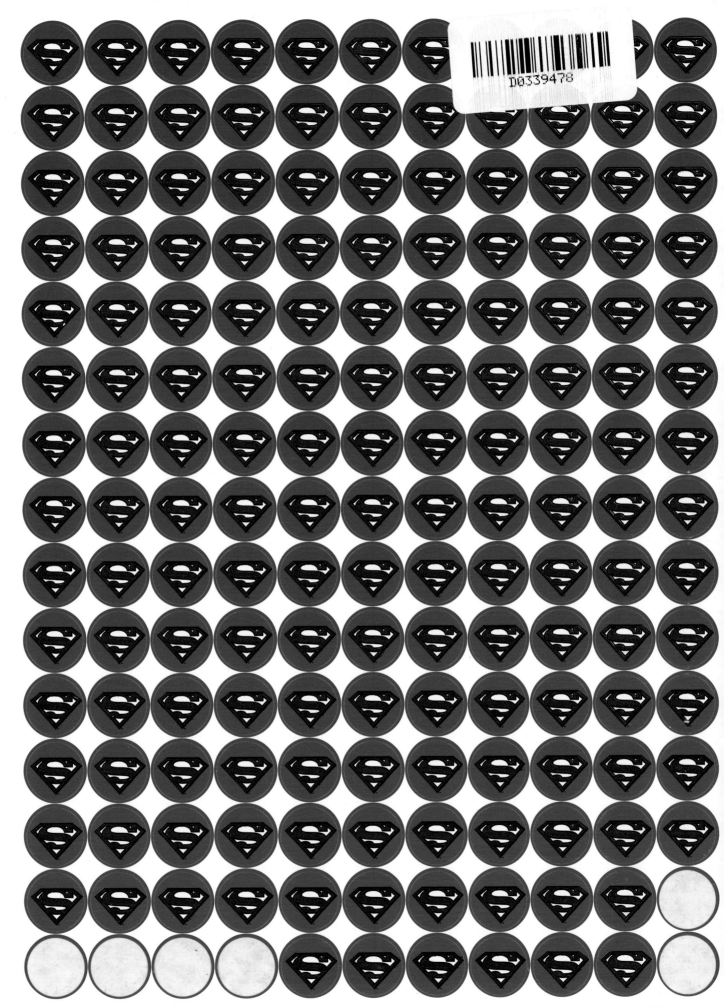

Progress Chart

This chart lists all the topics in the book. Once you have completed each page, stick a sticker in the correct box below.

Page	Topic	Sticker	Page	Topic	Sticker	Page	Topic	Sticker
2	Number		13	Ordering decimals		24	Word problems	
3	Place value		14	Adding		25	Word problems	
4	Multiplying by 10		15	Adding		26	Problems with measures	
5	Ordering		16	Subtracting		27	Telling time	
6	Rounding		17	Subtracting		28	Telling time	
7	Polygons		18	Choosing the operation		29	Tables and graphs	
8	Identifying patterns		19	Multiplying		30	Necessary information	
9	Odds and evens		20	Multiplying		31	Number pairs	
10	Addition fact families		21	Dividing		32	2 times table	
11	Fractions		22	Dividing		33	Multiplying by 2	
12	Fractions of shapes		23	Choosing the operation		34	Dividing by 2	

Well done! With the help of Superman, his friends, and his enemies, you can now count yourself a math expert!

Math
Made Easy

Level 3 Workbook

Metric Edition

Superman created by Jerry Siegel and Joe Shuster

Numbers

Write the number in words.

3,687 | Three thousand, six hundred eighty-seven

Write the number in standard form.

Four thousand, one hundred thirty-two. | 4,132

Write each number in words.

7,285   SIVIN THAWSIND TWO HUDERID ATIFFIVE

3,926

8,143

4,538

Write the numbers in standard form.

Four thousand, one hundred fifty-six.   4156

Five thousand, two hundred seventy-three.   5573

Six thousand, seven hundred ninety-three.   6793

Three thousand, nine hundred thirteen.   3913

Eight thousand, five hundred twenty-one.   8521

Eight thousand, seven hundred twenty-four.   8754

Write each number in words.

2,308

6,039

5,008

8,309

Write the numbers in standard form.

Eight thousand thirty-one.   8031

Four thousand, two hundred six.   4506

One thousand two.   1002

Place value

13,754 is the same as:
1 ten thousand, 3 thousands, 7 hundreds, 5 tens, 4 ones
or
13,754 is the same as 10,000 + 3,000 + 500 + 50 + 4

Write the correct number in the space.

3,462 = 3,000 + 400 + 60 +   *2*   1,392 = 1,000 +   *300*   + 90 + 2

6,839 = 6,000 + 800 + *30* + 9   5,799 = 5,000 + 700 + *40*   + 9

2,514 = 2,000 + *500* + 10 + 4   8,294 = 8,000 + *200*   + 90 + 4

7,476 = 7,000 + *400* + 70 + 6   2,176 = 2,000 + *100*   + 70 + 6

4,663 = *4000* + 600 + 60 + 4   7,264 = *7000*   + 200 + 60 + 4

Write the number that is the same as:

Eight thousand, one hundred eighty-eight   *8188*

Twelve thousand, three hundred sixty-one   *12361*

Fifteen thousand, nine hundred seventy-three   *15973*

Two thousand sixteen   *2450*

Eleven thousand, four hundred twenty   *11420*

Nine thousand forty-three   *9043*

Twenty-one thousand three   *21003*

Thirty thousand eight hundred   *30800*

Thirteen thousand thirty-eight   *13038*

YOU HAVE TO DO THESE ... FAST!

Look at these numbers: 6 8 3 0 7

Arrange these digits to make the largest number you can.   *87230*

Arrange these digits to make the smallest number you can.   *30678*

Multiplying by 10

Multiply each of these numbers by 10.

2 | 20 | 17 | 170 | 4 | 40 | 11 | 110

Multiply each of these numbers by 10.

5	50	12	120	9	90	17	170	23	230
3	30	28	280	11	110	19	190	2	20
4	40	1	10	27	270	21	210	14	140
8	80	13	130	24	240	7	70	25	250

Multiply each of these numbers by 10.

10	100	20	200	15	150	6	60	8	80
23	230	16	160	22	220	18	180	2	20
21	210	29	290	7	70	4	40	12	120
26	2020	3	30	13	130	5	50	17	170

Multiply each of these numbers by 10.

59	590	42	420	63	630	37	370	87	870
66	860	35	350	75	750	59	590	40	400
98	980	67	670	54	540	72	750	43	430

Multiply each of these numbers by 10.

32	320	63	630	48	480	56	560	74	740
38	380	69	690	82	820	63	630	95	950
47	47	57	570	99	990	40	400	77	770

Ordering

Write these numbers in order, from smallest to largest.

4,285	3,910	8,190	2,512
2,512	3,910	4,285	8,190

Write these numbers in order, from smallest to largest.

1,452	4,839	8,774	2,349
7,374	2,831	5,928	8,421
9,388	3,286	8,774	1,438
3,364	9,264	6,921	5,674
6,853	4,567	5,684	2,557
3,241	3,785	9,358	7,647

1452	2349	4839	8774
3241			

Write these numbers in order, from smallest to largest.

5,507	9,370	4,903	7,239
4,076	8,209	1,360	5,035
2,987	7,380	5,005	2,345
8,459	3,401	6,223	1,023
9,205	2,065	7,004	3,800

Write these numbers in order, from smallest to largest.

5,780	365	968	1,089
7,650	3,271	641	889
9,842	1,295	712	1,102
8,004	4,800	840	3,980
5,078	3,001	679	375

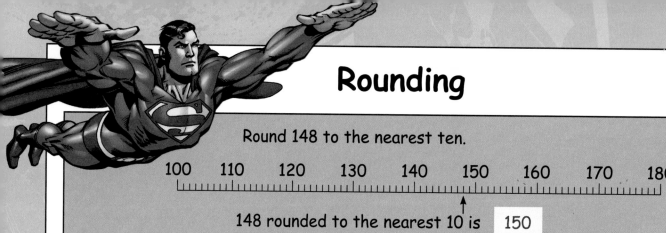

Rounding

Round 148 to the nearest ten.

100   110   120   130   140   150   160   170   180

148 rounded to the nearest 10 is   150

Round each number to the nearest ten.

378   380   231   230   483   480   854   850

767   770   623   620   389   390   235   240

Round each number to the nearest ten.

120   130   140   150   160   170   180   190   200   150

330   340   350   360   370   380   390   400   410   380

480   490   500   510   520   530   540   550   560   500

200   210   220   230   240   250   260   270   280   240

40   50   60   70   80   90   100   110   120   100

750   760   770   780   790   800   810   820   830   780

540   550   560   570   580   590   600   610   620   810

120   130   140   150   160   170   180   190   200   140

10   20   30   40   50   60   70   000   000   50

870   880   890   900   910   920   930   940   950   900

6

Polygons

Match the polygon with a solid figure.

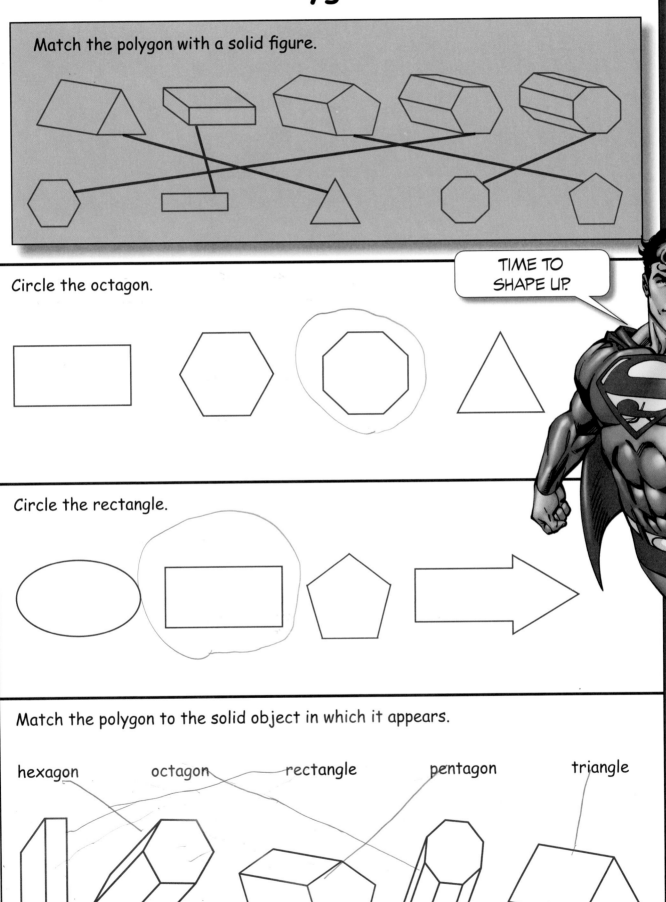

Circle the octagon.

Circle the rectangle.

TIME TO SHAPE UP.

Match the polygon to the solid object in which it appears.

hexagon   octagon   rectangle   pentagon   triangle

Identifying patterns

KEEP UP THE SEARCH.

Continue each pattern.

0	4	8	12	16	20
0	11	22	33	44	55
70	63	56	49	42	35

Continue each pattern.

2	7	12	17	22	27	32	37
3	10	17	24	31	38	45	52
1	11	21	31	41	51	61	61
5	7	9	11	13	15	17	19
6	9	12	15	18	21	24	27
7	12	17	22	27	32	37	42

Continue each pattern.

59	53	47	41	35	29	23	17
92	84	76	68	60	52	44	38
76	69	62	55	45	35	28	21
42	36	30	24	18	12	6	0
37	33	29	25	21	17	14	10

Continue each pattern.

46	53	65	80	93	112	151	95
93	87	81	75	89	83	57	51
0	7	14	21	28	34	45	49
5	15	22	35	45	55	65	75
4	12	20	28	36	44	55	80

Odds and evens

Multiply the odd number by the odd number. $3 \times 5 =$ 15

Multiply the even number by the even number. $8 \times 4 =$ 32

I'M VERY ODD!

Multiply the odd number by the odd number.

$3 \times 7 =$	$9 \times 9 =$	$7 \times 1 =$	$1 \times 1 =$
$7 \times 5 =$	$7 \times 9 =$	$1 \times 5 =$	$3 \times 1 =$
$5 \times 5 =$	$3 \times 5 =$	$7 \times 7 =$	$9 \times 7 =$
$1 \times 9 =$	$5 \times 9 =$	$9 \times 3 =$	$3 \times 3 =$

What do you notice about the numbers in your answer boxes?

_____

Multiply the even number by the even number.

$2 \times 4 =$	$4 \times 10 =$	$8 \times 6 =$	$10 \times 10 =$
$8 \times 10 =$	$6 \times 2 =$	$10 \times 2 =$	$6 \times 6 =$
$8 \times 2 =$	$8 \times 8 =$	$6 \times 4 =$	$12 \times 12 =$
$10 \times 6 =$	$4 \times 4 =$	$2 \times 2 =$	$4 \times 8 =$

What do you notice about the numbers in your answer boxes?

_____

Multiply the odd number by the even number.

$3 \times 6 =$	$7 \times 6 =$	$3 \times 8 =$	$3 \times 2 =$
$7 \times 4 =$	$3 \times 10 =$	$9 \times 4 =$	$8 \times 7 =$
$9 \times 6 =$	$8 \times 5 =$	$10 \times 9 =$	$4 \times 1 =$
$5 \times 8 =$	$4 \times 3 =$	$2 \times 7 =$	$12 \times 3 =$

What do you notice about the numbers in your answer boxes?

_____

Addition fact families

Circle the number sentence that is in the same fact family as the first pair.

14 - 9 = 5
5 + 9 = 14

14 + 2 = 16   (14 - 5 = 9)   9 - 7 = 00

12 - 4 = 8
4 + 8 = 12

8 - 4 = 4   (8 + 4 = 12)   12 - 9 = 3

Circle the number sentence that is in the same fact family as the first pair.

7 + 6 = 13
6 + 7 = 13

7 + 3 = 10   13 - 6 = 7   7 - 6 = 1

17 - 6 = 11
11 + 6 = 17

11 - 6 = 5   17 + 11 = 28   17 - 11 = 6

18 - 9 = 9
18 - 9 = 9

9 - 9 = 0   18 + 3 = 21   9 + 9 = 18

3 + 4 = 7
7 - 3 = 4

7 - 4 = 3   7 + 6 = 13   7 + 4 = 11

19 - 9 = 10
19 - 10 = 9

9 + 19 = 28   10 + 9 = 19   10 - 9 = 1

9 + 8 = 17
17 - 8 = 9

8 + 9 = 17   8 + 17 = 25   25 - 9 = 16

Write the fact family for each group of numbers.

3, 15, 18   6, 10, 4   4, 13, 9

LET'S GET THE
FACTS STRAIGHT.

Fractions

Write the fraction for the part that is shaded.

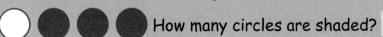 How many circles are shaded? **3**

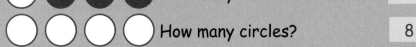 How many circles? **8**

So, the fraction of circles shaded = $\dfrac{3}{8}$ $\dfrac{\text{numerator}}{\text{denominator}}$

Circle the fraction that shows the part that is shaded.

$\dfrac{2}{3}$ $\dfrac{3}{5}$ $\dfrac{2}{5}$ $\dfrac{3}{7}$ $\dfrac{4}{9}$ $\dfrac{3}{4}$

Write the fraction for the part that is shaded.

___   ___   ___

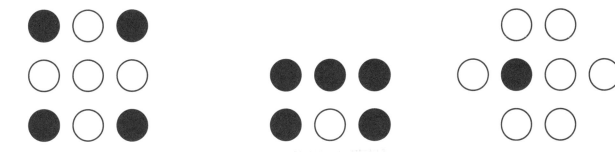

___   ___   ___

___   ___   ___

SANDER

Fractions of shapes

Shade $\frac{3}{5}$ of each shape.

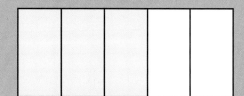
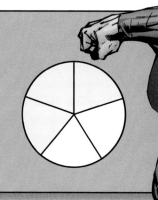

Shade $\frac{4}{5}$ of each shape.

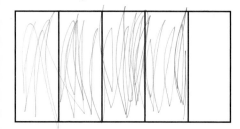
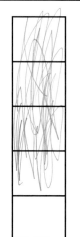

FLY THROUGH THESE!

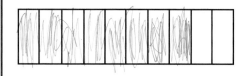
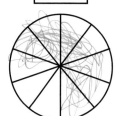

Shade the fraction shown of each shape.

$\frac{3}{10}$

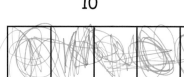

$\frac{8}{10}$

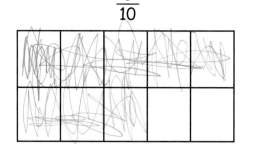

$\frac{3}{10}$

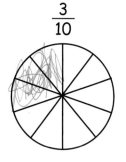

$\frac{7}{10}$

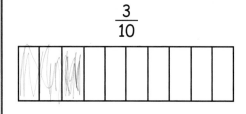

$\frac{6}{10}$

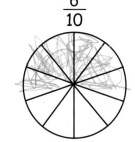

$\frac{9}{10}$

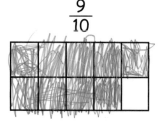

SANDER

Ordering decimals

Put these decimals in order from smallest to largest.

0.3   0.1   0.9   0.6   0.5 | 0.1 | 0.3 | 0.5 | 0.6 | 0.9 |

Put these decimals in order from smallest to largest.

0.3   0.5   0.7   0.8   0.4   0.3 0.4 0.5 0.7 0.8

0.6   0.1   0.7   0.3   0.4   0.1 0.3 0.4 0.6 0.7

0.9   0.7   0.8   0.2   0.6   0.2 0.6 0.7 0.8 0.9

0.1   0.3   0.2   0.8   0.7   0.1 0.2 0.3 0.7 0.8

0.8   0.2   0.4   0.6   0.5   0.2 0.4 0.5 0.6 0.8

Put these decimals in order from smallest to largest.

1.8   1.4   1.2   1.1   1.9

1.0   1.6   1.3   1.8   1.1

1.5   1.7   1.4   1.3   1.6

1.0   1.7   1.5   1.9   1.2

1.8   1.9   1.6   1.4   1.2

Put these decimals in order from smallest to largest.

2.8   2.3   2.0   2.5   2.6

3.2   3.8   3.0   3.1   3.7

5.2   7.8   2.6   3.4   1.9

0.9   6.8   9.9   1.8   4.3

5.1   8.1   6.2   3.1   3.6

13

Adding

Write the answer between the lines.

$$\begin{array}{r} 1 \\ 27 \\ + 53 \\ \hline 80 \end{array} \qquad \begin{array}{r} 30 \\ + 17 \\ \hline 47 \end{array} \qquad \begin{array}{r} 74 \\ + 23 \\ \hline 97 \end{array}$$

I CHALLENGE YOU TO DO THESE.

Write the answer between the lines.

$$\begin{array}{r} 24 \\ + 3 \\ \hline \end{array} \qquad \begin{array}{r} 41 \\ + 23 \\ \hline \end{array} \qquad \begin{array}{r} 12 \\ + 11 \\ \hline \end{array} \qquad \begin{array}{r} 74 \\ + 21 \\ \hline \end{array}$$

$$\begin{array}{r} 30 \\ + 28 \\ \hline \end{array} \qquad \begin{array}{r} 26 \\ + 13 \\ \hline \end{array} \qquad \begin{array}{r} 53 \\ + 34 \\ \hline \end{array} \qquad \begin{array}{r} 82 \\ + 17 \\ \hline \end{array}$$

$$\begin{array}{r} 65 \\ + 21 \\ \hline \end{array} \qquad \begin{array}{r} 13 \\ + 4 \\ \hline \end{array} \qquad \begin{array}{r} 72 \\ + 10 \\ \hline \end{array} \qquad \begin{array}{r} 67 \\ + 21 \\ \hline \end{array}$$

$$\begin{array}{r} 83 \\ + 6 \\ \hline \end{array} \qquad \begin{array}{r} 54 \\ + 33 \\ \hline \end{array} \qquad \begin{array}{r} 46 \\ + 21 \\ \hline \end{array} \qquad \begin{array}{r} 60 \\ + 36 \\ \hline \end{array}$$

$$\begin{array}{r} 24 \\ + 14 \\ \hline \end{array} \qquad \begin{array}{r} 36 \\ + 13 \\ \hline \end{array} \qquad \begin{array}{r} 61 \\ + 17 \\ \hline \end{array} \qquad \begin{array}{r} 36 \\ + 23 \\ \hline \end{array}$$

$$\begin{array}{r} 38 \\ + 21 \\ \hline \end{array} \qquad \begin{array}{r} 74 \\ + 25 \\ \hline \end{array} \qquad \begin{array}{r} 53 \\ + 39 \\ \hline \end{array} \qquad \begin{array}{r} 28 \\ + 31 \\ \hline \end{array}$$

$$\begin{array}{r} 68 \\ + 20 \\ \hline \end{array} \qquad \begin{array}{r} 57 \\ + 31 \\ \hline \end{array} \qquad \begin{array}{r} 46 \\ + 22 \\ \hline \end{array} \qquad \begin{array}{r} 35 \\ + 13 \\ \hline \end{array}$$

$$\begin{array}{r} 45 \\ + 32 \\ \hline \end{array} \qquad \begin{array}{r} 62 \\ + 22 \\ \hline \end{array} \qquad \begin{array}{r} 47 \\ + 11 \\ \hline \end{array} \qquad \begin{array}{r} 50 \\ + 37 \\ \hline \end{array}$$

Adding

Write the answer between the lines.

12	35	15
+ 40	+ 10	+ 4
52	45	19

Write the answer between the lines.

| 25 | 80 | 55 | 20 |
| + 10 | + 5 | + 35 | + 75 |

| 25 | 35 | 30 | 5 |
| + 40 | + 10 | + 20 | + 20 |

| 45 | 30 | 5 | 55 |
| + 45 | + 45 | + 15 | + 45 |

| 15 | 5 | 35 | 15 |
| + 30 | + 45 | + 30 | + 20 |

| 45 | 5 | 55 | 65 |
| + 25 | + 55 | + 15 | + 35 |

| 45 | 35 | 15 | 75 |
| +15 | + 45 | + 25 | + 10 |

| 80 | 45 | 50 | 5 |
| + 15 | + 45 | + 35 | + 95 |

| 75 | 15 | 75 | 25 |
| + 5 | + 20 | + 10 | + 35 |

Subtracting

I NEED THE ANSWERS... NOW!

Write the difference between the lines.
Start with the ones, then the tens.

```
  26          77          85
- 14        - 26        - 23
  12          51          62
```

Write the difference between the lines.

```
  13          48          29          84
- 11        - 32        - 17        - 20
_____       _____       _____       _____


  48          31          98          56
- 25        - 10        - 15        - 32
_____       _____       _____       _____


  46          76          65          33
- 12        - 46        - 54        - 23
_____       _____       _____       _____


  86          57          63          99
- 35        - 13        - 33        - 18
_____       _____       _____       _____


  75          76          45          79
- 12        - 43        - 21        - 38
_____       _____       _____       _____


  78          65          57          44
- 35        - 32        - 24        - 32
_____       _____       _____       _____


  54          47          73          56
- 32        - 25        - 40        - 35
_____       _____       _____       _____


  53          67          55          43
- 12        - 33        - 12        - 30
_____       _____       _____       _____
```

Subtracting

Write the difference between the lines.
Regroup if you need to.

$$
\begin{array}{r}
\overset{3\ 13}{4\cancel{3}} \\
-\ 18 \\
\hline
25
\end{array}
\qquad
\begin{array}{r}
\overset{2\ 12}{3\cancel{2}} \\
-\ 27 \\
\hline
5
\end{array}
\qquad
\begin{array}{r}
\overset{7\ 17}{8\cancel{7}} \\
-\ 58 \\
\hline
29
\end{array}
$$

DO WHAT YOU HAVE TO DO TO SOLVE THESE.

Write the difference between the lines.

56 − 38	86 − 39	12 − 9	31 − 19
62 − 48	97 − 18	61 − 17	54 − 39
83 − 29	64 − 55	56 − 28	46 − 33
47 − 17	54 − 39	37 − 18	42 − 36
68 − 51	62 − 45	35 − 18	44 − 26
80 − 45	48 − 36	56 − 47	73 − 34
83 − 29	25 − 17	70 − 45	54 − 38
35 − 18	63 − 46	37 − 15	45 − 18

Choosing the operation

Write either + or − in the box to make each problem correct.

18 [+] 32 [=] 50   45 [−] 22 [=] 23

Write either + or − in the box to make each problem correct.

85 [ ] 35 = 50   63 [ ] 23 = 86   66 [ ] 25 = 41

50 [ ] 12 = 62   28 [ ] 16 = 12   27 [ ] 35 = 62

14 [ ] 61 = 75   43 [ ] 10 = 33   72 [ ] 11 = 83

97 [ ] 53 = 44   14 [ ] 23 = 37   50 [ ] 36 = 14

Write either + or − in the box to make each problem correct.

28 m [ ] 21 m = 49 m   70 km [ ] 39 km = 31 km

37 km [ ] 14 km = 23 km   15 cm [ ] 11 cm = 4 cm

78 mm [ ] 48 mm = 30 mm   41 km [ ] 42 km = 83 km

18 m [ ] 33 m = 51 m   90 mm [ ] 78 mm = 12 mm

71 cm [ ] 10 cm = 61 cm   28 m [ ] 21 m = 49 m

40 m [ ] 51 m = 91 m   86 km [ ] 54 km = 32 km

YOU CHOOSE.

Write the answer in the box.

Superman starts with 8 capes and ends up with 10. How many has he added or subtracted?

A number is added to 12 and the result is 20. What number has been added?

Steel starts with 5 suits. He finishes up with 3. How many suits has he lost or gained?

I take a number away from 30 and have 12 left. What number did I take away?

18

Multiplying

Find the products. Regroup if you need to.

$$\begin{array}{r} 10 \\ \times\ 3 \\ \hline 30 \end{array} \qquad \begin{array}{r} \overset{1}{27} \\ \times\ 2 \\ \hline 54 \end{array} \qquad \begin{array}{r} 30 \\ \times\ 4 \\ \hline 120 \end{array} \qquad \begin{array}{r} \overset{1}{15} \\ \times\ 3 \\ \hline 45 \end{array}$$

SMASH YOUR WAY THROUGH THESE PROBLEMS!

Find the products.

$$\begin{array}{r} 24 \\ \times\ 2 \\ \hline \end{array} \qquad \begin{array}{r} 33 \\ \times\ 3 \\ \hline \end{array} \qquad \begin{array}{r} 14 \\ \times\ 2 \\ \hline \end{array} \qquad \begin{array}{r} 11 \\ \times\ 4 \\ \hline \end{array}$$

$$\begin{array}{r} 32 \\ \times\ 2 \\ \hline \end{array} \qquad \begin{array}{r} 12 \\ \times\ 4 \\ \hline \end{array} \qquad \begin{array}{r} 30 \\ \times\ 3 \\ \hline \end{array} \qquad \begin{array}{r} 40 \\ \times\ 2 \\ \hline \end{array}$$

$$\begin{array}{r} 41 \\ \times\ 4 \\ \hline \end{array} \qquad \begin{array}{r} 39 \\ \times\ 3 \\ \hline \end{array} \qquad \begin{array}{r} 91 \\ \times\ 1 \\ \hline \end{array} \qquad \begin{array}{r} 26 \\ \times\ 3 \\ \hline \end{array}$$

Find the products.

$$\begin{array}{r} 14 \\ \times\ 3 \\ \hline \end{array} \qquad \begin{array}{r} 15 \\ \times\ 4 \\ \hline \end{array} \qquad \begin{array}{r} 22 \\ \times\ 3 \\ \hline \end{array} \qquad \begin{array}{r} 60 \\ \times\ 2 \\ \hline \end{array}$$

$$\begin{array}{r} 31 \\ \times\ 3 \\ \hline \end{array} \qquad \begin{array}{r} 24 \\ \times\ 3 \\ \hline \end{array} \qquad \begin{array}{r} 51 \\ \times\ 2 \\ \hline \end{array} \qquad \begin{array}{r} 11 \\ \times\ 5 \\ \hline \end{array}$$

$$\begin{array}{r} 72 \\ \times\ 2 \\ \hline \end{array} \qquad \begin{array}{r} 16 \\ \times\ 2 \\ \hline \end{array} \qquad \begin{array}{r} 23 \\ \times\ 3 \\ \hline \end{array} \qquad \begin{array}{r} 50 \\ \times\ 4 \\ \hline \end{array}$$

$$\begin{array}{r} 25 \\ \times\ 2 \\ \hline \end{array} \qquad \begin{array}{r} 10 \\ \times\ 4 \\ \hline \end{array} \qquad \begin{array}{r} 31 \\ \times\ 2 \\ \hline \end{array} \qquad \begin{array}{r} 13 \\ \times\ 3 \\ \hline \end{array}$$

$$\begin{array}{r} 61 \\ \times\ 2 \\ \hline \end{array} \qquad \begin{array}{r} 19 \\ \times\ 3 \\ \hline \end{array} \qquad \begin{array}{r} 15 \\ \times\ 2 \\ \hline \end{array} \qquad \begin{array}{r} 48 \\ \times\ 2 \\ \hline \end{array}$$

Multiplying

Solve each problem.

14×3
$= (10 \times 3) + (4 \times 3)$
$= 30 + 12$
$= 42$

$$\begin{array}{r} 10 \\ \times\ 3 \\ \hline 30 \end{array} \qquad \begin{array}{r} 4 \\ \times\ 3 \\ \hline 12 \end{array}$$

$30 + 12 = 42$

Solve each problem.

16×4	11×6
15×5	31×3
19×3	12×4
21×4	22×5
32×7	14×6
34×4	27×3

Dividing

Write the answer to each division problem; "r" means remainder.

$17 \div 4 = $ 4 r 1 $58 \div 10 = $ 5 r 8

$$\begin{array}{r} 7\ r\ 2 \\ 3\overline{)23} \\ -21 \\ \hline 2 \end{array}$$

Write the answer to each division problem.

$31 \div 4 = $ $55 \div 5 = $ $29 \div 10 = $ $29 \div 2 = $

$47 \div 4 = $ $34 \div 5 = $ $57 \div 10 = $ $14 \div 2 = $

$18 \div 4 = $ $46 \div 5 = $ $35 \div 10 = $ $11 \div 2 = $

$25 \div 4 = $ $13 \div 5 = $ $90 \div 10 = $ $21 \div 2 = $

Write the answer to each division problem.

$4\overline{)25}$ $3\overline{)13}$ $5\overline{)38}$ $7\overline{)50}$ $6\overline{)15}$

$2\overline{)11}$ $8\overline{)20}$ $9\overline{)15}$ $6\overline{)29}$ $8\overline{)31}$

Write the answer in the box.

What is the remainder when 15 is divided by 2?

How many groups of 5 are there in 55?

How many groups of 4 are there in 24 and what is the remainder?

What is the remainder when 63 is divided by 10?

Divide 27 by 3.

How many groups of 3 are there in 17?

Dividing

Write the answer to each division problem.

$15 \div 4 =$ 3 r 3 $19 \div 2 =$ 9 r 1

$$\begin{array}{r} 2\ r\ 2 \\ 3\overline{)8} \\ -6 \\ \hline 2 \end{array}$$

I'M BRAINIAC. I CAN DIVIDE. CAN YOU?

Write the answer in the box.

$24 \div 4 =$ $80 \div 10 =$ $19 \div 3 =$ $29 \div 5 =$

$29 \div 4 =$ $38 \div 10 =$ $13 \div 3 =$ $31 \div 5 =$

$14 \div 4 =$ $17 \div 10 =$ $33 \div 3 =$ $12 \div 5 =$

$32 \div 4 =$ $24 \div 10 =$ $23 \div 3 =$ $38 \div 5 =$

Write the answer in the box.

$3\overline{)23}$ $4\overline{)31}$ $5\overline{)22}$ $2\overline{)29}$ $4\overline{)15}$

$4\overline{)45}$ $3\overline{)26}$ $2\overline{)59}$ $5\overline{)59}$ $3\overline{)17}$

Write the answer in the box.

What is the remainder when 36 is divided by 10?

How many whole sets of 5 are there in 16?

How many sets of 3 are there in 20 and what is the remainder?

What is the remainder when 44 is divided by 40?

22

Choosing the operation

Write either x or ÷ in the box to make each problem correct.

11 ⬚x⬚ 3 = 33   14 ⬚÷⬚ 2 = 7

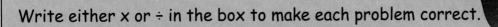

THIS IS HOW I OPERATE.

Write either x or ÷ in the box to make the product correct.

15 ⬚ 2 = 30   12 ⬚ 4 = 3   2 ⬚ 7 = 14

25 ⬚ 5 = 5   3 ⬚ 12 = 36   8 ⬚ 4 = 2

13 ⬚ 10 = 130   5 ⬚ 5 = 25   3 ⬚ 3 = 9

18 ⬚ 6 = 3   40 ⬚ 4 = 10   6 ⬚ 10 = 60

Write either x or ÷ in the box to make the product correct.

27 cm ⬚ 3 = 9 cm   50 mm ⬚ 10 = 5 mm   4 m ⬚ 3 = 12 m

16 mm ⬚ 2 = 8 mm   4 m ⬚ 5 = 20 m   40 m ⬚ 4 = 10 m

40 cm ⬚ 10 = 4 cm   50 m ⬚ 5 = 10 m   60 cm ⬚ 3 = 20 cm

6 m ⬚ 4 = 24 m   4 cm ⬚ 4 = 16 cm   15 cm ⬚ 2 = 30 cm

30 cm ⬚ 10 = 3 cm   20 mm ⬚ 5 = 4 mm   30 m ⬚ 3 = 10 m

12 m ⬚ 2 = 6 m   1 mm ⬚ 10 = 10 mm   3 cm ⬚ 2 = 6 cm

Write the answer in the box.

Which number multiplied by 3 equals 24?

Which number divided by 10 equals 7?

Which number divided by 8 equals 5?

Which number multiplied by 6 equals 6?

Which number multiplied by 9 equals 36?

Which number multiplied by 5 equals 30?

Word problems

Write the answer in the box.

I multiply a number by 4 and the answer is 20.
What number did I begin with? 5

FOR TRUTH
AND JUSTICE!

Write the answer in the box.

A number multiplied by 6 equals 24. What is the number?

I divide a number by 10 and the answer is 2. What number did I divide?

I multiply a number by 6 and the answer is 30. What is the number I multiplied?

After dividing a piece of wood into three equal sections, each section is 4 m long. How long was the piece of wood I started with?

A number multiplied by 6 gives the answer 36. What is the number?

Some money is divided into four equal amounts. Each amount is 10 cents. How much money was there before it was divided?

I multiply a number by 9 and the result is 45. What number was multiplied?

A number divided by 3 equals 5. What number was divided?

Three children share 18 peanuts equally among themselves. How many peanuts does each child receive?

A number divided by 4 is 8. What is the number?

I multiply a number by 6 and the answer is 36. What is the number?

Four sets of a number equal 16. What is the number?

A number divided by 5 is 5. What is the number?

A child divides a number by 8 and gets 2. What number was divided?

Three groups of a number equal 27. What is the number?

I multiply a number by 10 and the result is 100. What is the number?

Word problems

THIS IS THE MOMENT OF MY GREATEST TRIUMPH!

Write the answer in the box.

Lex Luther is given 3 dimes. How much money does he have altogether? | 30¢

Write the answer in the box.

Superman saves Jimmy Olsen 30 times in March, 40 times in April, and 20 times in May. How many times has Jimmy Olsen been saved altogether?

Four lifeboats carry a total of 100 people. How many people are in each boat?

Three women win the lottery and share $900 equally among themselves. How much does each woman receive?

Wayne has a collection of 120 Superman figures. He gives 40 of them to his friends. How many figures does he have now?

When Peter multiplies his apartment number by 3, the result is 75. What is his apartment number?

A copy of the *Daily Planet* costs $1.40. How much will two copies cost?

DAILY PLANET

Superman has captured some escaped animals. He has three cages. There are 12 animals in each cage. How many animals has Superman captured?

Lois Lane's car trip is supposed to be 70 kilometres long but the car breaks down half-way. How far has the car gone when it breaks down?

A teacher has 32 children in her class. 13 children are out with the flu. How many children are left in class?

Perry White employs 17 reporters at the *Daily Planet*. He fires 9 of them. How many reporters are left?

A safe contains 40 bars of gold. Lex Luthor steals 27 bars. How many bars are left in the safe?

Problems with measures

Which would be the best unit to use for the length of this girder?

metre

USE YOUR MENTAL POWERS TO FIGURE THESE OUT.

Choose the most appropriate unit for the measurements below.

metre   litre   kilometre   gram   kilogram   centimetre

Write the best unit for each of the following.

The length of
Lois Lane's car.

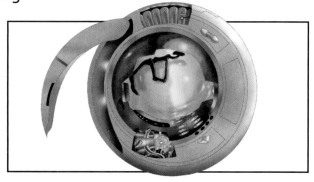

The weight
of a flyer pod.

The weight of Clark
Kent's glasses.

Xenon

Koron

The distance from
Koron to Xenon.

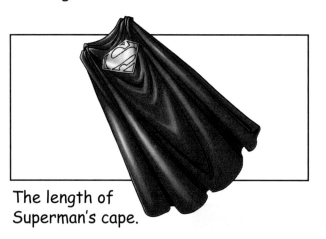

The length of
Superman's cape.

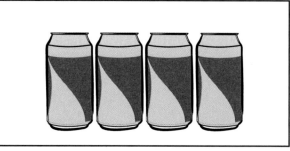

The capacity
of a soda can.

Telling time

What time is shown by these clocks?

18 minutes to 8

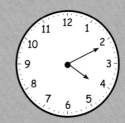

11 minutes after 4

What is the time shown by these clocks?

IT'S TIME TO GO!

Telling time

Draw the time on each clock face.

Twenty-six minutes after four.

Choose the most appropriate unit for the measurements below.

Eight minutes to twelve

Twenty to ten

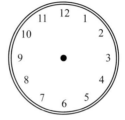 

Fourteen minutes after three

Eleven minutes to six

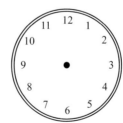 

Twenty-seven minutes after twelve

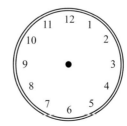

Tables and graphs

Look at this bar graph.

SUPERMAN'S POWERS

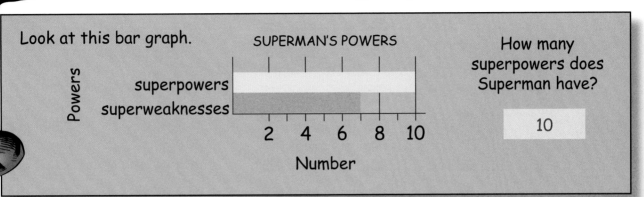

Powers
- superpowers
- superweaknesses

Number
2 4 6 8 10

How many superpowers does Superman have?

| 10 |

Look at this bar graph.

LEX LUTHOR'S SUITS

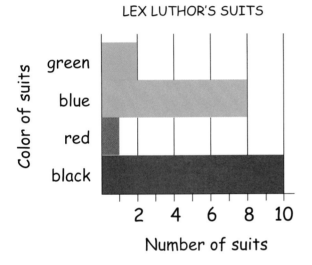

Color of suits
- green
- blue
- red
- black

Number of suits
2 4 6 8 10

How many green suits does Luthor have?

Luthor has 1 suit of which color?

How many blue suits does Luthor have?

Of which color does Luthor have the most suits?

How many suits does Luthor have altogether?

Complete the table.

FAVORITE SUPER HERO

Super heroes	tally marks	total
Superman	||||| |||	
Supergirl		4
Steel	|||	

Number of children

How many more children prefer Superman to Steel?

Which super hero is prefered by 4 children

WHOM DO YOU LIKE THE BEST?

Necessary information

Write the missing information you need to have to answer the questions.

Lex Luthor wants to build a fleet of satellites. Each satellite costs $1 million. How much will the fleet cost in all?

You need to know   how many satellites there will be in the fleet.

Write the missing information you need to have to answer the questions.

On Monday, 3,258 people bought the *Daily Planet*. How many people bought the newspaper in a whole week?

You need to know

Brainiac has $200. He wants to buy a computer for $180. He also wants a new computer mouse. Does he have enough money?

You need to know

Camera film costs 50¢, 75¢, or 90¢ depending on how many photographs it can take. Jimmy Olsen bought two films at the same price. How much money did he spend?

You need to know

Boss Moxie divides his gang into three teams. How many crooks in each team?

You need to know

Superman visits Metropolis, Coast City, Smallville, and all the other cities in Kansas. How many places did he visit.

You need to know

S.T.A.R. Labs bought a submarine for $2 million. It spent $3,500 on new lasers and $4,200 on a cloning machine. How much money was left?

You need to know

Number pairs

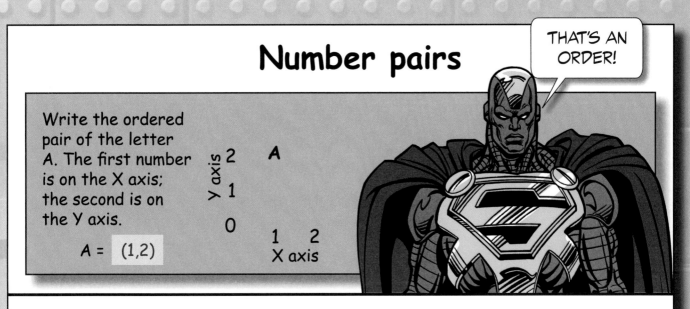

Write the ordered pair of the letter A. The first number is on the X axis; the second is on the Y axis.

A = (1,2)

Look at this grid and write the ordered pair of each letter.

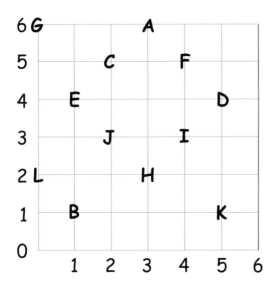

A =

B =

C =

D =

E =

F =

G =

H =

I =

J =

K =

L =

Use the grid to write the ordered pairs.

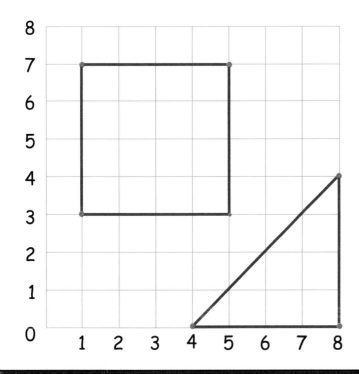

Write the ordered pair of each corner of the square.

Write the ordered pair of each corner of the triangle.

31

2 times table

YOU KNOW WHO I AM!

Color the multiples of 2. Find a pattern.

1	2	3	4	5
6	7	8	9	10
11	12	13	14	15
16	17	18	19	20
21	22	23	24	25

Write the answers.

1 x 2 = 2   2 x 2 =   3 x 2 =   4 x 2 =

5 x 2 =   6 x 2 =   7 x 2 =   8 x 2 =

9 x 2 =   10 x 2 =

How many horns?

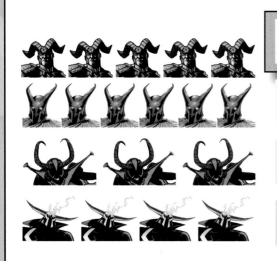

5	sets of 2	5	x 2 =	10	horns
	sets of 2		x 2 =		horns
	sets of 2		x 2 =		horns
	sets of 2		x 2 =		horns

Multiplying by 2

Write the problems.

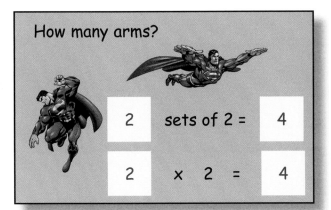

How many arms?

| 2 | sets of 2 = | 4 |
| 2 | x 2 = | 4 |

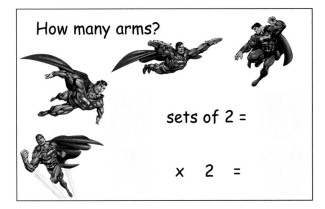

How many arms?

sets of 2 =

x 2 =

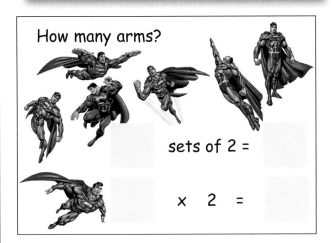

How many arms?

sets of 2 =

x 2 =

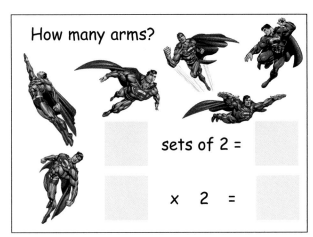

How many arms?

sets of 2 =

x 2 =

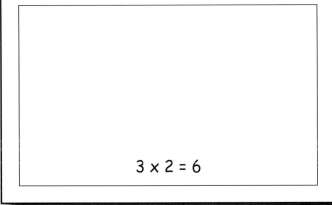

How many arms?

sets of 2 =

x 2 =

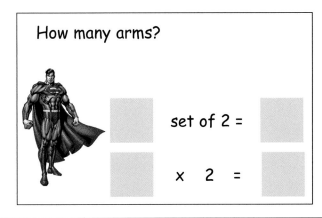

How many arms?

set of 2 =

x 2 =

Draw different pictures to go with these problems.

3 x 2 = 6

9 x 2 = 18

Dividing by 2

Share the kryptonite equally between the boxes.

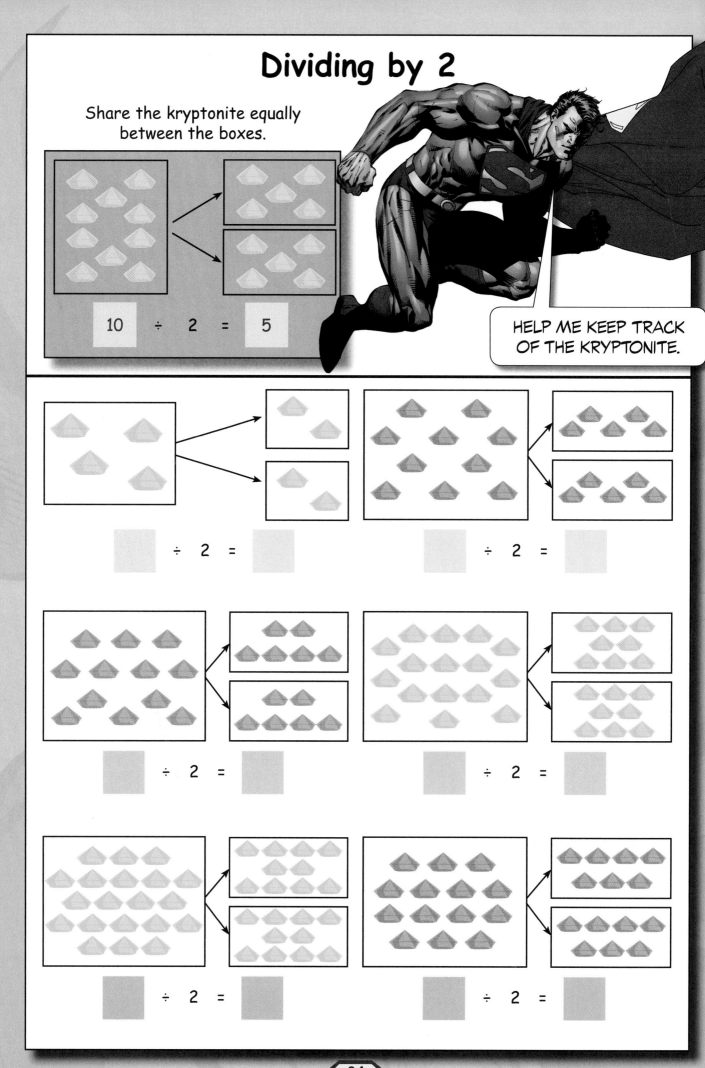

$$10 \div 2 = 5$$

HELP ME KEEP TRACK OF THE KRYPTONITE.

$$\boxed{} \div 2 = \boxed{}$$

$$\boxed{} \div 2 = \boxed{}$$

$$\boxed{} \div 2 = \boxed{}$$

$$\boxed{} \div 2 = \boxed{}$$

$$\boxed{} \div 2 = \boxed{}$$

$$\boxed{} \div 2 = \boxed{}$$

Using the 2 times table

Write the problems to match Superman's shields.

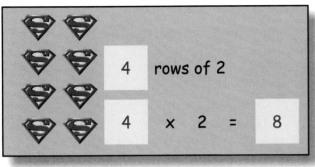

4 rows of 2

4 x 2 = 8

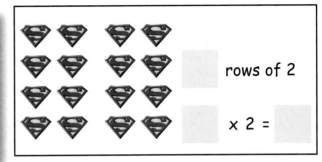

rows of 2

x 2 =

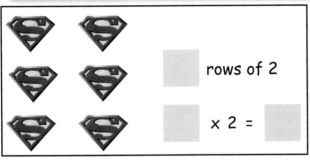

rows of 2

x 2 =

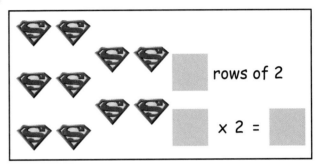

rows of 2

x 2 =

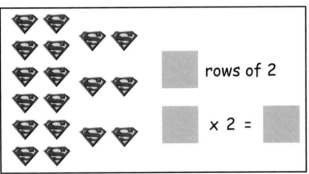

rows of 2

x 2 =

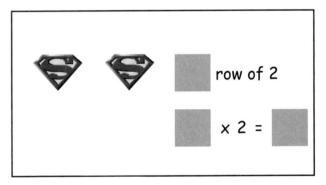

row of 2

x 2 =

Draw shields to match these problems.

3 x 2

4 x 2

2 x 2

7 x 2

Using the 2 times table

Each cape stands for 2. Join each set of capes to the correct number.

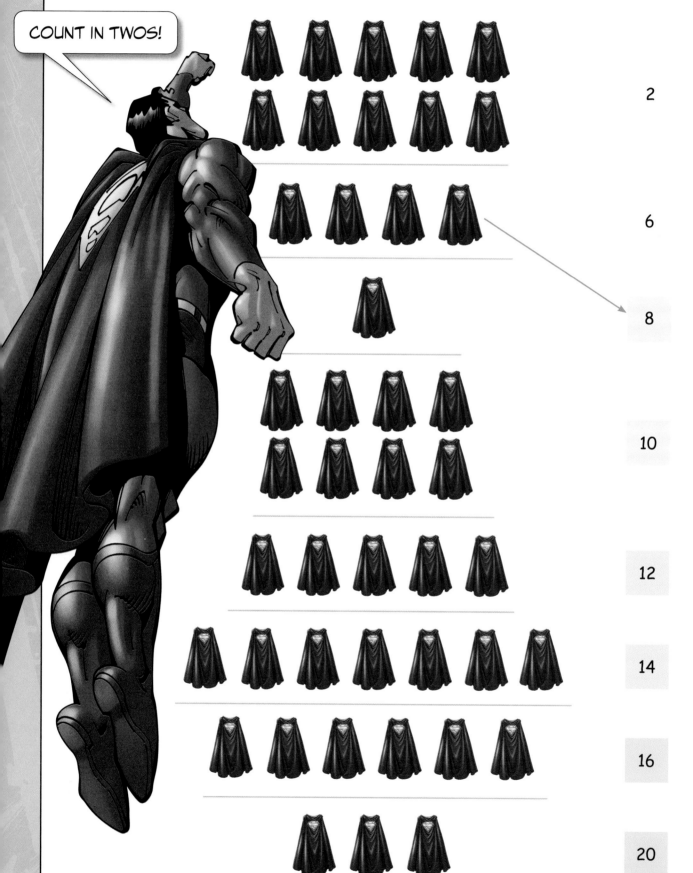

2

6

8

10

12

14

16

20

COUNT IN TWOS!

Using the 2 times table

How many eyes?

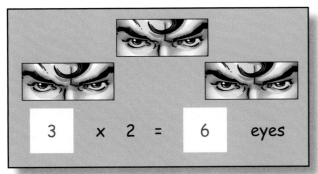

| 3 | x 2 = | 6 | eyes |

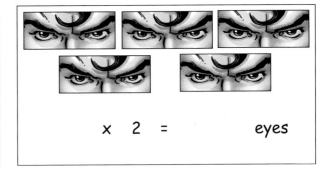

x 2 = eyes

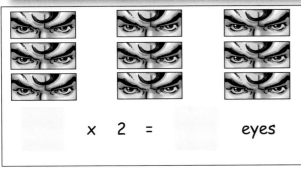

x 2 = eyes

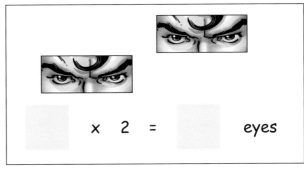

x 2 = eyes

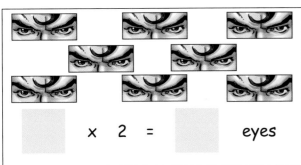

x 2 = eyes

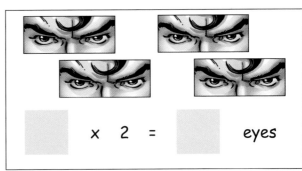

x 2 = eyes

Draw your own pictures to match these number sentences.

2 x 2 = 4

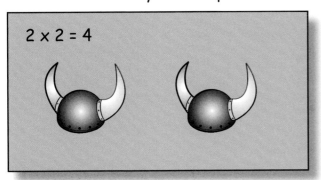

6 x 2 = 12

7 x 2 = 14

10 x 2 = 20

5 times table

YOU CAN DO IT!

Count in 5s, color the multiples of 5, and find a pattern.

1	2	3	4	5	6	7	8	9	10
11	12	13	14	15	16	17	18	19	20
21	22	23	24	25	26	27	28	29	30
31	32	33	34	35	36	37	38	39	40
41	42	43	44	45	46	47	48	49	50
51	52	53	54	55	56	57	58	59	60
61	62	63	64	65	66	67	68	69	70
71	72	73	74	75	76	77	78	79	80
81	82	83	84	85	86	87	88	89	90

Write the answers.

1 x 5 =   2 x 5 =   3 x 5 =   4 x 5 =

5 x 5 =   6 x 5 =   7 x 5 =   8 x 5 =

9 x 5 =   10 x 5 =

How many pieces of kryptonite?

3 sets of 5   x 5 =   crystals

2 sets of 5   x 5 =   crystals

4 sets of 5   x 5 =   crystals

6 sets of 5   x 5 =   crystals

Multiplying by 5

Draw a ring around rows of 5. Complete the problem.

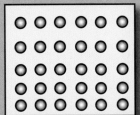

$3 \times 5 = 15$

PUNCH YOUR WAY THROUGH THESE!

Draw a ring around rows of 5.

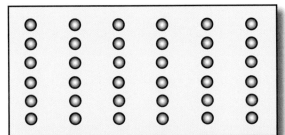

5 rings of 5 ___ $\times$ 5 = ___

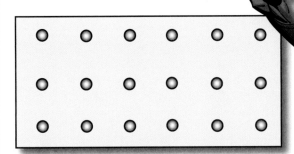

2 rings of 5 ___ $\times$ 5 = ___

1 ring of 5 ___ $\times$ 5 = ___

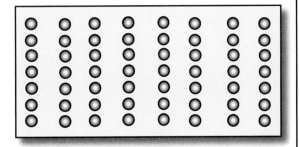

6 rings of 5 ___ $\times$ 5 = ___

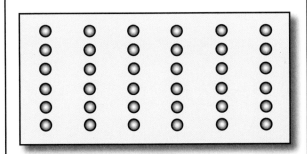

4 rings of 5 ___ $\times$ 5 = ___

3 rings of 5 ___ $\times$ 5 = ___

Dividing by 5

Write a number sentence to show how many cubes are in each stack.

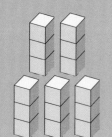

| 15 | cubes altogether |
| 5 | stacks |

$15 \div 5 = 3$

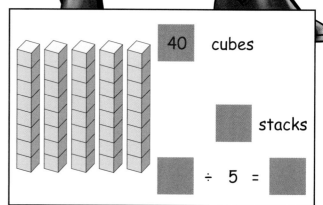

Write a number sentence to show how many cubes are in each stack.

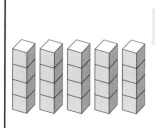 20 cubes

☐ stacks

☐ $\div$ 5 = ☐

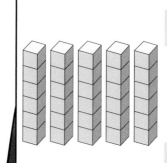 30 cubes

☐ stacks

☐ $\div$ 5 = ☐

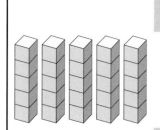 25 cubes

☐ stacks

☐ $\div$ 5 = ☐

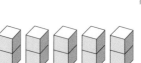 10 cubes

☐ stacks

☐ $\div$ 5 = ☐

 35 cubes

☐ stacks

☐ $\div$ 5 = ☐

 40 cubes

☐ stacks

☐ $\div$ 5 = ☐

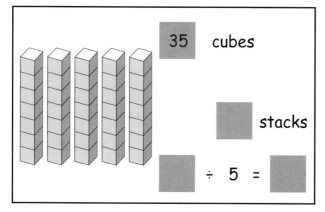

Using the 5 times table

I'LL USE MY POWERS TO SOLVE THESE PROBLEMS!

Write the number that is hiding under the star.

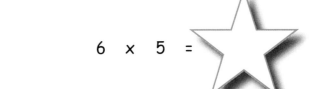
8 x 5 = 40

Write the number that is hiding under the star.

 x 5 = 25   6 x 5 = ☆

 x 5 = 5   10 x 5 = ☆

 x 5 = 35   4 x 5 = ☆

☆ x 5 = 45   3 x 5 = ☆

 x 5 = 10   0 x 5 = ☆

41

Using the 5 times table

Each shape stands for 5. Join each set of items to the correct number.

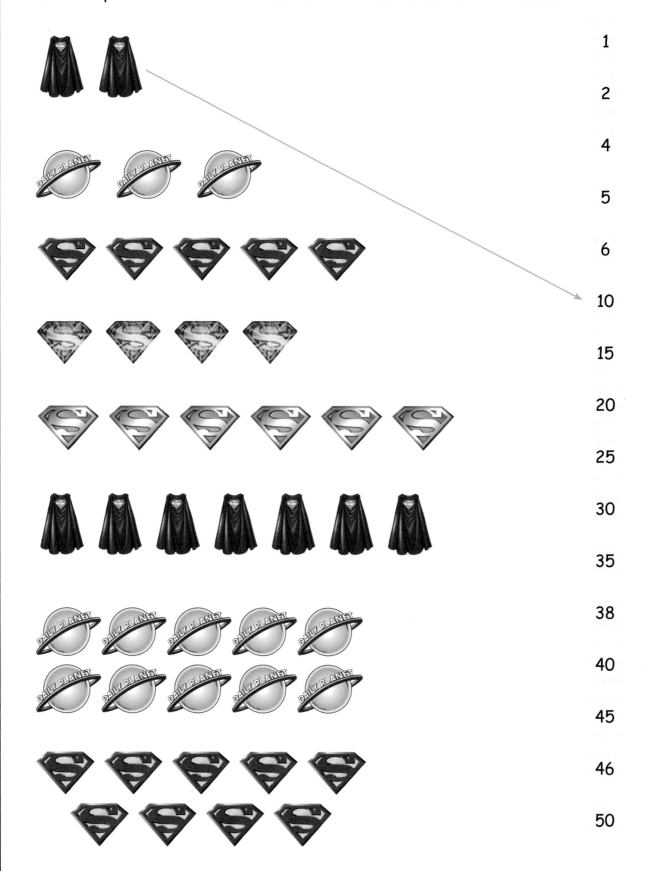

1

2

4

5

6

10

15

20

25

30

35

38

40

45

46

50

Using the 5 times table

How many altogether?

Lex Luthor has 7 jet airplanes. Each airplane has 5 seats. How many seats are there altogether?

7 x 5 = 35 seats

How many altogether?

Superman has 3 capes. Each cape has 5 pockets. How many pockets are there altogether?

x = pockets

Doomsday destroys 8 stars. Each star had 5 planets. How many planets are there altogether?

x = planets

Supergirl catches 6 gangs. Each gang contains 5 crooks. How many crooks are there altogether?

x = crooks

How many in each?

Lois Lane had 50 pens in 5 cases. How many pens were in each case?

50 ÷ 5 = 10 pens

How many in each?

Superman has 60 oxygen cartridges on 5 belts. How many cartridges are there on each belt?

÷ = cartridges

Jimmy Olsen has 35 photographs on 5 films. How many photos are there on each film?

÷ = photos

S.T.A.R. Labs has 25 clones in 5 buildings. How many clones are there in each building?

÷ = clones

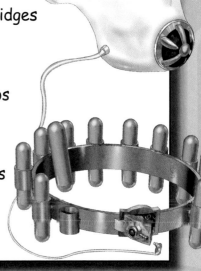

10 times table

Count in 10s, color the multiples of 10, and find a pattern.

1	2	3	4	5	6	7	8	9	10
11	12	13	14	15	16	17	18	19	20
21	22	23	24	25	26	27	28	29	30
31	32	33	34	35	36	37	38	39	40
41	42	43	44	45	46	47	48	49	50
51	52	53	54	55	56	57	58	59	60
61	62	63	64	65	66	67	68	69	70
71	72	73	74	75	76	77	78	79	80
81	82	83	84	85	86	87	88	89	90

I'M BRAINIAC. I CAN COUNT IN 10S. CAN YOU?

Find the products.

1 x 10 = 10   2 x 10 = ___   3 x 10 = ___   4 x 10 = ___

5 x 10 = ___   6 x 10 = ___   7 x 10 = ___   8 x 10 = ___

10 x 10 = ___   9 x 10 = ___

Each stack contains 10 cards. How many cards are there altogether?

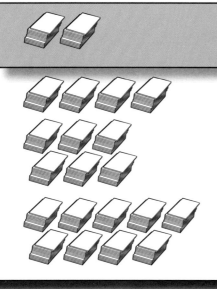

2 sets of 10   2 x 10 = 20 cards

___ sets of 10   ___ x 10 = ___ cards

___ sets of 10   ___ x 10 = ___ cards

___ sets of 10   ___ x 10 = ___ cards

Multiplying and dividing

Each belt has 10 tubes. How many tubes are there altogether?

How many belts? **2**

2 x **10** = **20** tubes

USE THE 10 TIMES TABLE.

Write how many tubes.

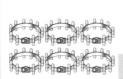 How many belts? ☐

☐ x ☐ = ☐ tubes

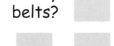 How many belts? ☐

☐ x ☐ = ☐ tubes

 How many belts? ☐

☐ x ☐ = ☐ tubes

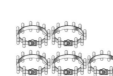 How many belts? ☐

☐ x ☐ = ☐ tubes

How many belts did these tubes come from?

30 ÷ **10** = **3** belts

Write how many belts.

☐ ÷ ☐ = ☐ belt

☐ ÷ ☐ = ☐ belts

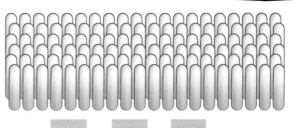

☐ ÷ ☐ = ☐ belts

45

Dividing by 10

HOW MANY DIMES DO I HAVE?

$1

One dollar is worth the same as 10 dimes.

One dime One dime One dime One dime One dime One dime One dime One dime One dime One dime

---

30 dimes

30 ÷ 10 = $ 3

---

60 dimes

÷ 10 = $

---

40 dimes

÷ 10 = $

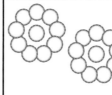

50 dimes

÷ 10 = $

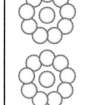

90 dimes

÷ 10 = $

100 dimes

÷ 10 = $

---

10 dimes

÷ 10 = $

---

20 dimes

÷ 10 = $

46

Using the 10 times table

How many altogether?

Steel has 3 tool boxes. Each box has 10 hammers. How many hammers are there altogether?

| 3 | x | 10 | = | 30 | hammers |

THIS MATH ISN'T AS TOUGH AS I AM!

How many altogether?

Clark Kent had 6 notebooks. There were 10 pages in each book. How many pages were there altogether?

x   =   pages

LexCorp had 2 offices. Each office had 10 desks. How many desks were there altogether?

x   =   desks

Project Cadmus had 5 tanks. Each tank had 10 guns on it. How many guns were there altogether?

x   =   guns

S.T.A.R. Labs built 7 rockets. Each rocket had 10 engines. How many engines were there altogether?

x   =   engines

How many in each?

Lois Lane had 20 lipsticks in 10 handbags. How many lipsticks were in each bag?

| 20 | ÷ | 10 | = | 2 | lipsticks |

How many in each?

There were 80 jewels in 10 safes. How many jewels were in each safe?

÷   =   jewels

There are 60 villains in 10 spaceships. How many villians in each spaceship?

÷   =   villains

Using the 10 times table

Match each cape to the correct shield.

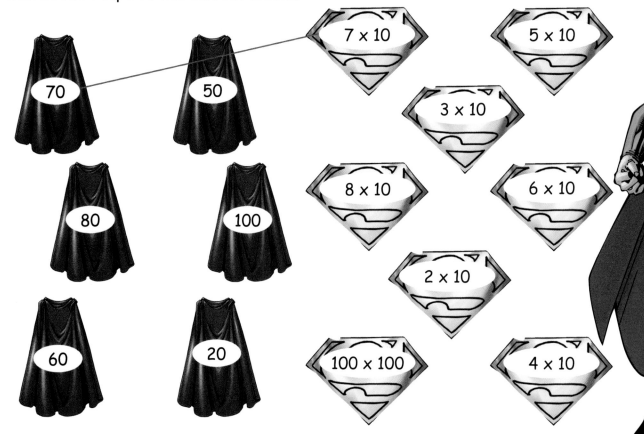

Match each shield to the correct cape.

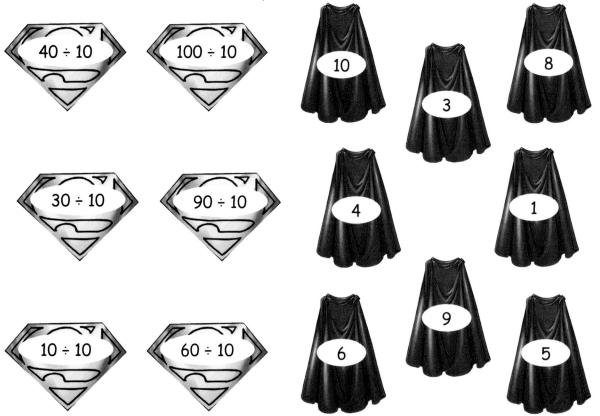

48

Using the 10 times table

Write in the missing numbers.

4 × 10 = 40

10	×	4	=	40
40	÷	10	=	4
40	÷	4	=	10

3 × 10 = 30

× =

÷ =

÷ =

9 × 10 = 90

× =

÷ =

÷ =

6 × 10 = 60

× =

÷ =

÷ =

5 × 10 = 50

× =

÷ =

÷ =

7 × 10 = 70

× =

÷ =

÷ =

2 × 10 = 20

× =

÷ =

÷ =

8 × 10 = 80

× =

÷ =

÷ =

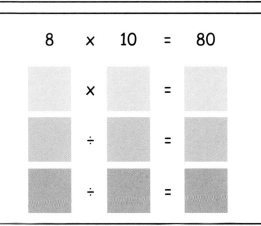

49

3 times table

Count in 3s, color the multiples of 3, and find a pattern.

1	2	3	4	5
6	7	8	9	10
11	12	13	14	15
16	17	18	19	20
21	22	23	24	25

RUN THROUGH THESE SUMS AS FAST AS YOU CAN!

Find the products.

1 x 3 = 3   2 x 3 =   3 x 3 =   4 x 3 =

Count each star as 3.

2 sets of 3   2 x 3 = 6

 sets of 3   x 3 =

 sets of 3   x 3 =

 sets of 3   x 3 =

Multiplying by 3

Write the number sentences to match the pictures.

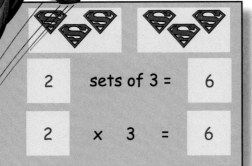

2	sets of 3 =	6
2	x 3 =	6

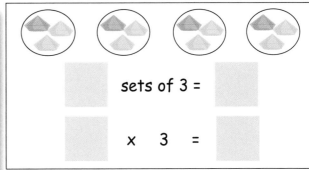

sets of 3 =

x 3 =

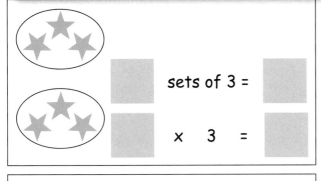

sets of 3 =

x 3 =

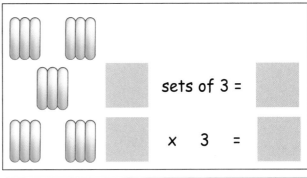

sets of 3 =

x 3 =

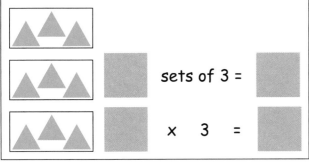

sets of 3 =

x 3 =

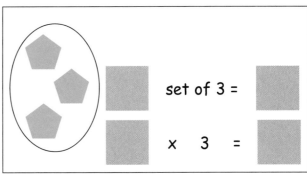

set of 3 =

x 3 =

Draw you own pictures to match these number sentences.

5 x 3 = 15

2 x 3 = 6

3 x 3 = 9

4 x 3 = 12

Dividing by 3

Divide the money equally among three people.
Write a problem to show what you have done.
You might find it easier to change all the money into 1¢ coins.

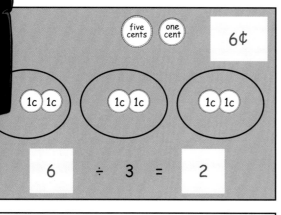

6¢

$6 \div 3 = 2$

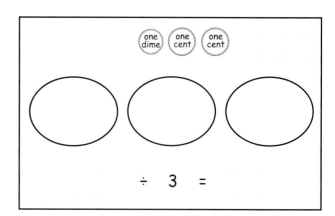

$\div\ 3\ =$

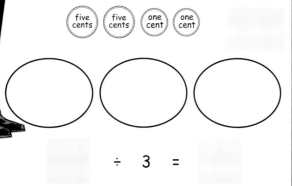

$\div\ 3\ =$

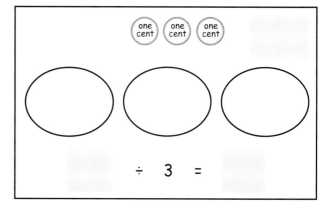

$\div\ 3\ =$

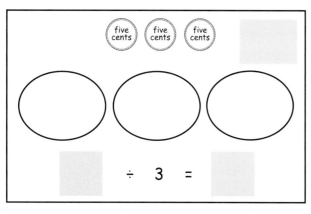

$\div\ 3\ =$

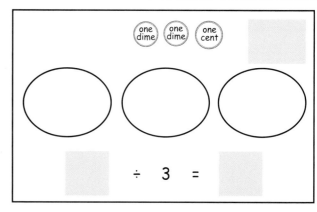

$\div\ 3\ =$

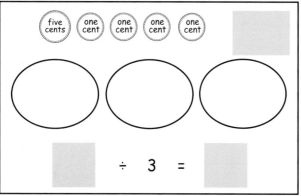

$\div\ 3\ =$

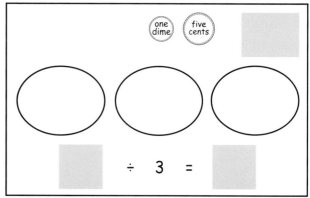

$\div\ 3\ =$

4 times table

Count in 4s, color the multiples
of 4, and find a pattern.

1	2	3	4	5
6	7	8	9	10
11	12	13	14	15
16	17	18	19	20
21	22	23	24	25

A JOB FOR
SUPERMAN...
AND FRIENDS!

Find the products.

1 x 4 = 4

2 x 4 =

3 x 4 =

4 x 4 =

Count each star as 4.

 4 sets of 4   4 x 4 = 16

   sets of 4   x 4 =

   sets of 4   x 4 =

   sets of 4   x 4 =

Multiplying by 4

Write number sentences to match the pictures.

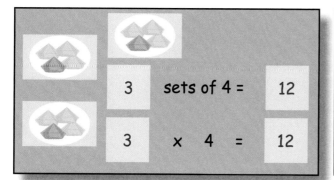

3 sets of 4 = 12

3 × 4 = 12

___ sets of 4 = ___

___ × 4 = ___

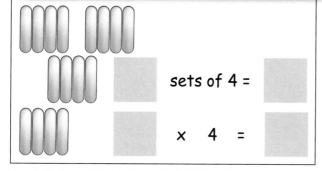

___ sets of 4 = ___

___ × 4 = ___

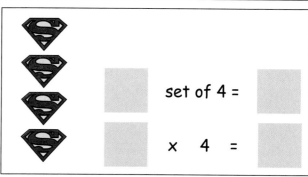

___ set of 4 = ___

___ × 4 = ___

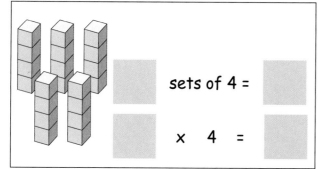

___ sets of 4 = ___

___ × 4 = ___

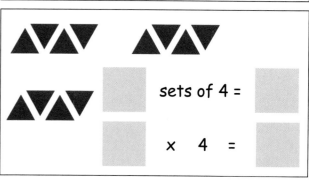

___ sets of 4 = ___

___ × 4 = ___

Draw different pictures to match these number sentences.

2 × 4 = 8

4 × 4 = 16

5 × 4 = 20

3 × 4 = 12

Dividing by 4

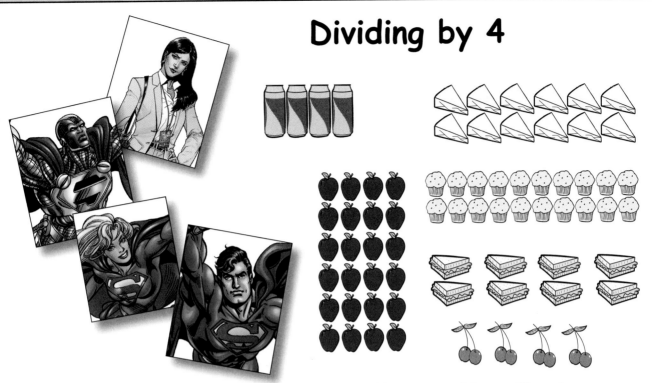

Superman and his friends are having a picnic. How many things will each super hero have? Draw the objects in the circles.

8 sandwiches

8 ÷ 4 = 2 each

12 cheeses

÷ 4 = each

4 drinks

÷ 4 = each

20 cakes

÷ 4 = each

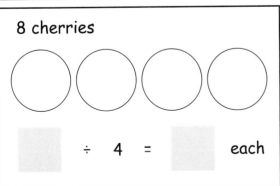

8 cherries

÷ 4 = each

24 apples

÷ 4 = each

Mixed tables

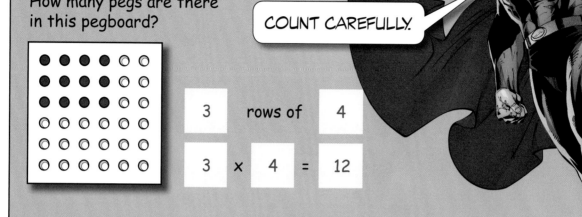

How many pegs are there in this pegboard?

COUNT CAREFULLY.

| 3 | rows of | 4 |

| 3 | x | 4 | = | 12 |

How many pegs are there in each pegboard?

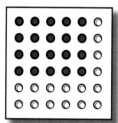   rows of

x   =

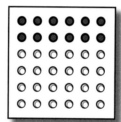   rows of

x   =

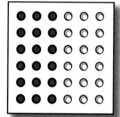   rows of

x   =

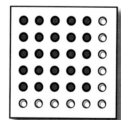   rows of

x   =

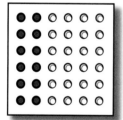   rows of

x   =

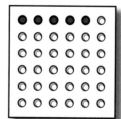   row of

x   =

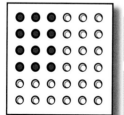   rows of

x   =

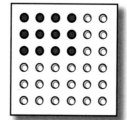   rows of

x   =

Mixed tables

Divide the 12 pennies equally. Draw the coins
and write the problem to show how many each character gets.

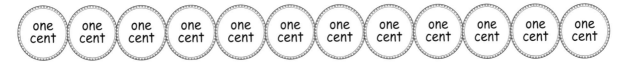

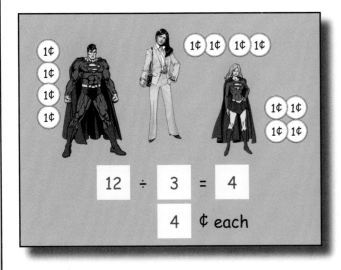

$$12 \div 3 = 4$$

$$4 \text{ ¢ each}$$

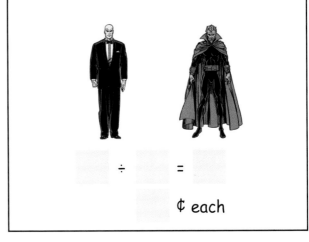

$$\boxed{} \div \boxed{} = \boxed{}$$

$$\boxed{} \text{ ¢ each}$$

$$\boxed{} \div \boxed{} = \boxed{}$$

$$\boxed{} \text{ ¢ each}$$

$$\boxed{} \div \boxed{} = \boxed{}$$

$$\boxed{} \text{ ¢}$$

$$\boxed{} \div \boxed{} = \boxed{} \text{ ¢ each}$$

Mixed tables

How much will Supergirl get paid?

IT'S A GOOD THING I DON'T DO THIS FOR THE MONEY!

Price List for Jobs	
Clean up neighborhood	2¢
Feed the homeless	5¢
Save the mayor	4¢
Mend a bridge	10¢
Put out a fire	7¢

Write a problem to show how much money Supergirl will get for these jobs.

Save the mayor 3 times.	3	x	4¢	=	12¢

Clean up the neighborhood 4 times.   ☐ x ☐ = ☐

Feed the homeless 2 times.   ☐ x ☐ = ☐

Put out a fire 5 times.   ☐ x ☐ = ☐

Mend a bridge 2 times.   ☐ x ☐ = ☐

How much will Supergirl get paid for these jobs?
Use the space to work out the problems.

Save the mayor twice and put out 3 fires.   ☐ + ☐ = ☐

Feed the homeless 6 times and mend 4 bridges.   ☐ + ☐ = ☐

58

Mixed tables

Write the numbers that the capes are hiding.

$4 \times 5 = 20$

$20 \div 4 = 5$

$2 \times 4 = $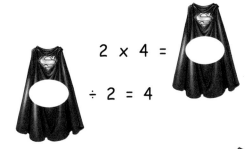

$\div 2 = 4$

$6 \div 3 = $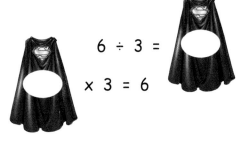

$\times 3 = 6$

$1 \times 3 = $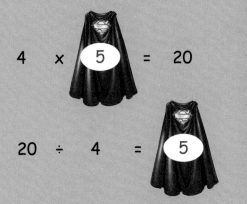

$3 \times = 9$

$5 \times = 45$

$45 \div 5 = $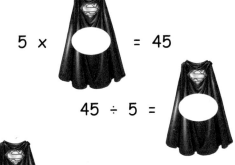

$8 \times 2 = $

$16 \div 2 = $

$60 \div = 6$

$10 \times = 60$

$\times 4 = 12$

$12 \div 4 = $

$7 \times 5 = $

$\div 5 = 7$

$5 \times = 50$

$50 \div = 5$

Mixed tables

10 → ÷ 2 → 5   15 → ÷ 5 → 3

12 → → □   30 → → □

2 → → □   50 → → □

8 → → □   35 → → □

9 → ÷ 3 → □   4 → ÷ 4 → □

12 → → □   8 → → □

15 → → □   12 → → □

6 → → □   16 → → □

70 → ÷ 10 → □

30 → → □   THIS LOOKS LIKE A JOB FOR SUPERMAN!

100 → → □

40 → → □

Mixed tables

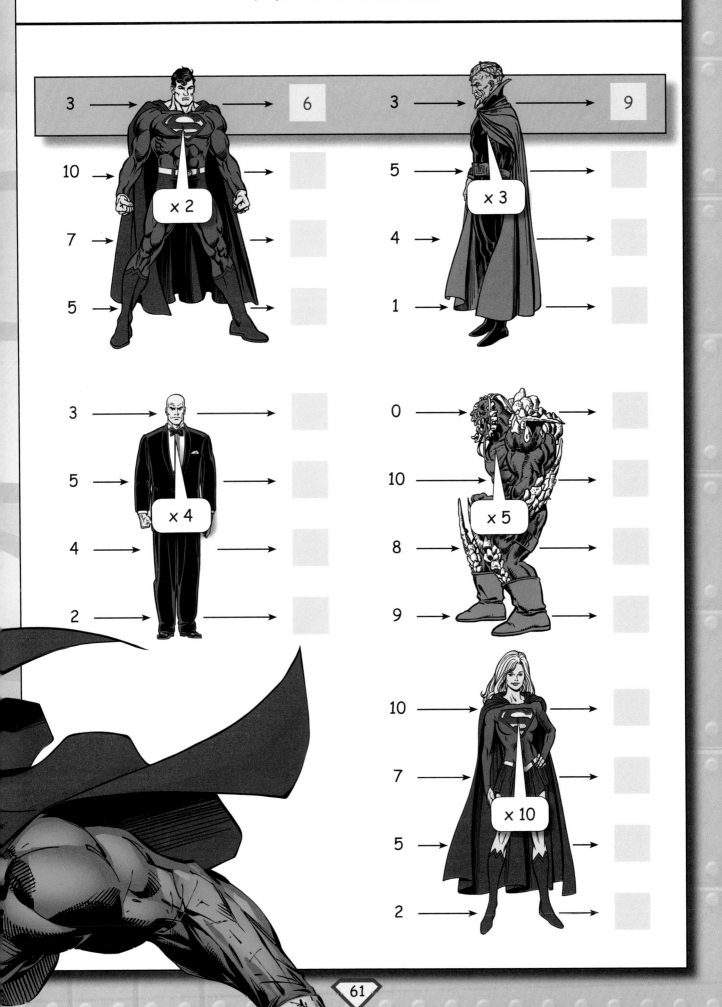

3 → → 6

3 → → 9

10 → **× 2** →

5 → **× 3** →

7 → →

4 → →

5 → →

1 → →

3 → →

0 → →

5 → **× 4** →

10 → **× 5** →

4 → →

8 → →

2 → →

9 → →

10 → →

7 → **× 10** →

5 → →

2 → →

Mixed tables

How many legs are in this group of four Superman characters?

| 4 | x | 2 | = | 8 | legs |

Work out how many:

People in 3 such groups? ___ x ___ = ___ people

Capes in 7 groups? ___ x ___ = ___ capes

Legs in 6 groups? ___ x ___ = ___ legs

Capes in 9 groups? ___ x ___ = ___ capes

Legs in 4 groups? ___ x ___ = ___ legs

Eyes on the men in 2 groups? ___ x ___ = ___ eyes

Hands in 5 groups? ___ x ___ = ___ hands

Capes and heads in 10 groups? ___ x ___ = ___ capes and heads

Number pairs

Put an X at (2,3).

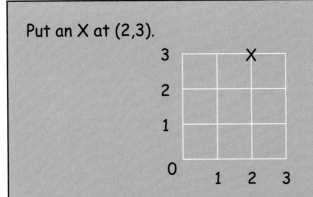

Put an X on this grid at each of these ordered pairs:
(1,1) (1,9) (3,9) (3,6) (7,6) (7,9) (9,9) (9,1) (7,1) (7,4) (3,4) (3,1) (1,1)

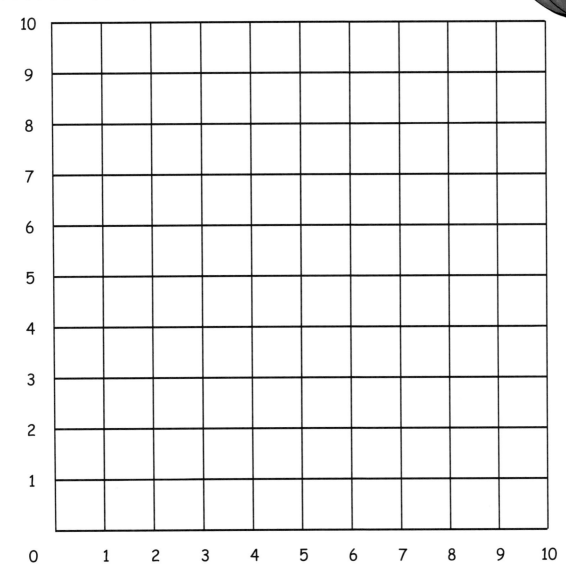

Join the Xs in the same order.
Which capital letter have you drawn?

Logic problems

Read the clues to find the secret number.

2 3 4 5 6 7

6
4   8
2

4   5
9   7

It is in both the rectangle and the oval.
It is not in the triangle. It is greater than 4.
What number is it?   6

Read the clues to find the secret number.

15
11   13
18   20

15   12
11   14
13

23   22   14
12   16   10

It is not in the square. It is an odd number.
It is greater than any number in the triangle.
What number is it?

11   10
16   19
15   14

13
15   11
12   8

14   15   12
7   21

It is in the rectangle and the oval.
It is greater than 10 and less than 17. It is an even number.
What number is it?

It is in the triangle.
It is not an even number.
It is in the big rectangle and
the small rectangle.
What number is it?

4   2
1   3   9
5   6   8 7

Dividing

Write the quotient in the box.

$$80 \div 10 = \boxed{8} \qquad 30 \div 10 = \boxed{3}$$

$$
\begin{array}{r}
\boxed{7} \\
10{\overline{\smash{\big)}\,70}} \\
-70 \\
\hline
0
\end{array}
$$

Write the quotient in the box.

$40 \div 10 =$	$320 \div 10 =$	$50 \div 10 =$
$130 \div 10 =$	$490 \div 10 =$	$100 \div 10 =$
$210 \div 10 =$	$10 \div 10 =$	$630 \div 10 =$
$20 \div 10 =$	$80 \div 10 =$	$220 \div 10 =$
$90 \div 10 =$	$200 \div 10 =$	$870 \div 10 =$
$60 \div 10 =$	$160 \div 10 =$	$30 \div 10 =$

Write the quotient in the box.

$$10{\overline{\smash{\big)}\,70}} \qquad 10{\overline{\smash{\big)}\,130}} \qquad 10{\overline{\smash{\big)}\,40}} \qquad 10{\overline{\smash{\big)}\,90}}$$

$$
\begin{array}{r} 26 \\ 10{\overline{\smash{\big)}\,260}} \end{array}
\qquad
\begin{array}{r} 1 \\ 10{\overline{\smash{\big)}\,10}} \end{array}
\qquad
\begin{array}{r} 30 \\ 10{\overline{\smash{\big)}\,300}} \end{array}
\qquad
\begin{array}{r} 42 \\ 10{\overline{\smash{\big)}\,420}} \end{array}
$$

Write the quotient in the box.

$1{,}560 \div 10 =$	$6{,}030 \div 10 =$	$4{,}020 \div 10 =$
$3{,}040 \div 10 =$	$8{,}750 \div 10 =$	$6{,}730 \div 10 =$
$4{,}700 \div 10 =$	$2{,}000 \div 10 =$	$1{,}010 \div 10 =$
$5{,}430 \div 10 =$	$3{,}980 \div 10 =$	$9{,}990 \div 10 =$

Rounding

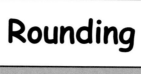

Round each amount to the nearest whole unit. If the number to the right of the <u>unit</u> is 5 or more, round up; if 4 or less, round down.

$<u>2</u>.70	$<u>1</u>.10	<u>3</u>.40 m	<u>1</u>.50 m
$3.00	$1.00	3 m	2 m

WHO CARES ABOUT THE CENTS?

Round each amount to the nearest dollar.

$1.35	$4.20	$15.50	$8.55
$4.25	$6.90	$3.75	$1.50
$5.80	$11.35	$9.90	$6.70
$12.55	$17.20	$2.45	$5.15
$10.10	$6.65	$13.40	$19.70

Round each amount to the nearest metre.

1.65 m	4.05 m	6.50 m	5.65 m
3.35 m	6.55 m	1.30 m	2.25 m
2.95 m	5.80 m	8.35 m	2.45 m
7.40 m	9.10 m	7.55 m	3.80 m
4.70 m	1.75 m	9.25 m	7.50 m

Round each amount to the nearest whole unit.

$4.95	20.65 m	2.85 m	$5.10
8.05 m	$9.15	$1.40	19.70 m
$12.40	$6.50	8.50 m	$7.10

Congruency

Figures that are the same size and shape are congruent.
Are these figures congruent?

yes   no   no   yes

Circle the congruent figures.

Identifying patterns

Complete each pattern.

| 88 | 78 | 68 | 58 | 48 | 38 | 28 | 18 |
| 38 | 35 | 32 | 29 | 26 | 23 | 20 | 17 |

Complete each pattern.

41	39	37					
67	61	55					
54	49	44					
77	73	69					
98	90	82					
27	25	23					
85	80	75					
64	56	48					
89	80	71					
50	44	38					
31	28	25					
46	41	36					
92	84	76					
19	17	15					
9	8	7					
59	52	45					
83	73	63					

Odds and evens

Add the even number to the even number.

2 + 4 =   12 + 4 =   2 + 20 =   8 + 18 =

8 + 14 =   10 + 22 =   30 + 40 =   12 + 14 =

8 + 2 =   28 + 4 =   6 + 6 =   2 + 12 =

What do you notice about each answer? _____

Add the odd number to the odd number.

3 + 7 =   1 + 15 =   9 + 9 =   11 + 9 =

3 + 3 =   5 + 7 =   1 + 1 =   19 + 13 =

9 + 13 =   3 + 17 =   5 + 33 =   11 + 3 =

What do you notice about each answer? _____

Add the odd number to the even number.

7 + 6 =   5 + 20 =   13 + 6 =   11 + 12 =

17 + 4 =   9 + 4 =   1 + 10 =   19 + 8 =

1 + 2 =   7 + 10 =   3 + 12 =   9 + 4 =

What do you notice about each answer? _____

Add the even number to the odd number.

10 + 7 =   4 + 1 =   12 + 13 =   28 + 5 =

2 + 3 =   2 + 17 =   20 + 3 =   2 + 11 =

8 + 7 =   6 + 3 =   32 + 7 =   14 + 7 =

What do you notice about each answer? _____

Probability

Look at the crystals in the oval.

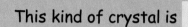

This kind of crystal is   least   likely to be picked from the oval.

This kind of crystal is   most   likely to be picked from the oval.

Look at this table.

TYPES OF JEWELS IN LEX LUTHOR'S SAFE

diamond	ruby	emerald	sapphire	jade
2	9	12	5	1

Which type of jewel is the least likely to be stolen?

Which type of jewel is the most likely to be stolen?

Look at the chart.

PENS IN LOIS'S HANDBAG

color	tally
blue	卌
green	|||
black	卌 ||
red	卌

Which color pen is most likely to be picked?

Which color pen is least likely to be picked?

Which color pen is as likely to be picked as a blue pen?

Place value

WORK IT OUT!

What is the value of each of the numbers in 492?

The value of 4 in 492 is	400	or	four hundred
The value of 9 in 492 is	90	or	ninety
The value of 2 in 492 is	2	or	two

What is the value of 6 in each of these numbers?

26　　　　　　　369　　　　　　　　13,697

961,782　　　　　　6,910　　　　　　8,461　　　　　12,946

Circle each number with a 5 having the value of fifty.

672,459　　　　　896,577　　　　　501,813　　　　　575,555

Circle each number with a 4 having the value of four hundred.

454,689　　　　　330,421　　　　　400,525　　　　　969,410

Write "increases" or "decreases" and by how much.

Change the 3 in 31 to 4. The value of the number _____ by _____

Change the 7 in 87 to 3. The value of the number _____ by _____

Change the 1 in 19 to 4. The value of the number _____ by _____

Change the 2 in 24 to 9. The value of the number _____ by _____

Change the 7 in 372 to 5. The value of the number _____ by _____

Change the 4 in 4,320 to 6. The value of the number _____ by _____

Fractions

Write the answer in the box.

$$\frac{1}{4} + \frac{1}{4}^{+1} = \frac{2}{4}^{\div 2}_{\div 2} = \frac{1}{2} \qquad \frac{1}{2} + \frac{1}{2} = \boxed{1}$$

DON'T WASTE A SECOND!

Write the answer in the box.

$\frac{3}{9} + \frac{3}{9} = \quad =$ $\frac{1}{8} + \frac{5}{8} = \quad =$ $\frac{3}{16} + \frac{5}{16} = \quad =$

$\frac{1}{5} + \frac{2}{5} =$ $\frac{4}{5} + \frac{1}{5} =$ $\frac{4}{8} + \frac{4}{8} =$

$\frac{2}{10} + \frac{3}{10} = \quad =$ $\frac{1}{15} + \frac{3}{15} =$ $\frac{4}{16} + \frac{8}{16} = \quad =$

$\frac{3}{12} + \frac{6}{12} = \quad =$ $\frac{1}{9} + \frac{8}{9} =$ $\frac{2}{9} + \frac{1}{9} = \quad =$

$\frac{2}{6} + \frac{1}{6} = \quad =$ $\frac{1}{15} + \frac{4}{15} = \quad =$ $\frac{1}{9} + \frac{3}{9} =$

Write the answer in the box.

$\frac{2}{6} + \frac{2}{6} = \quad =$ $\frac{1}{7} + \frac{5}{7} =$ $\frac{4}{16} + \frac{8}{16} = \quad =$

$\frac{1}{5} + \frac{3}{5} =$ $\frac{2}{4} + \frac{2}{4} =$ $\frac{2}{3} + \frac{1}{3} =$

$\frac{2}{12} + \frac{4}{12} = \quad =$ $\frac{3}{15} + \frac{5}{15} =$ $\frac{4}{19} + \frac{10}{19} =$

$\frac{1}{10} + \frac{8}{10} =$ $\frac{4}{4} + \frac{4}{4} =$ $\frac{4}{21} + \frac{3}{21} = \quad =$

$\frac{2}{15} + \frac{4}{15} = \quad =$ $\frac{2}{14} + \frac{5}{14} = \quad =$ $\frac{1}{10} + \frac{3}{10} =$

Write the answer in the box.

$2\frac{2}{5} + 1\frac{1}{5} =$ $3\frac{2}{5} + 3\frac{2}{5} =$ $3\frac{1}{5} + 1 =$

$3\frac{3}{5} + 2\frac{2}{5} =$ $1\frac{2}{5} + \frac{1}{5} =$ $4\frac{3}{5} + 1\frac{1}{5} =$

$\frac{3}{5} + \frac{3}{5} =$ $5\frac{1}{5} + 2\frac{2}{5} =$ $1\frac{1}{5} + \frac{4}{5} =$

Part of a whole

Write the fraction that shows the shaded part.

How many parts are shaded? | 3 parts
How many parts in all? | 4 parts

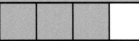

The shaded part is | $\frac{3}{4}$

Circle the fraction that shows the shaded part.

   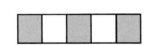

$\frac{1}{3}$ $\frac{1}{2}$ $\frac{1}{4}$ $\frac{3}{4}$ $\frac{2}{3}$ $\frac{3}{5}$ $\frac{7}{9}$ $\frac{7}{8}$ $\frac{4}{5}$

Write the fraction that shows the shaded part.

   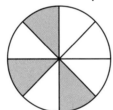   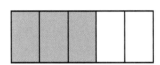

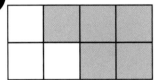   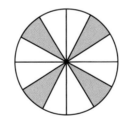   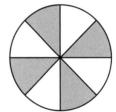

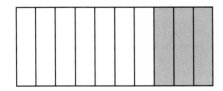   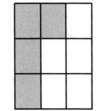   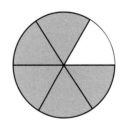

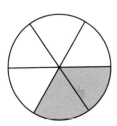   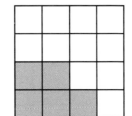   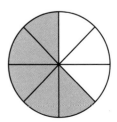

73

Decimals

Write these decimals in order, from least to greatest.

0.3	0.45	0.25	0.1	0.2	0.1	0.2	0.25	0.3	0.45

Write each row of decimals in order, from least to greatest.

0.42	0.48	0.41	0.49	0.45					
1.75	1.45	1.9	1.25	1.65					
4.73	4.83	4.23	4.13	4.33					
6.37	6.77	6.27	6.07	6.97					
8.31	6.31	1.31	9.31	4.31					
4.63	3.91	8.32	7.02	2.9					
3.25	8.2	5.9	1.33	4.32					
1.56	6.22	9.34	8.75	4.65					
4.6	2.38	6.32	8.2	7.32					

Write each row of decimals in order, from least to greatest.

2.67	5.28	1.73	4.92	2.56					
7.27	4.94	2.91	4.38	5.68					
8.27	4.56	8.42	9.28	8.44					
1.37	1.94	2.36	3.16	4.21					
4.36	7.27	5.25	6.28	5.29					
3.34	2.63	4.13	3.21	4.28					
7.35	6.48	7.21	6.22	4.46					
5.45	4.97	5.21	4.89	5.03					

Fractions and decimals

Write each fraction as a decimal.

$3 \frac{1}{2}$ = $2 \frac{1}{10}$ = $5 \frac{4}{10}$ = $4 \frac{1}{2}$ =

$5 \frac{2}{10}$ = $3 \frac{6}{10}$ = $8 \frac{1}{10}$ = $8 \frac{1}{2}$ =

$7 \frac{1}{10}$ = $1 \frac{3}{10}$ = $6 \frac{8}{10}$ = $10 \frac{9}{10}$ =

$9 \frac{6}{10}$ = $4 \frac{5}{10}$ = $9 \frac{1}{2}$ = $10 \frac{1}{2}$ =

Write each decimal as a fraction.

3.4   4.5   1.3   2.2

5.5   2.6   5.2   1.7

7.2   8.5   9.8   10.2

11.5   12.7   18.4   14.5

16.9   11.3   17.6   17.5

Write each fraction as a decimal.

$\frac{1}{2}$ = $\frac{2}{10}$ = $\frac{3}{10}$ =

Write each decimal as a fraction.

0.5   0.1   0.8

Adding

Write the sum between the lines. First, add the ones, then add the tens. Regroup if needed.

```
  1           1           1
 38          55          27
+13         +26         +25
 51          81          52
```

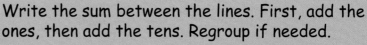

ADD 'EM UP, OR ELSE!

Write the sum between the lines.

56 + 17	18 + 14	28 + 14	47 + 26	58 + 15
16 + 16	47 + 34	56 + 38	34 + 19	57 + 37
29 + 16	19 + 14	33 + 19	48 + 27	33 + 18
27 + 14	19 + 14	23 + 16	57 + 15	68 + 13
26 + 35	34 + 48	13 + 27	18 + 32	25 + 45
17 + 44	33 + 58	29 + 53	32 + 53	23 + 48

Adding

Write the sum between the lines. First, add the ones, then add the tens. Regroup if needed.

$$
\begin{array}{r} \overset{1}{3}5 \\ + 15 \\ \hline 50 \end{array}
\qquad
\begin{array}{r} 56 \\ + 33 \\ \hline 89 \end{array}
\qquad
\begin{array}{r} \overset{1}{5}4 \\ + 18 \\ \hline 72 \end{array}
$$

GET ADDING!

Write the sum between the lines.

17 + 13	23 + 17	45 + 35	52 + 18	38 + 22
25 + 25	47 + 43	32 + 18	40 + 17	32 + 46
46 + 34	74 + 16	42 + 38	67 + 23	37 + 43
54 + 46	35 + 45	47 + 33	83 + 17	31 + 39
76 + 24	67 + 33	73 + 27	55 + 45	74 + 26
73 + 16	48 + 33	49 + 42	28 + 26	65 + 45

Subtracting

Write the difference between the lines. First, subtract the ones, then the tens. Regroup if needed.

```
    45          66          ³¹³43
  - 15        - 23        - 18
    30          43          25
```

YOU SHOULD FIND THESE EASY.

Write the difference between the lines.

```
    45          27          53          85          47
  - 23        - 14        - 20        - 41        - 25
  ▯           ▯           ▯           ▮           ▮


    29          53          82          37          44
  - 16        - 12        - 40        - 26        - 31
  ▯           ▯           ▯           ▮           ▮


    63          74          47          63          76
  - 21        - 32        - 36        - 42        - 35
  ▯           ▯           ▯           ▮           ▮


    85          83          95          67          86
  - 42        - 41        - 35        - 53        - 45
  ▯           ▯           ▯           ▮           ▮


    65          74          86          96          67
  - 35        - 54        - 66        - 86        - 17
  ▯           ▯           ▯           ▮           ▮


    59          48          46          78          67
  - 39        - 27        - 32        - 47        - 56
  ▯           ▯           ▮           ▮           ▮
```

Subtracting

Write the difference between the lines. First, subtract the ones, then the tens. Regroup if needed.

$$\overset{4\ 14}{\cancel{5}\cancel{4}}$$
$$-\ 28$$
$$\overline{26}$$

$$\overset{5\ 18}{\cancel{6}\cancel{8}}$$
$$-\ 39$$
$$\overline{29}$$

$$\overset{6\ 12}{\cancel{7}\cancel{2}}$$
$$-\ 24$$
$$\overline{48}$$

TAKE IT AWAY, LOIS!

Write the difference between the lines.

45	42	50	62	36
- 28	- 17	- 45	- 17	- 18

57	36	64	62	78
- 39	- 27	- 48	- 34	- 69

63	65	90	74	43
- 49	- 48	- 37	- 47	- 29

54	68	50	38	44
- 26	- 39	- 27	- 28	- 36

31	43	70	53	46
- 16	- 28	- 36	- 37	- 28

90	50	54	66	90
- 46	- 26	- 35	- 48	- 44

Real-life problems

Write the sum in the box.
Steel has two suits and makes four spares.
How many suits does he have now?

$2 + 4 = 6$

Write the answer in the box.

Superman has 14 oxygen cartridges but uses 8 in a fight with Parasite. How many oxygen cartridges does Superman have left?

After buying some candies for 50¢, Chris still has 45¢ left. How much did he have to begin with?

Supergirl saves 5 children from a runaway bus. There are 20 children still in the bus. How many children are there altogether?

Harry counts 150 stamps and his father counts 60 more. How many stamps does Harry have altogether?

Tom puts 15 toys in a box that already has 20 toys in it. How many toys are in the box now?

Lorna leaves 40¢ at home and takes 50¢ with her. How much money does Lorna have altogether?

Faruk gives some of his allowance to his brother. He gives his brother 85¢ and has 65¢ left. How much allowance did Faruk have in the first place?

Five letters of the alphabet are vowels. How many letters of the alphabet are not vowels?

MATH IS GETTING TOUGH IN METROPOLIS!

Multiplying

TIMES AND TIMES AGAIN.

Write the product between the lines. Multiply the ones, then multiply the tens and add any extra tens (regroup as needed).

$$\begin{array}{r} \overset{1}{34} \\ \times\ 3 \\ \hline 102 \end{array} \qquad \begin{array}{r} 71 \\ \times\ 6 \\ \hline 426 \end{array} \qquad \begin{array}{r} \overset{1}{26} \\ \times\ 3 \\ \hline 78 \end{array}$$

Write the answers between the lines.

$$\begin{array}{r} 66 \\ \times\ 2 \\ \hline \end{array} \qquad \begin{array}{r} 85 \\ \times\ 2 \\ \hline \end{array} \qquad \begin{array}{r} 72 \\ \times\ 2 \\ \hline \end{array} \qquad \begin{array}{r} 28 \\ \times\ 2 \\ \hline \end{array} \qquad \begin{array}{r} 46 \\ \times\ 2 \\ \hline \end{array}$$

$$\begin{array}{r} 55 \\ \times\ 3 \\ \hline \end{array} \qquad \begin{array}{r} 39 \\ \times\ 3 \\ \hline \end{array} \qquad \begin{array}{r} 53 \\ \times\ 3 \\ \hline \end{array} \qquad \begin{array}{r} 75 \\ \times\ 3 \\ \hline \end{array} \qquad \begin{array}{r} 43 \\ \times\ 3 \\ \hline \end{array}$$

$$\begin{array}{r} 36 \\ \times\ 4 \\ \hline \end{array} \qquad \begin{array}{r} 17 \\ \times\ 4 \\ \hline \end{array} \qquad \begin{array}{r} 75 \\ \times\ 4 \\ \hline \end{array} \qquad \begin{array}{r} 44 \\ \times\ 4 \\ \hline \end{array} \qquad \begin{array}{r} 62 \\ \times\ 4 \\ \hline \end{array}$$

$$\begin{array}{r} 75 \\ \times\ 5 \\ \hline \end{array} \qquad \begin{array}{r} 72 \\ \times\ 5 \\ \hline \end{array} \qquad \begin{array}{r} 94 \\ \times\ 5 \\ \hline \end{array} \qquad \begin{array}{r} 38 \\ \times\ 5 \\ \hline \end{array} \qquad \begin{array}{r} 64 \\ \times\ 5 \\ \hline \end{array}$$

$$\begin{array}{r} 94 \\ \times\ 6 \\ \hline \end{array} \qquad \begin{array}{r} 88 \\ \times\ 6 \\ \hline \end{array} \qquad \begin{array}{r} 72 \\ \times\ 6 \\ \hline \end{array} \qquad \begin{array}{r} 63 \\ \times\ 6 \\ \hline \end{array} \qquad \begin{array}{r} 46 \\ \times\ 6 \\ \hline \end{array}$$

$$\begin{array}{r} 85 \\ \times\ 7 \\ \hline \end{array} \qquad \begin{array}{r} 48 \\ \times\ 7 \\ \hline \end{array} \qquad \begin{array}{r} 93 \\ \times\ 7 \\ \hline \end{array} \qquad \begin{array}{r} 37 \\ \times\ 7 \\ \hline \end{array} \qquad \begin{array}{r} 55 \\ \times\ 7 \\ \hline \end{array}$$

Multiplying

Write the product between the lines.

$$\begin{array}{r} {}^{1}35 \\ \times\ 3 \\ \hline 105 \end{array}$$

$$\begin{array}{r} {}^{3}18 \\ \times\ 4 \\ \hline 72 \end{array}$$

$$\begin{array}{r} {}^{1}62 \\ \times\ 5 \\ \hline 310 \end{array}$$

I HAVE TO DO THESE BEFORE BRAINIAC.

Write the product between the lines.

42	64	53	22	38
× 9	× 9	× 9	× 9	× 9

33	26	84	65	27
× 4	× 4	× 4	× 4	× 4

35	92	52	98	43
× 8	× 8	× 8	× 8	× 8

47	36	23	58	29
× 5	× 5	× 5	× 5	× 5

84	39	96	26	56
× 4	× 5	× 6	× 7	× 8

29	59	39	69	79
× 4	× 5	× 6	× 7	× 8

Dividing

Write the quotient in the box.

$37 \div 6 =$ | 6 r 1 $27 \div 4 =$ | 6 r 3 $74 \div 8 =$ | 9 r 2

$$6\overline{)37}$$
$$\underline{-36}$$
$$1$$

$$4\overline{)27}$$
$$\underline{-24}$$
$$3$$

$$8\overline{)74}$$
$$\underline{-72}$$
$$2$$

Write the quotient between the lines.

$45 \div 6 =$	$35 \div 6 =$	$62 \div 6 =$
$22 \div 6 =$	$43 \div 6 =$	$66 \div 6 =$
$17 \div 6 =$	$25 \div 6 =$	$30 \div 6 =$
$31 \div 6 =$	$33 \div 6 =$	$49 \div 6 =$
$58 \div 7 =$	$15 \div 7 =$	$68 \div 7 =$
$29 \div 7 =$	$61 \div 7 =$	$77 \div 7 =$
$39 \div 7 =$	$35 \div 7 =$	$24 \div 7 =$
$76 \div 7 =$	$82 \div 7 =$	$64 \div 7 =$
$33 \div 8 =$	$57 \div 8 =$	$73 \div 8 =$
$42 \div 8 =$	$21 \div 8 =$	$46 \div 8 =$
$67 \div 8 =$	$38 \div 8 =$	$51 \div 8 =$
$49 \div 8 =$	$13 \div 8 =$	$64 \div 8 =$
$37 \div 9 =$	$59 \div 9 =$	$92 \div 9 =$
$24 \div 9 =$	$73 \div 9 =$	$100 \div 9 =$
$46 \div 9 =$	$35 \div 9 =$	$65 \div 9 =$
$22 \div 9 =$	$81 \div 9 =$	$50 \div 9 =$

Dividing

CLARK CAN'T DO THESE DIVISIONS, SO CAN YOU HELP HIM?

Write the answer in the box above the line.

4 r 3		6 r 2		8 r 1

$8\overline{)35}$
-32
3

$4\overline{)26}$
-24
2

$7\overline{)57}$
-56
1

Write the answer in the box above the line.

$6\overline{)45}$ $6\overline{)27}$ $6\overline{)37}$ $6\overline{)38}$ $6\overline{)41}$

$7\overline{)41}$ $7\overline{)29}$ $7\overline{)68}$ $7\overline{)51}$ $7\overline{)46}$

$8\overline{)52}$ $8\overline{)23}$ $8\overline{)69}$ $8\overline{)42}$ $8\overline{)31}$

$9\overline{)46}$ $9\overline{)21}$ $9\overline{)44}$ $9\overline{)74}$ $9\overline{)38}$

Choosing the operation

Write either x or ÷ in the box.

5 [x] 7 = 35   70 [÷] 7 = 10   6 [x] 7 = 42

MAKE YOUR MIND UP!

Write either x or ÷ in the box.

84 [ ] 7 = 12	8 [ ] 8 = 1	5 [ ] 9 = 45
27 [ ] 9 = 3	8 [ ] 7 = 56	4 [ ] 9 = 36
80 [ ] 10 = 8	70 [ ] 7 = 10	28 [ ] 4 = 7
21 [ ] 7 = 3	16 [ ] 4 = 4	54 [ ] 6 = 9
18 [ ] 3 = 6	64 [ ] 8 = 8	56 [ ] 7 = 8
40 [ ] 8 = 5	6 [ ] 8 = 48	3 [ ] 8 = 24
30 [ ] 5 = 6	63 [ ] 7 = 9	48 [ ] 8 = 6
28 [ ] 7 = 4	8 [ ] 8 = 64	81 [ ] 9 = 9
24 [ ] 8 = 3	4 [ ] 6 = 24	27 [ ] 3 = 9
7 [ ] 9 = 63	48 [ ] 6 = 8	7 [ ] 8 = 56
45 [ ] 9 = 5	36 [ ] 4 = 9	49 [ ] 7 = 7
30 [ ] 6 = 5	5 [ ] 8 = 40	54 [ ] 9 = 6
8 [ ] 6 = 48	9 [ ] 7 = 63	20 [ ] 6 = 120
700 [ ] 7 = 100	8 [ ] 8 = 1	84 [ ] 7 = 12
100 [ ] 5 = 20	400 [ ] 8 = 50	42 [ ] 6 = 7
5 [ ] 5 = 25	100 [ ] 10 = 10	6 [ ] 6 = 1

85

Real-life problems

Write the answer in the box.

A number multiplied by 7 is 56.
What is the number?

`8`

I divide a number by 9 and the result is 6.
What is the number?

`54`

Write the answer in the box.

A number multiplied by 8 is 48.
What is the number?

I divide a number by 4 and
the result is 9. What is the
number?

I divide a number by 7 and the
result is 6. What number did I
begin with?

A number multiplied by itself
gives the answer 16. What is
the number?

I divide a number by 7 and the
result is 7. What number did I
begin with?

A number multiplied by itself
gives the answer 49. What is
the number?

I multiply a number by 7 and
I end up with 63. What number
did I begin with?

Nine times a number is 72.
What is the number?

What do I have to multiply 7
by to get the result 63?

Nine times a number is 63.
What is the number?

When 6 is multiplied by a
number the result is 42. What
number was 6 multiplied by?

A number divided by 7 gives
the answer 10. What was the
starting number?

I multiply a number by 9 and
end up with 45. What number
did I multiply?

I multiply a number by 9 and
the result is 81. What number
did I begin with?

I MUST BREAK
FREE AND STOP
DOOMSDAY!

Real-life problems

A chain is 1.60 m long but Superman breaks 45 cm off. How much of the chain is left?

$$\begin{array}{r} \overset{5\ 10}{1\cancel{6}\cancel{0}} \\ -\ \ 45 \\ \hline 115 \end{array}$$ (1.60 m = 160 cm)

1.15 m

I HAVE ALL OF SUPERMAN'S POWERS!

Solve the problem. Write the answer in the box.

Mario is given 4 cans of juice. Each can contains 425 ml. How much does Mario have altogether?

A tower at Steel's SteelWorks is 145 m tall. Doomsday destroys 68 m of the tower. How much of the tower is left?

Lois's swimming pool is 947 cm deep at one end and 119 cm deep at the other. How much deeper is the deep end of the pool?

Lex Luthor's suits cost $8.30 to be cleaned. He pays with a $10.00 bill. How much change will he receive?

A galaxy has 472 planets. Doomsday destroys half the planets in the galaxy. How many planets are left?

Real-life problems

Superman weighs 40 kg more than Supergirl. Supergirl weighs 59 kg. How much does Superman weigh?

99 kg

$$\begin{array}{r} 59 \\ + \ 40 \\ \hline 99 \end{array}$$

Solve the problem. Write the answer in the box.

Two bags of money weigh a total of 70 kg. One bag weighs 40 kg. How much does the other bag weigh?

Encantadora has 34 lumps of kryptonite in each box. How many lumps will there be in 6 boxes?

Lex Luthor has $290, which is $140 more than his daughter. How much money does his daughter have?

Supergirl has a bottle of lemonade that contains 2 litres. She drinks 425 ml. How much drink is left?

Superman's capes can be measured in millimetres. How long is 1.80 m in mm?

Metropolis has 132 buildings in each precinct. How many buildings are there in 8 precincts?

Problems using time

Write the answer in the box.

What time will it be in 10 minutes?

6.30

TIME TO FLY!

Write the answer in the box.

What time will it be in 15 minutes?

What time will it be in 45 minutes?

What time was it 6 minutes ago?

Write the answer in the box.

What time was it 1 hour ago?

What time will it be in 40 minutes?

What time will it be in half an hour?

Write the answer in the box.

How many hours until 6.30?

What time was it 35 minutes ago?

What time will it be in 50 minutes?

Charts

	Period 1	Period 2	Period 3	Period 4
Monday	Math	Krypton	Spanish	Hypnotism
Tuesday	Math	English	Krypton	Flying practice
Wednesday	Math	Krypton	Laser-beam practice	Laser-beam practice
Thursday	Math	English	Science	Science
Friday	Krypton	Flying practice	Hypnotism	X-ray vision test

A.M   P.M

Write the answer in the box.

What subject does Supergirl have last period on Tuesday?

How many periods of Krypton does Supergirl have?

When does Supergirl have an afternoon of Science?

How many periods of Laser-beam practice does she have?

What subject comes before Spanish?

Which subject is taught third period on Friday?

Which day is the X-ray vision test?

What is the first period on Thursday?

When is Spanish?

What subject is taught second period on Tuesday?

Symmetry

The dotted line is the line of symmetry. Complete each shape.

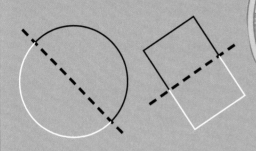

I USE MY X-RAY VISION TO SEE THE SHAPES.

Complete each shape.

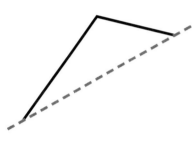

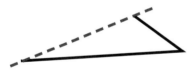

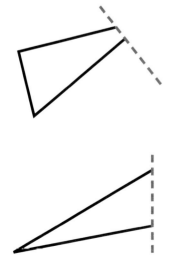

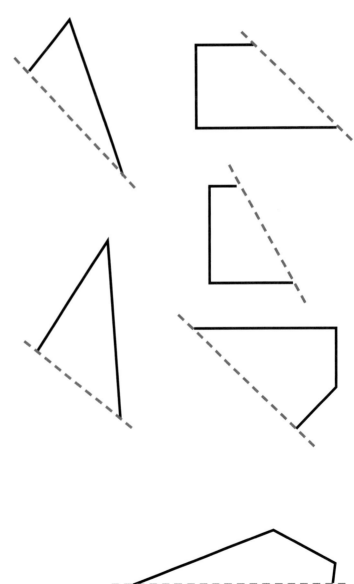

3-dimensional shapes

Draw a small circle around each vertex in this shape.

Draw a small circle around each vertex in this shape.

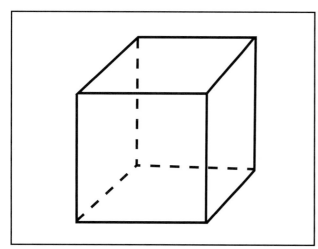

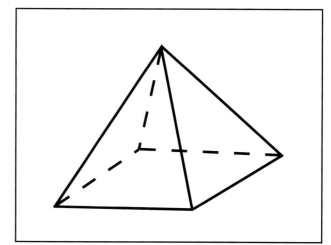

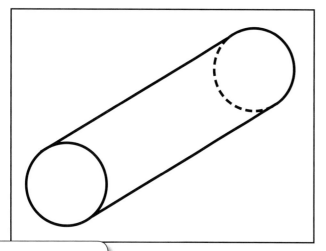

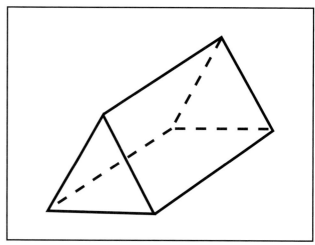

I DON'T LIKE TIGHT CORNERS.

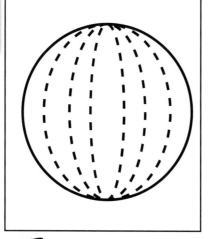

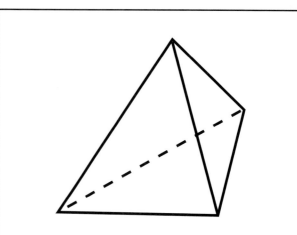

92

Number pairs

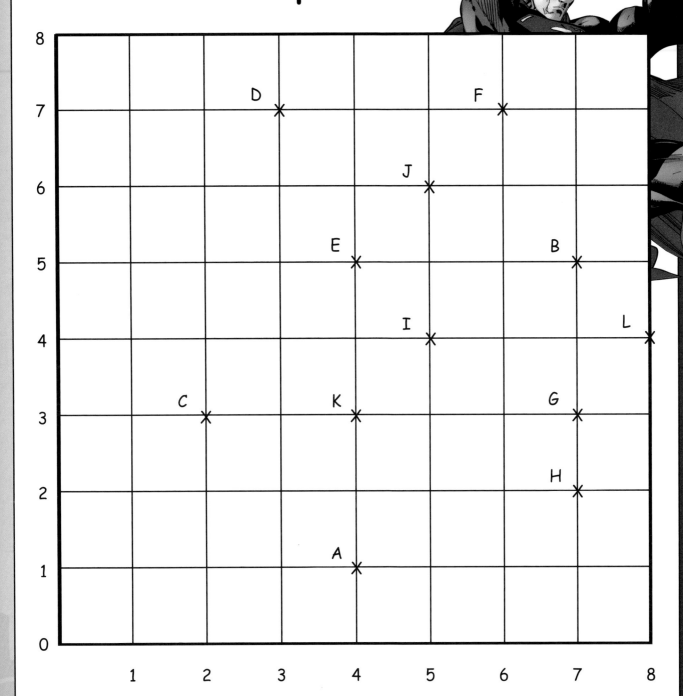

Write the coordinates of the x by each letter.

A =   D =   G =   J =

B =   E =   H =   K =

C =   F =   I =   L =

Adding and subtracting

Add 100 to 286.

386

Add 100 to 3,156.

3,256

Subtract 100 from 7,934.

7,834

Subtract 100 from 1,755.

1,655

Add 100 to each number.

824		318		529		224	
43		974		634		7,325	
3,890		25		827		4,236	

Add 100 to each number.

707		523		76		443	
34		6,021		5,897		2,890	
6,132		9,873		5,499		8,003	

Subtract 100 from each number.

672		189		343		682	
100		5,900		7,273		399	
106		1,378		201		9,546	

Subtract 100 from each number.

1,400		8,610		5,307		9,362	
2,834		1,452		8,445		1,423	
1,300		529		7,982		4,256	

Dividing by 10

I BET SUPERMAN CAN'T DO THESE. CAN YOU?

Divide each number by 10.

90		860		270		70	
200		330		10		300	
540		490		130		660	
60		170		20		110	
680		50		980		730	

Multiply each number by 10.

40		60		900		750	
50		10		560		840	
160		350		670		600	
420		70		20		100	
730		11		310		390	

Divide each number by 10.

700		2,300		4,100		3,650	
6,480		7,080		3,540		2,030	
1,030		9,670		6,320		1,400	
300		900		1,020		3,660	
20		18,000		13,600		17,890	

Length

Who lives farthest from LexCorp?

Lana lives farthest from Lex Corp.

Look at this map.

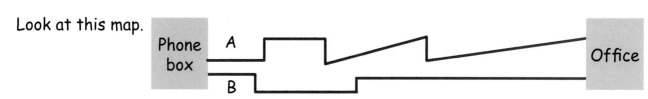

Which route between the newsroom and phone booth is shorter?

Look at this map.

Luthor Street

Clark Lane

City:
Smallville

Lois Road

Kent Avenue

Is the Lois Road to Smallville longer or shorter than Kent Avenue?

Which road to Smallville is longest?

Which road to Smallville is shorter than Kent Avenue?

Look at these pieces of rope.

Supergirl's

Superman's

Lois Lane's

Steel's

Whose rope is longest?

Whose rope is shorter than Steel's rope?

Whose rope is about the same length as Steel's rope?

Identifying patterns

Continue each pattern.

| 11 | 22 | 33 | 44 | 55 | 66 | 77 | 88 |
| 12 | 24 | 36 | 48 | 60 | 72 | 84 | 96 |

Continue each pattern.

8	20	32	44	56			
7	18	29	40	51			
25	36	47	58	69			
3	15	27	39	51			
1	12	23	34	45			
34	46	58	70	82			
5	16	27	38	49			
11	23	35	47	59			

Continue each pattern.

96	84	72	60	48			
99	88	77	66	55			
100	88	76	64	52			
78	67	56	45	34			
9	20	31	42	53			
7	19	31	43	55			
95	84	73	62	51			
10	22	34	46	58			

Properties of polygons

LET'S GET INTO SHAPE!

Circle the polygon that has 4 sides of the same length.

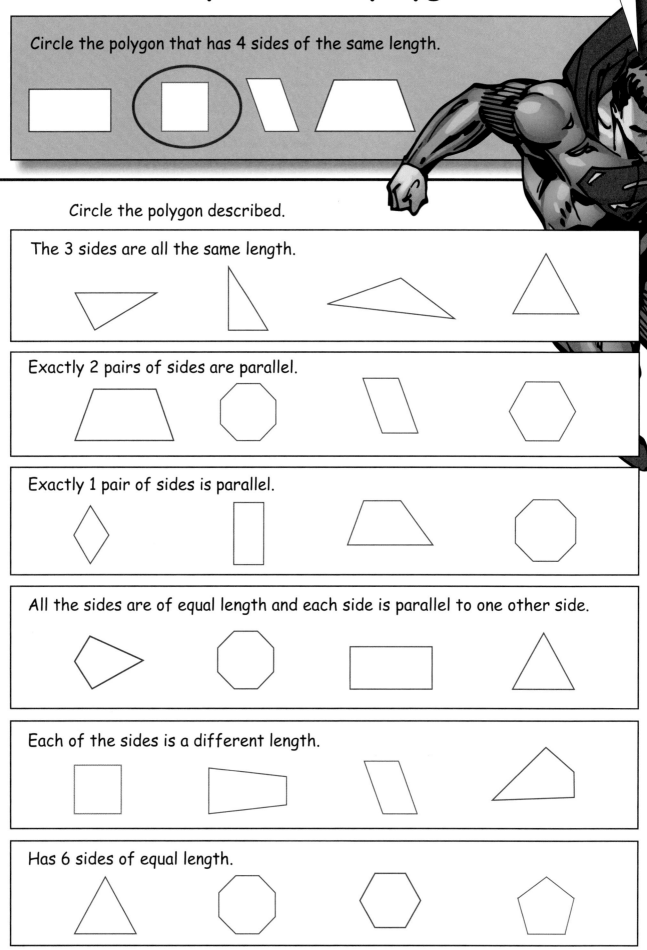

Circle the polygon described.

The 3 sides are all the same length.

Exactly 2 pairs of sides are parallel.

Exactly 1 pair of sides is parallel.

All the sides are of equal length and each side is parallel to one other side.

Each of the sides is a different length.

Has 6 sides of equal length.

Square numbers

This square has two rows and two columns. It is 2 x 2. How many dots are there?

4

Draw a picture like the one above to show each of these numbers.

3 x 3

How many dots are there?

4 x 4

How many dots are there?

5 x 5

How many dots are there?

6 x 6

How many dots are there?

7 x 7

How many dots are there?

8 x 8

How many dots are there?

9 x 9

How many dots are there?

10 x 10

How many dots are there?

Fractions and decimals

Write the fraction as a decimal.	Write the decimal as a fraction.
$\frac{1}{2}$ 0.5 $\frac{1}{10}$ 0.1	$0.25 = \frac{25}{100} = \frac{1}{4}$

WHAT FRACTION SHALL I BREAK DOOMSDAY INTO? YOU DECIDE!

Write each fraction as a decimal.

$\frac{1}{10}$ $\frac{1}{2}$ $\frac{7}{10}$ $\frac{2}{10}$

$\frac{8}{10}$ $\frac{3}{10}$ $\frac{9}{10}$ $\frac{3}{10}$

$\frac{6}{10}$ $\frac{4}{10}$ $\frac{1}{10}$ $\frac{5}{10}$

$\frac{2}{10}$ $\frac{5}{10}$ $\frac{6}{10}$ $\frac{4}{10}$

Write each decimal as a fraction.

0.2   0.7   0.3   0.4

0.1   0.6   0.2   0.75

0.5   0.4   0.5   0.9

0.25   0.8   0.6   0.8

Write the answer in the box.

Which of the two fractions above are the same as 0.5?

Which of the two fractions above are the same as 0.8?

Which of the two fractions above are the same as 0.2?

Which of the two fractions above are the same as 0.4?

Which of the two fractions above are the same as 0.6?

Fractions of shapes

Shade $\frac{3}{5}$ of each shape

 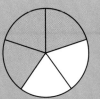

Shade $\frac{4}{5}$ of each shape

 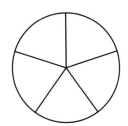 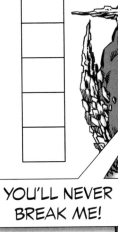

YOU'LL NEVER BREAK ME!

Shade $\frac{8}{10}$ of each shape

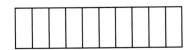 

Shade the fraction of each shape.

$\frac{4}{10}$ $\frac{8}{10}$ $\frac{3}{10}$

   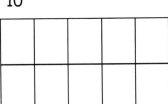

$\frac{7}{10}$ $\frac{6}{10}$ $\frac{9}{10}$

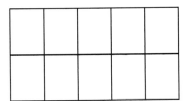   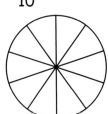   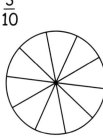

Comparing fractions

In each pair, circle the fraction with the greater value.

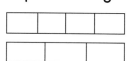 (①/③) or 1/5 ☐☐☐☐☐

In each pair, circle the fraction with the greater value.

$\frac{1}{4}$ or $\frac{1}{3}$ $\frac{1}{5}$ or $\frac{1}{7}$ $\frac{1}{6}$ or $\frac{1}{3}$ $\frac{1}{4}$ or $\frac{1}{5}$

$\frac{1}{2}$ or $\frac{1}{4}$ $\frac{1}{12}$ or $\frac{1}{4}$ $\frac{1}{4}$ or $\frac{1}{9}$ $\frac{1}{10}$ or $\frac{1}{100}$

$\frac{1}{3}$ or $\frac{2}{3}$ $\frac{3}{5}$ or $\frac{4}{5}$ $\frac{2}{5}$ or $\frac{1}{5}$ $\frac{1}{4}$ or $\frac{3}{4}$

$\frac{5}{8}$ or $\frac{3}{8}$ $\frac{1}{12}$ or $\frac{3}{12}$ $\frac{5}{8}$ or $\frac{3}{8}$ $\frac{1}{6}$ or $\frac{5}{6}$

In each pair, circle the fraction with the greater value.

$1\frac{2}{3}$ or $1\frac{1}{3}$ $1\frac{1}{4}$ or $1\frac{1}{2}$ $2\frac{2}{5}$ or $1\frac{3}{5}$ $2\frac{3}{4}$ or $2\frac{1}{4}$

$3\frac{1}{2}$ or $4\frac{1}{4}$ $1\frac{3}{4}$ or $1\frac{1}{2}$ $5\frac{2}{3}$ or $4\frac{2}{3}$ $6\frac{5}{8}$ or $6\frac{3}{8}$

$\frac{3}{4}$ or $\frac{1}{3}$ $\frac{3}{5}$ or $\frac{2}{3}$ $\frac{5}{6}$ or $\frac{3}{4}$

 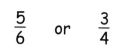

$3\frac{1}{2}$ or $3\frac{2}{3}$ $4\frac{3}{5}$ or $4\frac{5}{6}$

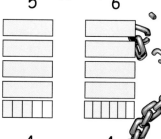 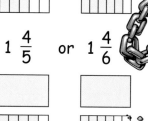

$2\frac{6}{10}$ or $2\frac{4}{5}$ $1\frac{4}{5}$ or $1\frac{4}{6}$

 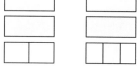  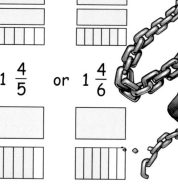

LITTLE PIECES!

Rounding decimals

ROUND EM UP!

Write each amount to the nearest dollar.

$1.76	$3.56	$1.23	$2.43
$2.00	$4.00	$1.00	$2.00

Write each amount to the nearest dollar.

$2.86	$3.29		$6.82		$7.12	
$8.63	$4.96		$8.32		$2.78	
$4.33	$8.70		$6.65		$5.30	
$7.02	$6.74		$7.89		$12.89	
$11.64	$10.64		$15.67		$21.37	

Write each amount to the nearest metre.

1.65 m	4.42 m		6.80 m		4.84 m	
7.5 m	3.18 m		7.92 m		9.63 m	
5.42 m	12.82 m		18.09 m		16.45 m	
10.53 m	20.65 m		17.45 m		14.95 m	
12.46 m	19.05 m		15.51 m		27.47 m	

Write each amount to the nearest dollar or metre.

6.34 m	$3.50		$5.01		6.50 m	
12.50 m	18.99 m		$12.50		23.50 m	
$61.67	$45.52		50.50 m		67.50 m	
$15.11	$21.56		$98.59		$14.99	
$91.50	$78.03		$63.56		$95.50	

Adding

Write the sum between the lines.

$$\begin{array}{r} 77 \\ + 22 \\ \hline 99 \end{array} \qquad \begin{array}{r} {}^{1} \\ 39 \\ + 34 \\ \hline 73 \end{array} \qquad \begin{array}{r} {}^{1} \\ 46 \\ + 36 \\ \hline 82 \end{array}$$

Write the sum between the lines.

47 + 13	28 + 13	56 + 14	78 + 16	45 + 13
54 + 19	47 + 16	84 + 13	54 + 17	36 + 25
45 + 27	70 + 14	64 + 29	28 + 14	45 + 35
14 + 54	18 + 44	14 + 56	17 + 54	18 + 43
82 + 9	46 + 27	74 + 18	45 + 34	26 + 36
45 + 35	43 + 28	57 + 44	59 + 37	57 + 36
32 + 45	28 + 46	34 + 19	71 + 19	39 + 38

104

Adding

Write the sum between the lines.

¹
45 cm
+ 35 cm
80 cm

¹
34 cm
+ 28 cm
62 cm

¹
35 cm
+ 48 cm
83 cm

Write the sum between the lines.

28 cm
+ 36 cm

56 cm
+ 36 cm

68 cm
+ 45 cm

49 cm
+ 27 cm

37 cm
+ 46 cm

38 m
+ 44 m

55 m
+ 37 m

29 m
+ 34 m

56 m
+ 35 m

47 m
+ 45 m

36 kg
+ 17 kg

47 kg
+ 27 kg

43 kg
+ 18 kg

52 kg
+ 17 kg

65 kg
+ 27 kg

43 L
+ 29 L

66 L
+ 27 L

44 L
+ 18 L

48 L
+ 24 L

57 L
+ 42 L

Write the sum between the lines.

$33.00
+ $19.00

$46.00
$13.00

$75.00
+ $26.00

$37.00
+ $15.00

Adding

Write the sum between the lines.

1	2	1
23	29	56
17	38	19
+ 16	+ 17	+ 24
56	**84**	**99**

Write the sum between the lines.

19	12	17
10	14	10
+ 11	+ 12	+ 12

THIS ADDS UP
TO BIG TROUBLE!

19	12	17	19	16
32	25	26	13	21
+ 12	+ 33	+ 13	+ 14	+ 32

32	45	60	50	30
20	26	14	21	42
+ 26	+ 25	+ 8	+ 31	+ 25

65	55	45	35	25
15	35	5	25	15
+ 5	+ 5	+ 5	+ 10	+ 5

62	56	45	34	23
12	16	32	16	45
+ 5	+ 7	+ 13	+ 9	+ 32

Subtracting

Write the difference between the lines.

```
          2 12        5 18
   68      3̶2̶         6̶8̶
 - 15    - 26       - 29
 ┌────┐  ┌────┐     ┌────┐
 │ 53 │  │  6 │     │ 39 │
 └────┘  └────┘     └────┘
```

Write the difference between the lines.

```
   90        50        70        40
 - 27      - 18      - 23      - 19
 _____


   71        64        85        62
 - 36      - 45      - 37      - 15
 _____


   85        97        75        65        45
 - 48      - 49      - 65      - 34      - 17
 _____


   70        63        73        53        47
 - 26      -  7      - 56      - 26      - 43
 _____


   73        53        61        53        61
 - 44      - 23      - 19      - 16      - 14
 _____


   64        81        74        82        73
 - 47      - 39      - 47      - 38      - 27
 _____
```

107

Subtracting

KEEP ON TAKING AWAY.

| 85 cm | 74 cm | 73 cm | 60 cm | 45 cm |
| - 47 cm | - 39 cm | - 48 cm | - 47 cm | - 26 cm |

| 40 cm | 74 cm | 82 cm | 63 cm | 45 cm |
| - 17 cm | - 38 cm | - 29 cm | - 44 cm | - 23 cm |

| 43 cm | 83 cm | 62 cm | 81 cm | 61 cm |
| - 17 cm | - 36 cm | - 27 cm | - 36 cm | - 27 cm |

Write the answer between the lines.

| 90 m | 84 m | 75 m | 37 m | 50 m |
| - 37 m | + 29 m | - 39 m | - 18 m | - 28 m |

Write the answer between the lines.

| 56 kg | 79 kg | 64 kg | 47 kg | 68 kg |
| - 45 kg | + 27 kg | - 27 kg | - 38 kg | - 39 kg |

Real-life problems

Superman has to fly 81 km. He's traveled 49 km. How many more kilometres has he left to go?

$$\begin{array}{r} 7\ 11 \\ \cancel{81} \\ -\ 49 \\ \hline 32 \end{array}$$

32 km

Solve the problem and then write the answer in the box.

Steel has 47 hammers. He makes another 24 before one battle but then loses 18 in a second battle. How many hammers does Steel have now?

Lois has 70 pens and gives 26 of them to Clark. She buys 12 new pens to replace the ones she has given away. How many pens does Lois have now?

Clark Kent empties his trouser pockets and finds 26¢ in one pocket, 13¢ in another pocket, and 37¢ in another one. How much money has Clark found altogether?

Supergirl has 64 french fries with her burger. She eats 16 fries and gives 6 to Superboy. How many fries does Supergirl have left?

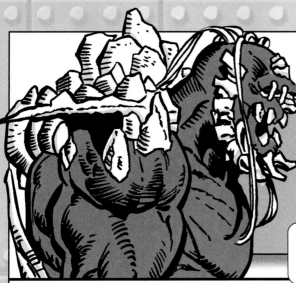

Multiplying

Write the answers between the lines.

$$\begin{array}{r} {}^{4} \\ 29 \\ \times\ 5 \\ \hline 145 \end{array}$$
$$\begin{array}{r} 51 \\ \times\ 4 \\ \hline 204 \end{array}$$
$$\begin{array}{r} {}^{1} \\ 36 \\ \times\ 3 \\ \hline 108 \end{array}$$

Write the answers between the lines.

78 × 2	57 × 2	94 × 2	85 × 2	64 × 2
94 × 3	32 × 3	58 × 3	41 × 3	19 × 3
74 × 4	18 × 4	67 × 4	43 × 4	26 × 4
33 × 5	49 × 5	67 × 5	28 × 5	63 × 5
15 × 6	53 × 6	64 × 6	85 × 6	72 × 6
47 × 8	84 × 8	51 × 8	85 × 8	37 × 8

Multiplying

Write the answers between the lines.

¹
23
× 5
115

²
66
× 4
264

⁴
38
× 5
190

²
97
× 3
291

Write the answers between the lines.

37
× 4

47
× 5

87
× 6

17
× 7

97
× 8

43
× 7

50
× 7

37
× 7

29
× 7

16
× 7

61
× 9

14
× 9

36
× 9

58
× 9

27
× 9

45
× 10

67
× 10

12
× 10

31
× 10

98
× 10

58
× 6

38
× 7

78
× 8

28
× 9

18
× 10

69
× 9

89
× 8

59
× 7

29
× 6

49
× 5

Dividing

I'LL SOON DIVIDE THESE UP!

Write the answer in the box.

$25 \div 3 =$ $20 \div 3 =$ $32 \div 3 =$

$13 \div 3 =$ $35 \div 4 =$ $13 \div 4 =$

$47 \div 4 =$ $4 \div 4 =$ $37 \div 5 =$

$12 \div 5 =$ $15 \div 5 =$ $24 \div 5 =$

$43 \div 6 =$ $6 \div 5 =$ $49 \div 5 =$

Write the answer in the box.

$$8\overline{)32}$$ $$8\overline{)50}$$ $$8\overline{)10}$$ $$8\overline{)63}$$ $$8\overline{)27}$$

$$3\overline{)30}$$ $$3\overline{)14}$$ $$3\overline{)25}$$ $$2\overline{)5}$$ $$2\overline{)18}$$

Write the answer in the box.

$45 \div 8 =$ $73 \div 8 =$ $56 \div 8 =$

$73 \div 9 =$ $41 \div 9 =$ $50 \div 9 =$

$54 \div 10 =$ $89 \div 10 =$ $42 \div 10 =$

Dividing

Write the answer in the box.

$41 \div 4 =$ ☐ 10 r 1

$$4\overline{)41}$$
$$40$$
$$1$$

☐ 3 r 1

$$6\overline{)19}$$
$$18$$
$$1$$

☐ 3 r 4

$$9\overline{)31}$$
$$27$$
$$4$$

Write the answer in the box.

$47 \div 9 =$

$78 \div 8 =$

$53 \div 7 =$

$18 \div 4 =$

$36 \div 8 =$

$28 \div 7 =$

$32 \div 3 =$

$67 \div 9 =$

$25 \div 4 =$

$42 \div 7 =$

$42 \div 9 =$

$12 \div 9 =$

$36 \div 4 =$

$34 \div 10 =$

$56 \div 11 =$

Write the answer in the box.

$$7\overline{)45}$$ $$8\overline{)56}$$ $$9\overline{)43}$$ $$9\overline{)30}$$ $$9\overline{)35}$$

$$9\overline{)53}$$ $$9\overline{)76}$$ $$9\overline{)54}$$ $$8\overline{)43}$$ $$7\overline{)27}$$

Write the answer in the box.

$8 \div 6 =$

$13 \div 10 =$

$70 \div 10 =$

$12 \div 10 =$

$17 \div 7 =$

$70 \div 7 =$

$11 \div 9 =$

$23 \div 8 =$

$54 \div 6 =$

Choosing the operation

Write x or ÷ in the box to make the number sentence true.

6 $\times$ 7 = 42   24 ÷ 6 = 4   10 ÷ 2 = 5

Write either x or ÷ in the box to make the number sentence true.

7 ☐ 5 = 35	35 ☐ 5 = 7	35 ☐ 7 = 5
5 ☐ 7 = 35	9 ☐ 6 = 54	54 ☐ 6 = 9
54 ☐ 9 = 6	6 ☐ 9 = 54	8 ☐ 4 = 32
32 ☐ 4 = 8	32 ☐ 8 = 4	4 ☐ 8 = 32
9 ☐ 4 = 36	4 ☐ 9 = 36	36 ☐ 9 = 4
36 ☐ 9 = 4	80 ☐ 10 = 8	8 ☐ 10 = 80
9 ☐ 7 = 63	81 ☐ 9 = 9	9 ☐ 9 = 81
8 ☐ 8 = 64	64 ☐ 8 = 8	25 ☐ 5 = 5
5 ☐ 5 = 25	16 ☐ 4 = 4	4 ☐ 4 = 16
7 ☐ 7 = 49	49 ☐ 7 = 7	9 ☐ 3 = 3
3 ☐ 3 = 9	100 ☐ 10 = 10	10 ☐ 10 = 100
50 ☐ 10 = 5	5 ☐ 8 = 40	40 ☐ 4 = 10
20 ☐ 5 = 4	2 ☐ 10 = 20	36 ☐ 6 = 6
3 ☐ 7 = 21	21 ☐ 7 = 3	7 ☐ 4 = 28
10 ☐ 14 = 140	140 ☐ 2 = 70	70 ☐ 10 = 7
140 ☐ 2 = 70	140 ☐ 10 = 14	72 ☐ 8 = 9
9 ☐ 2 = 18	7 ☐ 12 = 84	50 ☐ 5 = 10
20 ☐ 4 = 5	8 ☐ 3 = 24	42 ☐ 6 = 7

Real-life problems

A chain is 1.60 m long but
Superman breaks 45 cm off.
How much of the chain is left?

$$\begin{array}{r} 510 \\ 1\cancel{6}\cancel{0} \\ -\ \ 45 \\ \hline 115 \end{array}$$

115 cm

Write the answer in the box.

Boss Moxie shares 62 stolen
jewels equally among 5 henchmen
and gives the rest to Lex Luthor.
How many jewels does Luthor get?

Supergirl catches a gang of
8 crooks. Each crook has robbed
3 banks. How many banks have
been robbed in all?

Wendy has 56 building blocks and
puts them in stacks of 11. How
many stacks of of 11 can
Wendy make?

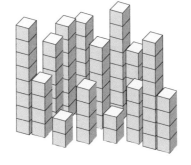

Ashley has seven dimes, four
nickels, and four pennies. How
much does he have altogether?

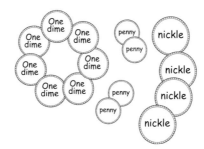

Perimeter

Write the perimeter in the box. To find the perimeter, add up all the sides.

2 cm

7 cm

7 cm
2 cm
7 cm
+ 2 cm
18 cm

WHERE'S SUPERGIRL WHEN I NEED HER?

Write the perimeter of each shape in the answer box. Label your answer with the correct units.

5 cm

1 cm

3 cm

2 cm

5 cm

3 cm

5 cm

5 cm

2 cm

8 cm

6 cm

4 cm

3 cm

7 cm

10 cm

10 cm

12 cm

5 cm

20 cm

4 cm

Area

Write the area of the shape in the box. To find the area, multiply the length by the width.

1 cm

7 cm

$1 \times 7 = 7$

7 cm²

Write the area of each shape in the answer box. Label your answer with the units.

Area

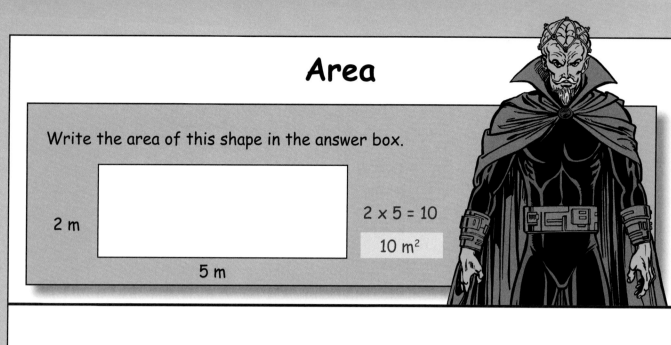

Write the area of this shape in the answer box.

2 m

5 m

2 x 5 = 10

10 m²

7 m

3 m

8 m

2 m

1 m

5 m

6 m

5 m

7 m

6 m

9 m

10 m

20 m

10 m

25 m

4 m

118

Problems using time

Write the answer in the box.

How many minutes until 11 o'clock?

25 minutes

TIME TO GET GOING!

Write the answer in the box.

What time will it be in 20 minutes?

What time was it half an hour ago?

How many minutes until 9.45?

The clock is 10 minutes fast.
What is the real time?

Write the answer in the box.

What time will it be in half an hour?

How many minutes until 4 o'clock?

How long until a quarter to 4?

How many minutes since 2 o'clock?

Write the answer in the box.

How many minutes since 12.40?

How many minutes until 2 o'clock?

What time was it one hour ago?

How many hours until 4.15?

Reading timetables

	Metropolis	Smallville	Coast City	Krypton
Superman	8:00	8:02	8:06	8:25
Kryptonian skyship	8:10	8:23	No stop	8:53
Warsuit	8:30	9:05	10:20	No stop
Phantom zone portal	8:00	No stop	No stop	8:03

The timetable shows the time it takes different things to travel between Metropolis and Krypton.

Write the answer in the box.

How long does Superman take between Metropolis and Krypton?

When does the Warsuit arrive at Smallville?

Where does the Kryptonian skyship not stop?

Where is Superman at 8:02?

Does the Warsuit stop at Krypton?

How long does it take to travel to Krypton using the Phantom Zone portal?

How long does it take the skyship to travel from Smallville to Krypton?

How long does the Warsuit take between Metropolis and Coast City?

Which vehicle arrives at Krypton at 8:53?

Where is Superman at 8:25?

120

Averages

| 4 | 2 | 2 | 2 | 3 | 6 | 2 |

The average is   3

I'M NOT AVERAGE
AT ANYTHING.

Write the average of each row in the box.

2	3	7	4	2	7	2	5	
7	4	5	4	8	5	3	4	
5	3	5	3	5	2	4	5	
7	5	9	7	2	4	8	6	
4	3	4	3	4	3	4	7	
1	4	2	7	3	8	2	5	
3	2	1	2	2	3	2	1	
8	3	6	8	3	2	8	2	

Write the average of each row in the box.

6	6	9	3	6	8	4	
3	1	9	6	2	9	5	
6	5	1	6	8	3	6	
4	9	5	7	6	8	3	
4	6	2	4	3	8	1	
9	7	4	7	8	5	9	
2	2	1	3	2	3	1	
6	4	5	4	7	3	6	

Estimating

Superman flies between 10 and 16 kilometres every minute. If Superman flew for 10 minutes, about how many kilometres would he have traveled? Estimate to find the answer. You will need to figure out Superman's average speed.

I MUST GET TO THE FORTRESS AS FAST AS I CAN.

Superman flew about | 130 kilometres |

Estimate to find the answer.

Superman prevents 5 disasters a day. He saves between 30 and 50 people each time. About how many people does Superman rescue in a day?

About

Boss Moxie's gang steals between $30 and $70 during each robbery. If the gang makes 9 robberies, about how much will they steal?

About

Rocks weigh between 2 and 4 kilograms. If Superman moves 300 rocks, about how heavy will the rocks be altogether?

About

Supergirl's capes are between 100 and 160 cm long. If she has 12 capes, how long will they be altogether?

About

Lois Lane writes between 10 and 20 news stories a week. About how many stories does she write in ten weeks?

About

Calculating change

Circle the correct change.

Supergirl bought a ball costing 45 cents.

How much change did she get?

She paid one dollar

 quarter quarter one dime one dime   (quarter quarter five cents)   quarter quarter quarter   quarter one dime

---

Circle the correct change.

Menu	
Banana	25¢
Pear	75¢
Apple	60¢

> I'M USED TO QUICK CHANGES. HOW ABOUT YOU?

Superman bought an apple. He paid one dollar

How much change did he get?

 one dime one dime one dime    one dime one dime one dime one dime   quarter quarter one dime one dime

---

Supergirl bought a banana. She paid one dollar

How much change did she get?

 quarter quarter quarter one dime   quarter quarter five cents one dime one dime

Lois Lane bought a pear. She paid one dollar

How much change did she get?

 quarter quarter quarter five cents   quarter quarter quarter   quarter

Counting money

Count the coins. Write the total amount.

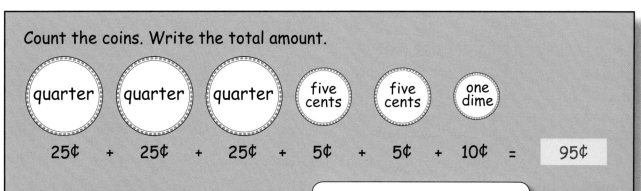

quarter	quarter	quarter	five cents	five cents	one dime		
25¢ +	25¢ +	25¢ +	5¢ +	5¢ +	10¢ =		95¢

BUT DON'T TAKE ANY CASH! I'M WATCHING YOU!

Count the coins. Write the total amount.

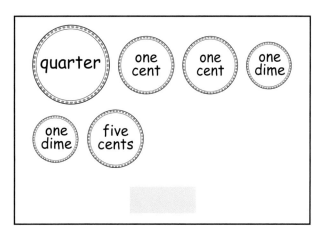

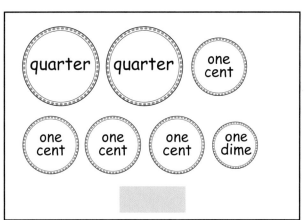

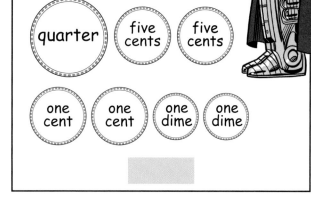

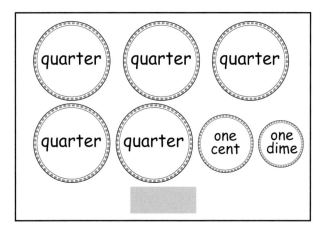

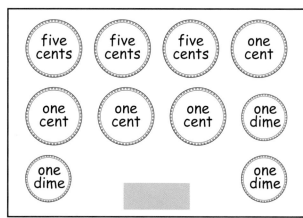

124

Number pairs

Look at the grid and then answer the questions below.

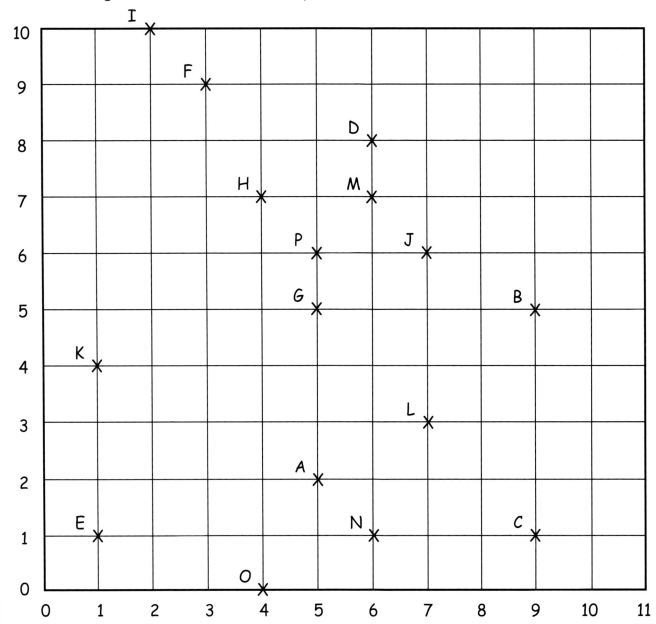

Give the coordinates of each letter.

A =   E =   I =   M =

B =   F =   J =   N =

C =   G =   K =   O =

D =   H =   L =   P =

Multiply or divide?

Write x or ÷ in the box.

6 ☒ 5 = 30   16 ☒ 4 = 4   6 ☒ 10 = 60

Write x or ÷ in the box.

8		5	= 40	5		2	= 10	10		5	= 2

8 ☐ 5 = 40   5 ☐ 2 = 10   10 ☐ 5 = 2

25 ☐ 5 = 5   35 ☐ 5 = 7   3 ☐ 8 = 24

18 ☐ 2 = 9   10 ☐ 10 = 100   6 ☐ 10 = 60

40 ☐ 10 = 4   36 ☐ 6 = 6   5 ☐ 12 = 60

6 ☐ 7 = 42   3 ☐ 12 = 36   90 ☐ 9 = 10

80 ☐ 8 = 10   14 ☐ 7 = 2   18 ☐ 6 = 3

Write the answer in the box.

A number divided by 3 is 10. What is the number?

I multiply a number by 6 and the answer is 30. What is the number?

A number multiplied by 10 gives the answer 200. What is the number?

I divide a number by 8 and the answer is 5. What is the number?

A number divided by 7 is 5. What is the number?

I multiply a number by 2 and the answer is 18. What is the number?

A number multiplied by 5 is 45. What is the number?

I divide a number by 2 and the answer is 1. What is the number?

Write x or ÷ in the box.

7 ☐ 10 = 70   7 ☐ 7 = 49   10 ☐ 10 = 1

5 ☐ 5 = 1   9 ☐ 3 = 27   50 ☐ 5 = 10

15 ☐ 5 = 3   20 ☐ 5 = 100   3 ☐ 3 = 9

20 ☐ 5 = 4   4 ☐ 2 = 8   50 ☐ 5 = 10

Lines of symmetry

Draw the line of symmetry on each shape.

YOU'VE GOT TO DRAW
THE LINE SOMEWHERE!

Draw the line of symmetry on each shape.

A   B   C

D   E   I

K   M   T

Half of each shape is drawn along with the line of symmetry. Draw the other half.

127

Counting by 3s, 4s, and 5s

Find the pattern. Continue each row.

Count by 3s.	9	12	15	18	21	24	27
Count by 4s.	8	12	16	20	24	28	32
Count by 5s.	55	50	45	40	35	30	25

DARKSEID'S DAYS ARE NUMBERED!

Write the answer in each box.

0	4	8					
10	15	20					
27	30	33					
32	36	40					
105	110	115					
45	48	51					
6	10	14					
28	24	20					
38	43	48					
83	80	77					
55	51	47					
85	80	75					50
49	46	43					
73	69	65					45
39	34						4

Multiples

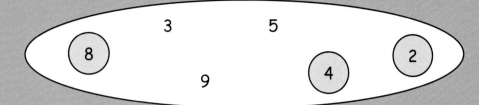

Circle the numbers that are in the 2 times table.

3   5
8   4   2
9

Circle the numbers that are in the 2 times table.

16   27   13
19   12
22   20
21

Circle the numbers that are in the 2 times table.

36   70   25
57   18
44   57
73

Circle the numbers that are in the 5 times table.

45   25   51
20   11
34   10
54

Circle the numbers that are in the 5 times table.

7   80   56
53   81
5   65   50

Circle the numbers that are in the 10 times table.

20   24   1
40   44
58   60
15

Circle the numbers that are in the 10 times table.

327   605   275
485   260
110   99   70

Comparing and ordering

Write these numbers in order, starting with the smallest.

| 482 | 597 | 632 | 382 | 382 | 482 | 597 | 632 |

KEEP THEM IN ORDER!

Write these numbers in order, starting with the smallest.

291	103	775	453
536	237	439	333
638	950	475	969
195	483	520	681
473	374	937	793
406	560	460	650
738	837	378	783
473	374	734	347
206	620	602	260
634	364	436	463
47	740	74	704
401	140	41	104
290	92	209	29
803	380	83	38
504	450	54	45

Rounding

What is 428 rounded to the nearest 100?

400   420   440   460   480   500

428

400

LET'S TIDY UP.

What is each number rounded to the nearest 100?

569		342		142		439	
371		873		934		555	
812		240		854		444	
548		639		299		146	
161		427		307		732	

What is 250 rounded to the nearest 100?

200 210 220 230 240 250 260 270 280 290 300 310

250

300

What is each number rounded to the nearest 100?

350		850		45		827	
71		405		87		450	
655		540		280		208	
750		250		90		59	
550		105		855		120	

Fractions

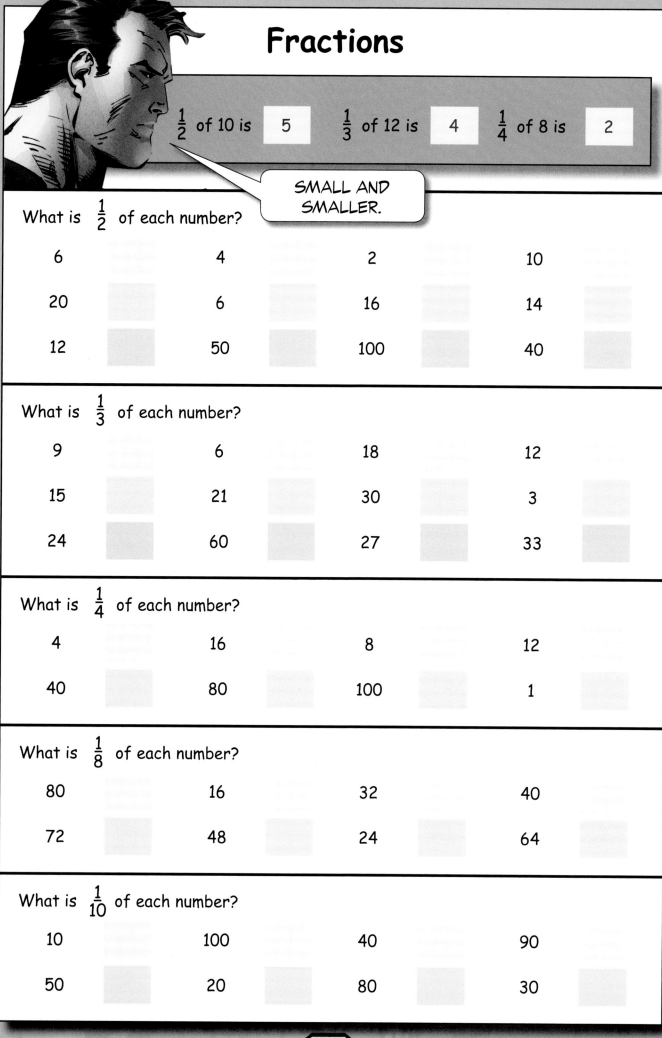

$\frac{1}{2}$ of 10 is 5 $\frac{1}{3}$ of 12 is 4 $\frac{1}{4}$ of 8 is 2

SMALL AND SMALLER.

What is $\frac{1}{2}$ of each number?

6		4		2		10	
20		6		16		14	
12		50		100		40	

What is $\frac{1}{3}$ of each number?

9		6		18		12	
15		21		30		3	
24		60		27		33	

What is $\frac{1}{4}$ of each number?

| 4 | | 16 | | 8 | | 12 | |
| 40 | | 80 | | 100 | | 1 | |

What is $\frac{1}{8}$ of each number?

| 80 | | 16 | | 32 | | 40 | |
| 72 | | 48 | | 24 | | 64 | |

What is $\frac{1}{10}$ of each number?

| 10 | | 100 | | 40 | | 90 | |
| 50 | | 20 | | 80 | | 30 | |

132

Multiplying

Write the answer in the box.

6 x 3 = 18   8 x 5 = 40   7 x 10 = 70

I'M GONNA TURN THE TABLES ON MY ENEMIES!

Write the answer in the box.

6 x 6 =   2 x 3 =   6 x 4 =   4 x 3 =

5 x 8 =   7 x 3 =   6 x 9 =   10 x 4 =

3 x 2 =   9 x 4 =   7 x 5 =   5 x 4 =

0 x 8 =   5 x 3 =   4 x 4 =   0 x 7 =

9 x 3 =   10 x 7 =   3 x 3 =   9 x 5 =

Write the answer in the box.

Four times a number is 12. What is the number?

A child draws 8 squares. How many sides have been drawn?

Lois Lane works for 5 days every week. How many days does she work in 9 weeks?

A girl is given 3 stickers for every point she gains in a spelling test. How many stickers will she receive if she gets 10 points?

A box contains 4 pieces of kryptonite. Lex Luthor has 7 of these boxes. How many pieces of kryptonite does Luthor have?

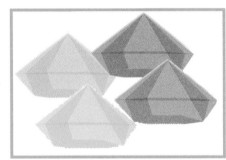

Mari is given eight 5¢ coins. How much money is she given?

Five times a number is 30. What is the number?

The *Daily Planet* has 20 pages. Each page has 3 stories on it. How many stories does the *Daily Planet* have in all?

Six times a number is 42. What is the number?

Dividing

Work out each division problem.
Some will have remainders, some will not.

$18 \div 3 =$ 6

$12 \div 5 =$ 2 r 2

```
      8 r 1           3 r 1
   2)17            3)10
    - 16             - 9
      1               1
```

Work out each division problem.

$18 \div 3 =$ $36 \div 4 =$ $16 \div 4 =$ $24 \div 6 =$

$20 \div 5 =$ $36 \div 9 =$ $30 \div 10 =$ $27 \div 3 =$

$8 \div 2 =$ $24 \div 4 =$ $35 \div 7 =$ $100 \div 10 =$

$4 \div 1 =$ $33 \div 11 =$ $48 \div 6 =$ $36 \div 6 =$

Work out each division problem. Some will have remainders, some will not.

```
  4)20        3)32        5)12        10)10
```

```
  4)17        3)24        5)25        10)33
```

Work out the answer to each problem.

Superman has 23 kryptonite crystals to share equally between four of his friends. How many crystals does each person get, and how many are left over for Superman?

Superman divides 36 coins between five sacks. How many coins go in each sack, and how many are left over?

Bar graphs

LOIS'S PENS

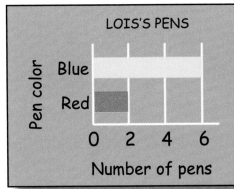

How many pens does Lois Lane have?

8

CHECK THE DATA!

Pen color

Blue

Red

0   2   4   6

Number of pens

Look at this bar graph. Then answer the questions.

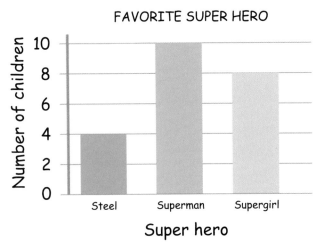

FAVORITE SUPER HERO

Number of children

10
8
6
4
2
0

Steel   Superman   Supergirl

Super hero

This graph shows the favorite super hero of some children.

How many children were asked which super hero they liked best?

How many children liked Steel best?

Which super hero did 8 children like?

Who was the favorite super hero?

Look at this bar graph. Then answer the questions.

This graph shows the most useful superpower of a group of super heroes.

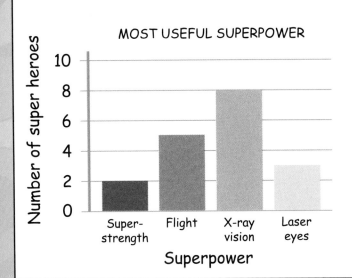

MOST USEFUL SUPERPOWER

Number of super heroes

10
8
6
4
2
0

Super-strength   Flight   X-ray vision   Laser eyes

Superpower

How many super heroes were asked which of their powers was most useful?

Which superpower did 5 super heroes think is most useful?

How many more super heroes thought X-ray vision was more useful than superstrength?

Symmetry

Draw the lines of symmetry on each shape.

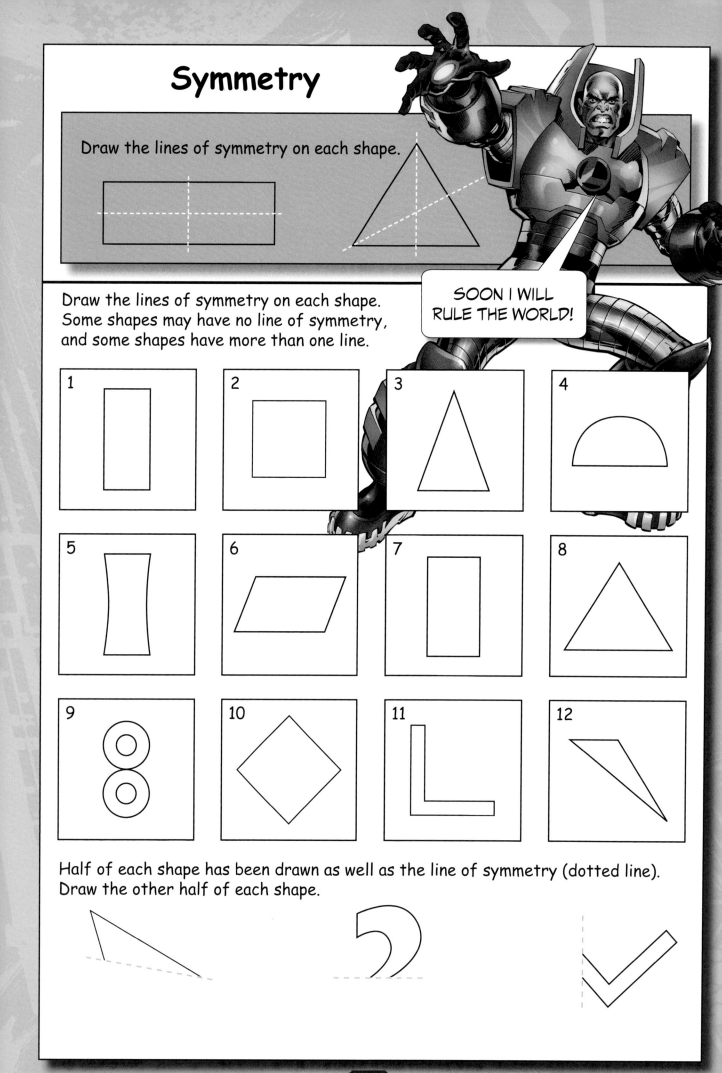

SOON I WILL RULE THE WORLD!

Draw the lines of symmetry on each shape. Some shapes may have no line of symmetry, and some shapes have more than one line.

1

2

3

4

5

6

7

8

9

10

11

12

Half of each shape has been drawn as well as the line of symmetry (dotted line). Draw the other half of each shape.

Ordering

Write these numbers in order starting with the smallest.

560	506	650	605
506	560	605	650

LET'S GET SOME ORDER INTO PROCEEDINGS!

Write these numbers in order starting with the smallest.

340	403	304	430

702	270	720	207

901	910	190	109

560	650	605	506

489	849	984	948

726	672	762	267

890	980	809	908

486	684	864	648

405	450	540	504

76	104	200	92

440	66	177	781

632	236	77	407

74	12	101	800

842	587	99	88

842	99	587	72

600	304	403	89

500	486	395	288

78	9	302	470

2	1	201	38

186	168	158	184

Fractions of shapes

Shade half of each shape.

Shade half of each shape.

Shade a third of each shape.

Choosing the operation

Write the answer in the box.

31 is added to a number and the sum is 56. What number did I begin with?

I take 12 piles of paper from the desk and end up with 19 piles. How many piles of paper did I start with?

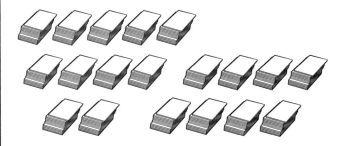

I add 15 to a number and the total of the two numbers is 28. What number did I begin with?

After adding 22 to a number the total is 45. What is the number?

When 26 is subtracted from a number, the difference is 14. What is the number?

What number must you subtract from 19 to find a difference of 8?

I start with 29 and take away a number. The difference is 14. What number did I subtract?

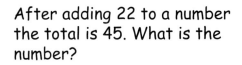

Leon starts with 60¢ but spends some money in a shop. He goes home with 14¢. How much did Leon spend?

Bridget starts out with 32¢ but is given some money by her aunt. Bridget then has 44¢. How much was she given?

Debra gives 35¢ to charity. If she started with 75¢, how much has she left?

A tower is made up of 20 blocks. 35 more are put on top. How many blocks are in the tower now?

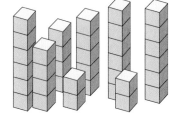

A box contains 72 pins and then some are added so that the new total is 93. How many pins have been added?

Tim has a 350 ml can of soda. He drinks 150 ml. How many ml does he have left?

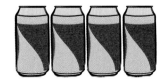

Choosing the operation

Write the answer in the box.

I divide a number by 5 and the answer is 6. What number did I begin with? `30`

A number is multiplied by 7 and the result is 28. What is the number? `4`

Write the answer in the box.

A number is multiplied by 7 and the result is 35. What is the number?

When a number is divided by 4 the result is 4. What is the number?

I multiply a number by 10, and the final number is 90. What number did I multiply?

After dividing a number by 9, I am left with 4. What number did I divide?

When 40 is multiplied by a number the result is 80. What number is used to multiply?

I divide a number by 3 and the result is 8. What is the number?

After multiplying a number by 2, I have 36. What was the number I started with?

I multiply a number by 9 and the result is 54. What number was multiplied?

After dividing a number by 4, I am left with 15. What number was divided?

$55 is shared equally by some super heroes. Each super hero receives $11. How many super heroes are there?

Each box contains 12 pens. I have 36 pens altogether. How many boxes do I have?

$9 = 3$ 12×6 $\times -?$

A bag contains 8 chocolate bars. In all I have 72 chocolate bars. How many bags do I have?

100 nuts are shared equally between 2 squirrels. How many nuts does each squirrel receive?

Clark Kent gives $20 to each charity. He gives away $120. How many charities did Clark give money to?

Bar graphs and pictographs

BRAVERY AWARDS

Number of awards: 5, 4, 3, 2, 1, 0
Superman — Supergirl
Super hero

Look at the bar graph and answer the question.

Which super hero has 3 bravery awards?

Supergirl

GET THE PICTURE?

Look at the bar graph and answer the questions.

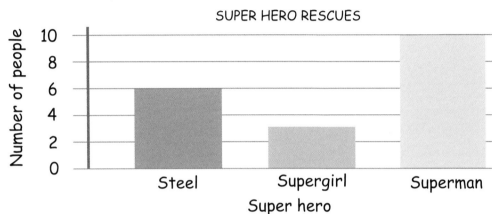

SUPER HERO RESCUES

Number of people: 10, 8, 6, 4, 2, 0
Steel — Supergirl — Superman
Super hero

Which super hero rescued three people?

Which super hero rescued the most people?

How many people did Steel rescue?

Look at the pictograph and answer the questions.

CHILDREN'S WORST SUPER VILLAINS

Super villains:
Parasite
Doomsday
Lex Luthor
Darkseid

Number of children

Each shield stands for 2 children.

Which super villain is disliked by 3 children?

Which is the most disliked super villain?

How many more children dislike Darkseid than dislike Parasite?

141

Adding two numbers

Find each sum.

```
  211      482
+ 214    + 573
  425    1,055
```

Remember to regroup if you have to.

JUST FIGURE IT OUT.
I KNOW YOU CAN DO IT!

Find each sum.

```
  224        452        612        843
+ 365      + 227      + 345      + 291
_____      _____      _____      _____


  485        563        535        481
+ 606      + 147      + 187      + 377
_____      _____      _____      _____
```

Write the answer in the box.

313 + 237 = [ ]   635 + 267 = [ ]

Write the missing number in the box.

```
  3 6 2      2   6       7   1        7 3 9
+ 4 1 9    + 5 8 1     + 2 6 4      + 2 4
  7   1      8 4 7       9 6            7 9
```

Find each sum.

Doomsday has 207 bony spikes on
one arm and 143 spikes on the other.
How many bony spikes does he have
on his arms altogether?

Doomsday has 164 bony spikes on his left
leg and 341 spikes on his right leg. How
many spikes does he have on both legs?

Adding two numbers

Find each sum.

$$\begin{array}{r} 1,234 \\ + 5,642 \\ \hline 6,876 \end{array} \qquad \begin{array}{r} 3,794 \\ + 5,125 \\ \hline 8,919 \end{array}$$

Remember to regroup if you need to.

GET THESE RIGHT BEFORE I FLY.

Find each sum.

$$\begin{array}{r} 2,552 \\ + 3,214 \\ \hline \end{array} \qquad \begin{array}{r} 5,325 \\ + 2,653 \\ \hline \end{array} \qquad \begin{array}{r} 2,471 \\ + 4,238 \\ \hline \end{array}$$

$$\begin{array}{r} 3,749 \\ + 2,471 \\ \hline \end{array} \qquad \begin{array}{r} 4,675 \\ + 3,916 \\ \hline \end{array} \qquad \begin{array}{r} 8,482 \\ + 1,349 \\ \hline \end{array}$$

Write the answer in the box.

2,431 + 4,621 =

1,342 + 3,264 =

1,738 + 4,261 =

2,013 + 3,642 =

Write the missing number in the box.

$$\begin{array}{r} \boxed{}\,7\,4\,1 \\ + 2,9\,\boxed{}\,4 \\ \hline 6,6\,8\,4 \end{array} \qquad \begin{array}{r} \boxed{}\,6\,5\,2 \\ + 3,2\,\boxed{}\,4 \\ \hline 4,9\,2\,6 \end{array} \qquad \begin{array}{r} 3,6\,4\,2 \\ + \boxed{}\,8\,3 \\ \hline 8,4\,7\,3 \end{array}$$

Find each sum.

On Monday, Superman saved 2,521 people from death, and Supergirl saved 2,443 people. How many people did they save on Monday?

On Saturday, Supergirl rescued 4,476 people, and Steel rescued 3,478 people on Sunday. How many people did they rescue that weekend?

Subtracting three-digit numbers

Write the difference between the lines.

$$\begin{array}{r} 644 \\ - 223 \\ \hline 421 \end{array} \qquad \begin{array}{r} \overset{6\ 11}{4\cancel{7}1}\text{ cm} \\ - 252 \text{ cm} \\ \hline 219 \text{ cm} \end{array}$$

DO YOU KNOW THE DIFFERENCE?

Write the difference between the lines.

$$\begin{array}{r} 363 \\ - 151 \\ \hline \end{array} \qquad \begin{array}{r} 578 \\ - 334 \\ \hline \end{array} \qquad \begin{array}{r} 745 \\ - 524 \\ \hline \end{array} \qquad \begin{array}{r} 693 \\ - 481 \\ \hline \end{array}$$

$$\begin{array}{r} 480 \text{ m} \\ - 130 \text{ m} \\ \hline \end{array} \qquad \begin{array}{r} 559 \text{ m} \\ - 218 \text{ m} \\ \hline \end{array} \qquad \begin{array}{r} 750 \text{ m} \\ - 640 \text{ m} \\ \hline \end{array} \qquad \begin{array}{r} 472 \text{ m} \\ - 362 \text{ m} \\ \hline \end{array}$$

Write the difference in the box.

$364 - 122 =$

$799 - 354 =$

$\$776 - \$515 =$

$\$840 - \$730 =$

$\$684 - \$574 =$

$\$220 - \$120 =$

Write the difference between the lines.

$$\begin{array}{r} 463 \\ - 145 \\ \hline \end{array} \qquad \begin{array}{r} 584 \\ - 237 \\ \hline \end{array} \qquad \begin{array}{r} 661 \\ - 342 \\ \hline \end{array} \qquad \begin{array}{r} 494 \\ - 185 \\ \hline \end{array}$$

$$\begin{array}{r} 325 \\ - 116 \\ \hline \end{array} \qquad \begin{array}{r} 837 \\ - 719 \\ \hline \end{array} \qquad \begin{array}{r} 468 \\ - 209 \\ \hline \end{array} \qquad \begin{array}{r} 852 \\ - 329 \\ \hline \end{array}$$

Find the answer to each problem.

Metallo shoots 234 missiles, but 127 are destroyed. How many missiles are left?

The city of Kandor has 860 palaces. 420 are knocked down. How many palaces remain?

Subtracting three-digit numbers

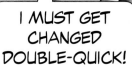

Write the difference between the lines.

$$\begin{array}{r} {\scriptstyle 6\ 11}\\ 7\cancel{1}5 \\ -\ 152 \\ \hline 563 \end{array}$$

$$\begin{array}{r} {\scriptstyle 10}\\ {\scriptstyle 6\ \cancel{0}\ \cancel{1}1}\\ 7\cancel{1}1\ \text{m} \\ -\ 292\ \text{m} \\ \hline 419\ \text{m} \end{array}$$

I MUST GET CHANGED DOUBLE-QUICK!

Write the difference between the lines.

$$\begin{array}{r} 624\ \text{m} \\ -\ 263\ \text{m} \\ \hline \end{array}$$
$$\begin{array}{r} 419\ \text{m} \\ -\ 137\ \text{m} \\ \hline \end{array}$$
$$\begin{array}{r} 747\ \text{m} \\ -\ 456\ \text{m} \\ \hline \end{array}$$
$$\begin{array}{r} 815\ \text{m} \\ -\ 193\ \text{m} \\ \hline \end{array}$$

$$\begin{array}{r} 614 \\ -\ 407 \\ \hline \end{array}$$
$$\begin{array}{r} 826 \\ -\ 727 \\ \hline \end{array}$$
$$\begin{array}{r} 521 \\ -\ 355 \\ \hline \end{array}$$
$$\begin{array}{r} 915 \\ -\ 786 \\ \hline \end{array}$$

Write the difference in the box.

516 - 308 =

748 - 339 =

631 - 542 =

477 - 198 =

Write the difference between the lines.

$$\begin{array}{r} 535 \\ -\ 247 \\ \hline \end{array}$$
$$\begin{array}{r} 715 \\ -\ 518 \\ \hline \end{array}$$
$$\begin{array}{r} 312 \\ -\ 113 \\ \hline \end{array}$$
$$\begin{array}{r} 924 \\ -\ 528 \\ \hline \end{array}$$

Write the missing numbers in the box.

$$\begin{array}{r} 7\ 2\ 3 \\ -\ \ 1\ 2\ \square \\ \hline 5\ 9\ 5 \end{array}$$
$$\begin{array}{r} 6\ \square\ 2 \\ -\ 3\ 1\ 7 \\ \hline 3\ 4\ 5 \end{array}$$
$$\begin{array}{r} 4\ \square\ 6 \\ -\ 3\ 1\ 7 \\ \hline 9\ 9 \end{array}$$
$$\begin{array}{r} 5\ 3\ 2 \\ -\ \square\ \ 5 \\ \hline 3\ 4\ 7 \end{array}$$

Find the answer to each problem.

A theater holds 745 people. 357 people buy tickets. How many seats are empty?

There are 664 people in a park. 276 are boating on a lake. How many are taking part in other activities?

Multiplying by one digit numbers

Find each product.

$$22 \times 2 = 44$$

$$\overset{1}{26} \times 3 = 78$$

$$\overset{1}{44} \times 4 = 176$$

I'VE GOT A FAVOR TO ASK! HELP ME FIND EACH ANSWER.

Find each product.

37 × 2	19 × 2	16 × 4	32 × 3
21 × 3	25 × 4	16 × 6	33 × 5
39 × 2	24 × 2	41 × 2	36 × 3
29 × 3	35 × 2	28 × 3	26 × 6
10 × 6	30 × 2	20 × 4	50 × 3

Find the answer to each problem.

Brainiac blasts 26 cities, but Doomsday destroys twice as many. How many cities does Doomsday destroy?

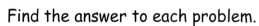

A gas canister is 30 cm long. How long will 4 canisters be?

Multiplying by one-digit numbers

Find each product.

$$
\begin{array}{r} 43 \\ \times\ 3 \\ \hline 129 \end{array}
\qquad
\begin{array}{r} \overset{3}{7}6 \\ \times\ 6 \\ \hline 456 \end{array}
\qquad
\begin{array}{r} \overset{3}{3}5 \\ \times\ 7 \\ \hline 245 \end{array}
$$

GET ME THE PRODUCTS NOW!

Find each product.

$$
\begin{array}{r} 46 \\ \times\ 8 \\ \hline \end{array}
\qquad
\begin{array}{r} 48 \\ \times\ 5 \\ \hline \end{array}
\qquad
\begin{array}{r} 40 \\ \times\ 7 \\ \hline \end{array}
\qquad
\begin{array}{r} 32 \\ \times\ 6 \\ \hline \end{array}
\qquad
\begin{array}{r} 36 \\ \times\ 9 \\ \hline \end{array}
$$

$$
\begin{array}{r} 54 \\ \times\ 4 \\ \hline \end{array}
\qquad
\begin{array}{r} 55 \\ \times\ 6 \\ \hline \end{array}
\qquad
\begin{array}{r} 58 \\ \times\ 7 \\ \hline \end{array}
\qquad
\begin{array}{r} 96 \\ \times\ 3 \\ \hline \end{array}
\qquad
\begin{array}{r} 42 \\ \times\ 9 \\ \hline \end{array}
$$

$$
\begin{array}{r} 82 \\ \times\ 3 \\ \hline \end{array}
\qquad
\begin{array}{r} 24 \\ \times\ 9 \\ \hline \end{array}
\qquad
\begin{array}{r} 81 \\ \times\ 7 \\ \hline \end{array}
\qquad
\begin{array}{r} 64 \\ \times\ 4 \\ \hline \end{array}
\qquad
\begin{array}{r} 52 \\ \times\ 6 \\ \hline \end{array}
$$

$$
\begin{array}{r} 37 \\ \times\ 7 \\ \hline \end{array}
\qquad
\begin{array}{r} 40 \\ \times\ 8 \\ \hline \end{array}
\qquad
\begin{array}{r} 50 \\ \times\ 3 \\ \hline \end{array}
\qquad
\begin{array}{r} 30 \\ \times\ 7 \\ \hline \end{array}
\qquad
\begin{array}{r} 20 \\ \times\ 9 \\ \hline \end{array}
$$

$$
\begin{array}{r} 27 \\ \times\ 5 \\ \hline \end{array}
\qquad
\begin{array}{r} 36 \\ \times\ 4 \\ \hline \end{array}
\qquad
\begin{array}{r} 21 \\ \times\ 6 \\ \hline \end{array}
\qquad
\begin{array}{r} 42 \\ \times\ 9 \\ \hline \end{array}
\qquad
\begin{array}{r} 57 \\ \times\ 2 \\ \hline \end{array}
$$

Find the answer to the problem.

Superman flies 48 kilometres in an hour. How many kilometres does he fly in 6 hours?

A canister belt can hold 7 gas canisters. How many canisters can 28 belts hold?

147

Division with remainders

Find each quotient.

$$3\overline{)17} \quad \begin{array}{r} 5\,r\,2 \\ \underline{15} \\ 2 \end{array}$$

$$4\overline{)30} \quad \begin{array}{r} 7\,r\,2 \\ \underline{28} \\ 2 \end{array}$$

DIVIDE AND
YOU WILL RULE!

Find each quotient.

$3\overline{)35}$ $4\overline{)46}$ $3\overline{)22}$ $5\overline{)38}$

$4\overline{)50}$ $5\overline{)37}$ $5\overline{)63}$ $4\overline{)58}$

$2\overline{)37}$ $4\overline{)67}$ $7\overline{)75}$ $2\overline{)99}$

$4\overline{)59}$ $5\overline{)84}$ $3\overline{)76}$ $5\overline{)94}$

Write the answer in the box.

What is 37 divided by 4?   What is 78 divided by 5?

What is 46 divided by 3?   What is 53 divided by 2?

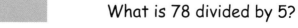

Division with remainders

Find each quotient.

$$\begin{array}{r} 5\ r\ 3 \\ 6\overline{)33} \\ 30 \\ \hline 3 \end{array}$$

$$\begin{array}{r} 7\ r\ 2 \\ 7\overline{)51} \\ 49 \\ \hline 2 \end{array}$$

I'M ON THE CASE.

Find each quotient.

$6\overline{)43}$ $9\overline{)40}$ $8\overline{)75}$ $6\overline{)98}$

$7\overline{)53}$ $7\overline{)82}$ $9\overline{)53}$ $6\overline{)94}$

$7\overline{)65}$ $8\overline{)63}$ $6\overline{)26}$ $8\overline{)45}$

$9\overline{)92}$ $7\overline{)85}$ $8\overline{)66}$ $7\overline{)27}$

Write the answer in the box.

What is 97 divided by 7?

What is 84 divided by 8?

What is 75 divided by 6?

What is 64 divided by 9?

Appropriate units of measure

Choose the best units to measure the length of each item.

millimetres	centimetres	metres

pen nib	notebook	swimming pool
millimetres	centimetres	metres

Choose the best units to measure the length of each item.

millimetres	centimetres	metres

TV set	flea	toothbrush	football field

shoe	backyard	kayak	cat's claw

The height of a door is about 2

The length of a pencil is about 18

The height of a flagpole is about 7

Choose the best units to measure the weight of each item.

grams	kilograms	tonnes

dog	ship	apple	pants

hamburger	elephant	refrigerator

The weight of a tennis ball is about 60

The weight of a bag of potatoes is about 2

The weight of a truck is about 4

TO THE RESCUE!

Real-life problems

Perry White spent $4.68 at the store and had $4.77 left. How much did he start with?

$9.45

```
  1 1
  4.77
- 4.68
  9.45
```

Talia Head saves $30.00 a week. How much will she have if she saves all of it for 8 weeks?

$240

```
  30.00
×     8
 240.00
```

Smallville theater charges $4 for each matinee ticket. If it sells 560 tickets for a matinee performance, how much money does it take in?

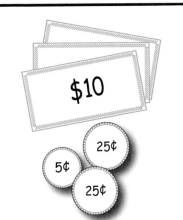

Steel has saved $9.69. His niece has saved $3.24 less. How much does his niece have?

The cost for 9 children to see a Superman film is $54. How much does each child pay? If only 6 children go, what will the total cost be?

Steel has $12.95. Supergirl gives him another $3.64, and he goes out and buys a hammer for $3.25. How much does he have left?

Lex Luthor has $60 in savings. He decides to spend $\frac{1}{4}$ of it. How much will he have left?

LET'S SOLVE THESE PROBLEMS.

151

Perimeters of squares and rectangles

Find the perimeter of the white rectangle. To find the perimeter, add the lengths of the four sides:
8 cm + 8 cm + 5 cm + 5 cm = 26 cm

You can also do this with multiplication:
(2 x 8) cm + (2 x 5) cm
= 16 cm + 10 cm
= 26 cm

8 cm

5 cm

26 cm

PROJECT CADMUS NEEDS YOUR HELP. FIND THE PERIMETERS – FAST!

Find the perimeters of these rectangles and squares.

3 mm

3 mm

4 m

6 m

3 cm

2 cm

1 mm

1 mm

5 cm

3 cm

5 m

5 m

4 m

3 m

2 cm

2 cm

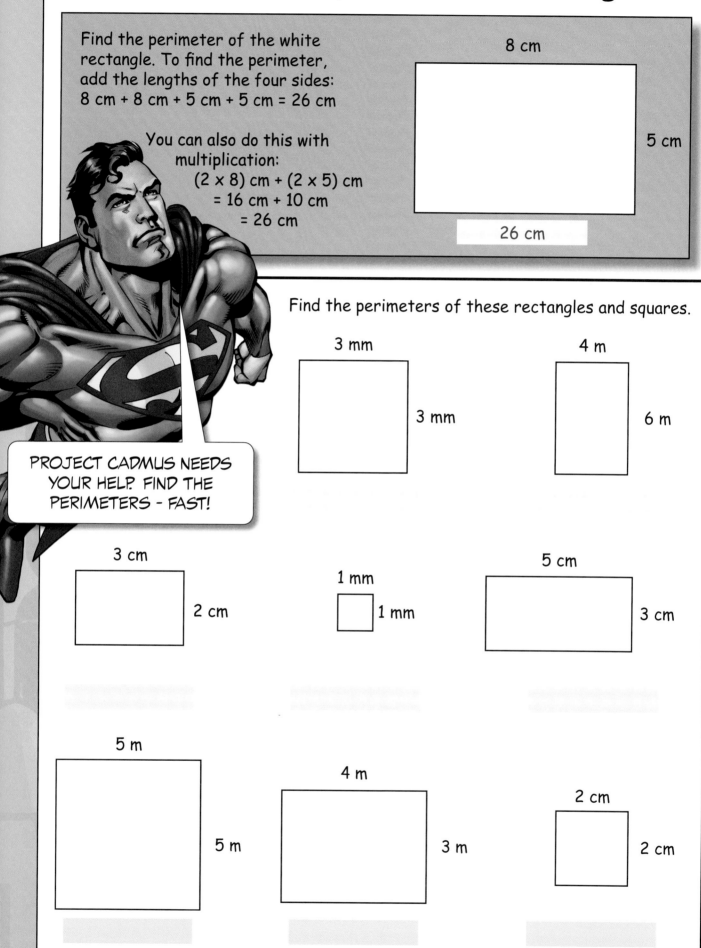

Comparing areas

Write how many units are in each figure. Then circle the figure with the greatest area in each group.

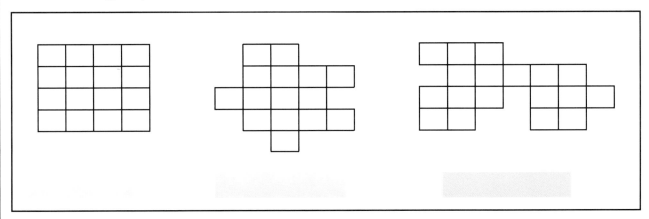

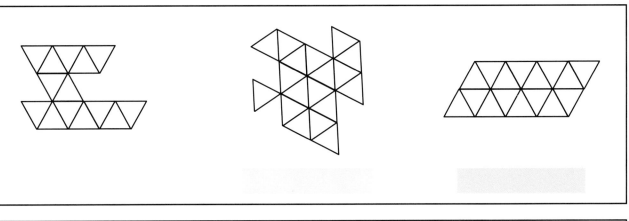

Adding fractions

Write the sum in the simplest form.

$\dfrac{1}{3} + \dfrac{1}{3} = \dfrac{\ }{\ }$

$\dfrac{1}{4} + \dfrac{1}{4} = \dfrac{\ }{\ } = \dfrac{\ }{\ }$

$\dfrac{2}{3} + \dfrac{1}{3} = \dfrac{\ }{\ } = \boxed{\ }$

$\dfrac{3}{7} + \dfrac{2}{7} = \dfrac{\ }{\ }$

$\dfrac{2}{5} + \dfrac{2}{5} = \dfrac{\ }{\ }$

$\dfrac{5}{16} + \dfrac{7}{16} = \dfrac{\ }{\ } = \dfrac{\ }{\ }$

$\dfrac{3}{8} + \dfrac{5}{8} = \dfrac{\ }{\ } = \boxed{\ }$

$\dfrac{7}{13} + \dfrac{5}{13} = \dfrac{\ }{\ }$

$\dfrac{5}{16} + \dfrac{3}{16} = \dfrac{\ }{\ } = \dfrac{\ }{\ }$

$\dfrac{2}{10} + \dfrac{3}{10} = \dfrac{\ }{\ } = \dfrac{\ }{\ }$

$\dfrac{2}{5} + \dfrac{3}{5} = \dfrac{\ }{\ } = \boxed{\ }$

$\dfrac{7}{12} + \dfrac{3}{12} = \dfrac{\ }{\ } = \dfrac{\ }{\ }$

$\dfrac{3}{11} + \dfrac{5}{11} = \dfrac{\ }{\ }$

$\dfrac{8}{14} + \dfrac{5}{14} = \dfrac{\ }{\ }$

$\dfrac{2}{9} + \dfrac{4}{9} = \dfrac{\ }{\ } = \dfrac{\ }{\ }$

$\dfrac{5}{7} + \dfrac{1}{7} = \dfrac{\ }{\ }$

$\dfrac{1}{12} + \dfrac{3}{12} = \dfrac{\ }{\ } = \dfrac{\ }{\ }$

$\dfrac{5}{11} + \dfrac{3}{11} = \dfrac{\ }{\ }$

$\dfrac{5}{18} + \dfrac{4}{18} = \dfrac{\ }{\ } = \dfrac{\ }{\ }$

$\dfrac{1}{9} + \dfrac{2}{9} = \dfrac{\ }{\ } = \dfrac{\ }{\ }$

$\dfrac{4}{15} + \dfrac{7}{15} = \dfrac{\ }{\ }$

$\dfrac{2}{5} + \dfrac{2}{5} = \dfrac{\ }{\ }$

$\dfrac{1}{6} + \dfrac{5}{6} = \dfrac{\ }{\ } = \boxed{\ }$

$\dfrac{1}{4} + \dfrac{1}{4} = \dfrac{\ }{\ } = \dfrac{\ }{\ }$

$\dfrac{1}{8} + \dfrac{5}{8} = \dfrac{\ }{\ } = \dfrac{\ }{\ }$

$\dfrac{3}{10} + \dfrac{2}{10} = \dfrac{\ }{\ } = \dfrac{\ }{\ }$

$\dfrac{9}{15} + \dfrac{1}{15} = \dfrac{\ }{\ } = \dfrac{\ }{\ }$

$\dfrac{1}{20} + \dfrac{6}{20} = \dfrac{\ }{\ }$

Subtracting fractions

Write the sum in the simplest form.

$$\frac{5}{6} - \frac{4}{6} = \frac{1}{6}$$

$$\frac{5}{8} - \frac{3}{8} = \frac{2 \div 2}{8 \div 2} = \frac{1}{4}$$

Write the sum in the simplest form.

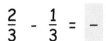

KEEP IT SIMPLE!

$$\frac{2}{3} - \frac{1}{3} = \frac{\ }{\ }$$

$$\frac{1}{4} - \frac{1}{4} = \frac{\ }{\ }$$

$$\frac{7}{12} - \frac{5}{12} = \frac{\ }{\ } = \frac{\ }{\ }$$

$$\frac{6}{7} - \frac{5}{7} = \frac{\ }{\ }$$

$$\frac{18}{30} - \frac{15}{30} = \frac{\ }{\ } = \frac{\ }{\ }$$

$$\frac{3}{6} - \frac{1}{6} = \frac{\ }{\ } = \frac{\ }{\ }$$

$$\frac{13}{16} - \frac{7}{16} = \frac{\ }{\ } = \frac{\ }{\ }$$

$$\frac{7}{13} - \frac{5}{13} = \frac{\ }{\ }$$

$$\frac{12}{13} - \frac{8}{13} = \frac{\ }{\ }$$

$$\frac{9}{10} - \frac{7}{10} = \frac{\ }{\ } = \frac{\ }{\ }$$

$$\frac{8}{17} - \frac{4}{17} = \frac{\ }{\ }$$

$$\frac{4}{5} - \frac{3}{5} = \frac{\ }{\ }$$

$$\frac{7}{8} - \frac{5}{8} = \frac{\ }{\ } = \frac{\ }{\ }$$

$$\frac{7}{12} - \frac{5}{12} = \frac{\ }{\ } = \frac{\ }{\ }$$

$$\frac{9}{10} - \frac{3}{10} = \frac{\ }{\ } = \frac{\ }{\ }$$

$$\frac{7}{9} - \frac{4}{9} = \frac{\ }{\ } = \frac{\ }{\ }$$

$$\frac{5}{7} - \frac{1}{7} = \frac{\ }{\ }$$

$$\frac{5}{11} - \frac{3}{11} = \frac{\ }{\ }$$

$$\frac{9}{12} - \frac{5}{12} = \frac{\ }{\ } = \frac{\ }{\ }$$

$$\frac{4}{5} - \frac{2}{5} = \frac{\ }{\ }$$

$$\frac{7}{8} - \frac{1}{8} = \frac{\ }{\ } = \frac{\ }{\ }$$

$$\frac{5}{9} - \frac{2}{9} = \frac{\ }{\ } = \frac{\ }{\ }$$

$$\frac{14}{15} - \frac{4}{15} = \frac{\ }{\ } = \frac{\ }{\ }$$

$$\frac{4}{5} - \frac{1}{5} = \frac{\ }{\ }$$

$$\frac{5}{6} - \frac{1}{6} = \frac{\ }{\ } = \frac{\ }{\ }$$

$$\frac{11}{18} - \frac{8}{18} = \frac{\ }{\ } = \frac{\ }{\ }$$

$$\frac{9}{11} - \frac{5}{11} = \frac{\ }{\ }$$

$$\frac{3}{14} - \frac{2}{14} = \frac{\ }{\ }$$

$$\frac{8}{16} - \frac{5}{16} = \frac{\ }{\ }$$

$$\frac{17}{19} - \frac{6}{19} = \frac{\ }{\ }$$

Volumes of cubes

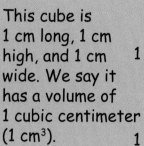
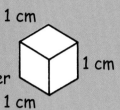

I THINK OUR MISSION IS ACCOMPLISHED.

These shapes are made of 1 cm³ cubes. What are their volumes?

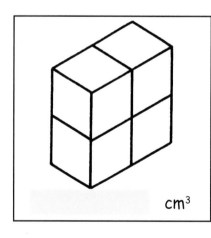 cm³

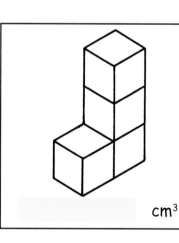 cm³

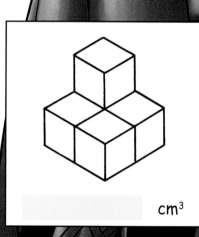 cm³

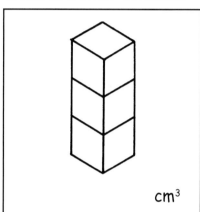 cm³

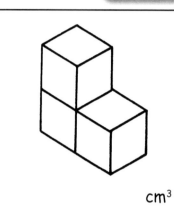 cm³

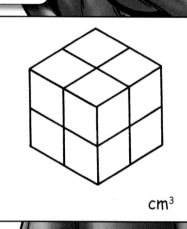 cm³

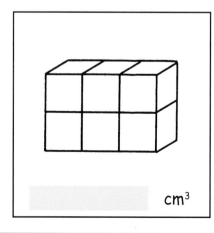 cm³

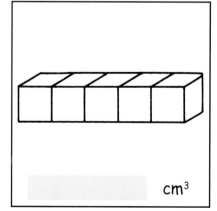 cm³

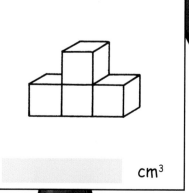 cm³

Answer Section with Parents' Notes

Level 3 Workbook

This section provides answers to all the activities in this book. These pages will enable you to mark your children's work, or they can be used by your children if they prefer to do their own marking.

The notes for each page help explain common errors and problems and, where appropriate, indicate the kind of practice needed to ensure that your children understand where and how they have made errors.

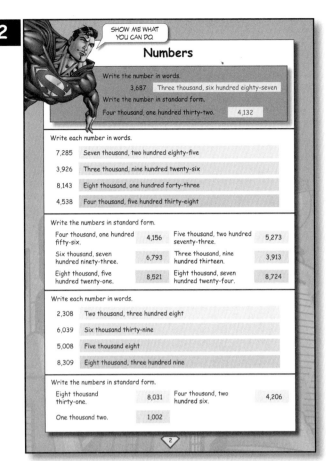

Children may use zeros incorrectly in numbers. In word form, zeros are omitted, but children should take care to include them when writing numbers in standard form.

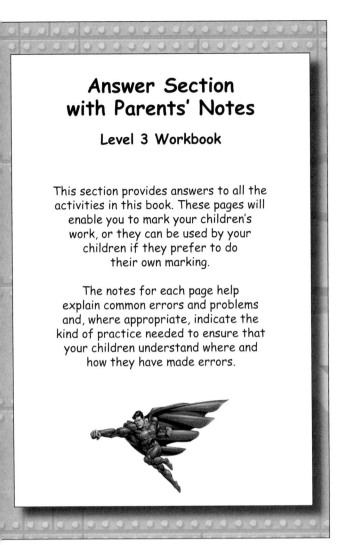

Again, make sure that children understand the use of zeros in numbers.

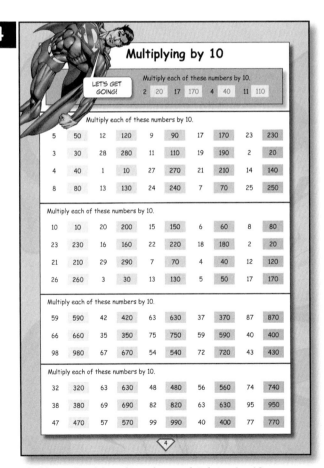

Children should realize that multiplying by 10 means adding a zero to a number. The ones become tens and the tens become hundreds, leaving a blank space—the zero—in the ones column.

Ordering

Write these numbers in order, from smallest to largest.

4,285	3,910	8,190	2,512
2,512	3,910	4,285	8,190

SMALL OR LARGE? I NEED TO KNOW!

Write these numbers in order, from smallest to largest.

1,452	4,839	8,774	2,349		1,452	2,349	4,839	8,774
7,374	2,831	5,928	8,421		2,831	5,928	7,374	8,421
9,388	3,286	8,774	1,438		1,438	3,286	8,774	9,388
3,364	9,264	6,921	5,674		3,364	5,674	6,921	9,264
6,853	4,567	5,684	2,557		2,557	4,567	5,684	6,853
3,241	3,785	9,358	7,647		3,241	3,785	7,647	9,358

Write these numbers in order, from smallest to largest.

5,507	9,370	4,903	7,239		4,903	5,507	7,239	9,370
4,076	8,209	1,360	5,035		1,360	4,076	5,035	8,209
2,987	7,380	5,005	2,345		2,345	2,987	5,005	7,380
8,459	3,401	6,223	1,023		1,023	3,401	6,223	8,459
9,205	2,065	7,004	3,800		2,065	3,800	7,004	9,205

Write these numbers in order, from smallest to largest.

5,780	365	968	1,089		365	968	1,089	5,780
7,650	3,271	641	889		641	889	3,271	7,650
9,842	1,295	712	1,102		712	1,102	1,295	9,842
8,004	4,800	840	3,980		840	3,980	4,800	8,004
5,078	3,001	679	375		375	679	3,001	5,078

5

Children who do not understand the place value of digits may make errors in thinking that a "hundreds" number is bigger than a "thousands" number because the first digit is bigger.

Rounding

Round 148 to the nearest ten.

100 110 120 130 140 150 160 170 180

148 rounded to the nearest 10 is 150

Round each number to the nearest ten.

378	380	231	230	483	480	854	850
767	770	623	620	389	390	235	240

Round each number to the nearest ten.

Number line	Answer
120 130 140 150 160 170 180 190 200	160
330 340 350 360 370 380 390 400 410	380
480 490 500 510 520 530 540 550 560	500
200 210 220 230 240 250 260 270 280	240
40 50 60 70 80 90 100 110 120	100
750 760 770 780 790 800 810 820 830	780
540 550 560 570 580 590 600 610 620	610
120 130 140 150 160 170 180 190 200	140
10 20 30 40 50 60 70 000 000	50
870 880 890 900 910 920 930 940 950	910

6

Children should remember that numbers ending in 5 or greater are rounded up.

Polygons

Match the polygon with a solid figure.

Circle the octagon.

TIME TO SHAPE UP

Circle the rectangle.

Match the polygon to the solid object in which it appears.

hexagon   octagon   rectangle   pentagon   triangle

7

Children can count the sides of the polygons to match them with other polygons or with the names that identify them.

KEEP UP THE SEARCH.

Identifying patterns

Continue each pattern.

0	4	8	12	16	20
0	11	22	33	44	55
70	63	56	49	42	35

Continue each pattern.

2	7	12	17	22	27	32	37
3	10	17	24	31	38	45	52
1	11	21	31	41	51	61	71
5	7	9	11	13	15	17	19
6	9	12	15	18	21	24	27
7	12	17	22	27	33	40	47

Continue each pattern.

59	53	47	41	35	29	23	17
92	84	76	68	60	52	44	36
76	69	62	55	48	41	34	27
42	36	30	24	18	12	6	0
37	33	29	25	21	17	13	9

Continue each pattern.

46	53	60	67	74	81	88	95
93	87	81	75	69	63	57	51
0	7	14	21	28	35	42	49
5	15	25	35	45	55	65	75
4	12	20	28	36	44	52	60

8

It may help to point out that some patterns show an increase and some a decrease. Children should double check that the operation that turns the first number into the second also turns the second number into the third. They can then continue the pattern.

Odds and evens

IM VERY ODD!

Multiply the odd number by the odd number.   3 x 5 = 15
Multiply the even number by the even number. 8 x 4 = 32

Multiply the odd number by the odd number.

3 x 7 = 21	9 x 9 = 81	7 x 1 = 7	1 x 1 = 1
7 x 5 = 35	7 x 9 = 63	1 x 5 = 5	3 x 1 = 3
5 x 5 = 25	3 x 5 = 15	7 x 7 = 49	9 x 7 = 63
1 x 9 = 9	5 x 9 = 45	9 x 3 = 27	3 x 3 = 9

What do you notice about the numbers in your answer boxes?
They are all odd numbers.

Multiply the even number by the even number.

2 x 4 = 8	4 x 10 = 40	8 x 6 = 48	10 x 10 = 100
8 x 10 = 80	6 x 2 = 12	10 x 2 = 20	6 x 6 = 36
8 x 2 = 16	8 x 8 = 64	6 x 4 = 24	12 x 12 = 144
10 x 6 = 60	4 x 4 = 16	2 x 2 = 4	4 x 8 = 32

What do you notice about the numbers in your answer boxes?
They are all even numbers.

Multiply the odd number by the even number.

3 x 6 = 18	7 x 6 = 42	3 x 8 = 24	3 x 2 = 6
7 x 4 = 28	3 x 10 = 30	9 x 4 = 36	8 x 7 = 56
9 x 6 = 54	8 x 5 = 40	10 x 9 = 90	4 x 1 = 4
5 x 8 = 40	4 x 3 = 12	2 x 7 = 14	12 x 3 = 36

What do you notice about the numbers in your answer boxes?
They are all even numbers.

9

If children fail to notice any similarity in the products, suggest that they check to see if all of the products are even or if all are odd.

Addition fact families

Circle the number sentence that is in the same fact family as the first pair.

14 - 9 = 5
5 + 9 = 14   14 + 2 = 16   (14 - 5 = 9)   9 - 7 = 00

12 - 4 = 8
4 + 8 = 12   8 - 4 = 4   (8 + 4 = 12)   12 - 9 = 3

Circle the number sentence that is in the same fact family as the first pair.

7 + 6 = 13
6 + 7 = 13   7 + 3 = 10   (13 - 6 = 7)   7 - 6 = 1

17 - 6 = 11
11 + 6 = 17   11 - 6 = 5   17 + 11 = 28   (17 - 11 = 6)

18 - 9 = 9
18 - 9 = 9   9 - 9 = 0   18 + 3 = 21   (9 + 9 = 18)

3 + 4 = 7
7 - 3 = 4   (7 - 4 = 3)   7 + 6 = 13   7 + 4 = 11

19 - 9 = 10
19 - 10 = 9   9 + 19 = 28   (10 + 9 = 19)   10 - 9 = 1

9 + 8 = 17
17 - 8 = 9   (8 + 9 = 17)   8 + 17 = 25   25 - 9 = 16

Write the fact family for each group of numbers.

3, 15, 18	6, 10, 4	4, 13, 9
3 + 15 = 18	6 + 4 = 10	4 + 9 = 13
15 + 3 = 18	4 + 6 = 10	9 + 4 = 13
18 - 15 = 3	10 - 6 = 4	13 - 9 = 4
18 - 3 = 15	10 - 4 = 6	13 - 4 = 9

LET'S GET THE FACTS STRAIGHT.

10

Children should understand that subtraction "undoes" addition. You may want to use counters to show the addition fact families.

EVERY SECOND COUNTS!

Fractions

Write the fraction for the part that is shaded.

How many circles are shaded?   3
How many circles?   8

So, the fraction of circles shaded = $\frac{3}{8}$ numerator / denominator

Circle the fraction that shows the part that is shaded.

$\frac{2}{3}$ $\frac{3}{5}$ $\left(\frac{2}{5}\right)$ $\left(\frac{3}{7}\right)$ $\frac{4}{9}$ $\frac{3}{4}$

Write the fraction for the part that is shaded.

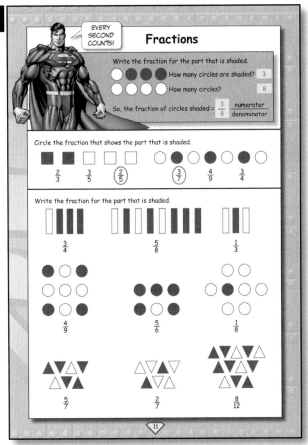

$\frac{3}{4}$ $\frac{5}{8}$ $\frac{1}{3}$

$\frac{4}{9}$ $\frac{5}{6}$ $\frac{1}{8}$

$\frac{5}{7}$ $\frac{2}{7}$ $\frac{8}{12}$

11

If children have difficulty, point out that the denominator (the bottom number of the fraction) is the total number of parts, and the numerator (the top number of the fraction) is the number of shaded parts.

Fractions of shapes

Shade $\frac{3}{5}$ of each shape.

Shade $\frac{4}{5}$ of each shape.

FLY THROUGH THESE!

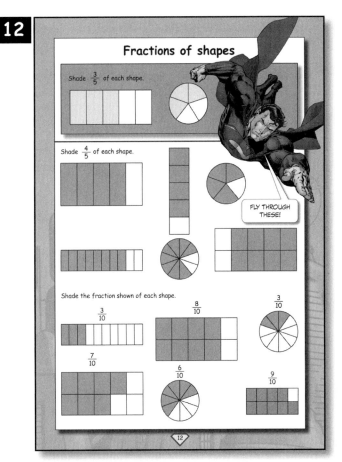

Shade the fraction shown of each shape.

$\frac{3}{10}$ $\frac{8}{10}$ $\frac{3}{10}$

$\frac{7}{10}$ $\frac{6}{10}$ $\frac{9}{10}$

12

Children may shade in any combination of the sections as long as the total shaded area represents the fraction.

Ordering decimals

Put these decimals in order from smallest to largest.

| 0.3 | 0.1 | 0.9 | 0.6 | 0.5 | | 0.1 | 0.3 | 0.5 | 0.6 | 0.9 |

Put these decimals in order from smallest to largest.

0.3	0.5	0.7	0.8	0.4		0.3	0.4	0.5	0.7	0.8
0.6	0.1	0.7	0.3	0.4		0.1	0.3	0.4	0.6	0.7
0.9	0.7	0.8	0.2	0.6		0.2	0.6	0.7	0.8	0.9
0.1	0.3	0.2	0.8	0.7		0.1	0.2	0.3	0.7	0.8
0.8	0.2	0.4	0.6	0.5		0.2	0.4	0.5	0.6	0.8

Put these decimals in order from smallest to largest.

1.8	1.4	1.2	1.1	1.9		1.1	1.2	1.4	1.8	1.9
1.0	1.6	1.3	1.8	1.1		1.0	1.1	1.3	1.6	1.8
1.5	1.7	1.4	1.3	1.6		1.3	1.4	1.5	1.6	1.7
1.0	1.7	1.5	1.9	1.2		1.0	1.2	1.5	1.7	1.9
1.8	1.9	1.6	1.4	1.2		1.2	1.4	1.6	1.8	1.9

Put these decimals in order from smallest to largest.

2.8	2.3	2.0	2.5	2.6		2.0	2.3	2.5	2.6	2.8
3.2	3.8	3.0	3.1	3.7		3.0	3.1	3.2	3.7	3.8
5.2	7.8	2.6	3.4	1.9		1.9	2.6	3.4	5.2	7.8
0.9	6.8	9.9	1.8	4.3		0.9	1.8	4.3	6.8	9.9
5.1	8.1	6.2	3.7	3.6		3.6	3.7	5.1	6.2	8.1

13

In the final section, children must compare not only the decimal parts of the numbers but also the whole number parts. For example, they should realize that 3.4 is greater than 1.8.

Adding

Write the answer between the lines.

27	30	74
+ 53	+ 17	+ 23
80	47	97

I CHALLENGE YOU TO DO THESE.

Write the answer between the lines.

24	41	12	74
+ 3	+ 23	+ 11	+ 21
27	64	23	95

30	26	53	82
+ 28	+ 13	+ 34	+ 17
58	39	87	99

65	13	72	67
+ 21	+ 4	+ 10	+ 21
86	17	82	88

83	54	46	60
+ 6	+ 33	+ 21	+ 36
89	87	67	96

24	36	61	36
+ 14	+ 13	+ 17	+ 23
38	49	78	59

38	74	53	28
+ 21	+ 25	+ 39	+ 31
59	99	92	59

68	57	46	35
+ 20	+ 31	+ 22	+ 13
88	88	68	48

45	62	47	50
+ 32	+ 22	+ 11	+ 37
77	84	58	87

14

Children must remember that when they regroup, they must add 1 to the tens column.

Adding

Write the answer between the lines.

12	35	15
+ 40	+ 10	+ 4
52	45	19

Write the answer between the lines.

25	80	55	20
+ 10	+ 5	+ 35	+ 75
35	85	90	95

25	35	30	5
+ 40	+ 10	+ 20	+ 20
65	45	50	25

45	30	5	55
+ 45	+ 45	+ 15	+ 45
90	75	20	100

15	5	35	15
+ 30	+ 45	+ 30	+ 20
45	50	65	35

45	5	55	65
+ 25	+ 55	+ 15	+ 35
70	60	70	100

45	35	15	75
+15	+ 45	+ 25	+ 10
60	80	40	85

80	45	50	5
+ 15	+ 45	+ 35	+ 95
95	90	85	100

75	15	75	25
+ 5	+ 20	+ 10	+ 35
80	35	85	60

15

Children must remember that when they regroup, they must add 1 to the tens column.

Subtracting

I NEED THE ANSWERS... NOW!

Write the difference between the lines. Start with the ones, then the tens.

26	77	85
- 14	- 26	- 23
12	51	62

Write the difference between the lines.

13	48	29	84
- 11	- 32	- 17	- 20
2	16	12	64

48	31	98	56
- 25	- 10	- 15	- 32
23	21	83	24

46	76	65	33
- 12	- 46	- 54	- 23
34	30	11	10

86	57	63	99
- 35	- 13	- 33	- 18
51	44	30	81

75	76	45	79
- 12	- 43	- 21	- 38
63	33	24	41

78	65	57	44
- 35	- 32	- 24	- 32
43	33	33	12

54	47	73	56
- 32	- 25	- 40	- 35
22	23	33	21

53	67	55	43
- 12	- 33	- 12	- 30
41	34	43	13

16

Children will not need to regroup to subtract the numbers on this page. Discuss any mistakes with them to determine whether they are due to lapses of concentration or a basic misunderstanding of subtraction.

Subtracting

Write the difference between the lines.
Regroup if you need to.

43	32	87
- 18	- 27	- 58
25	**5**	**29**

DO WHAT YOU HAVE TO DO TO SOLVE THESE.

Write the difference between the lines.

56	86	12	31
- 38	- 39	- 9	- 19
18	**47**	**3**	**12**

62	97	61	54
- 48	- 18	- 17	- 39
14	**79**	**44**	**15**

83	64	56	46
- 29	- 55	- 28	- 33
54	**9**	**28**	**13**

47	54	37	42
- 17	- 39	- 18	- 36
30	**15**	**19**	**6**

68	62	35	44
- 51	- 45	- 18	- 26
17	**17**	**17**	**18**

80	48	56	73
- 45	- 36	- 47	- 34
35	**12**	**9**	**39**

83	25	70	54
- 29	- 17	- 45	- 38
54	**8**	**25**	**16**

35	63	37	45
- 18	- 46	- 15	- 18
17	**17**	**22**	**27**

Most of the problems on this page require regrouping. Make sure that children do not neglect to regroup when necessary.

Choosing the operation

Write either + or − in the box to make each problem correct.

18 **+** 32 = 50   45 **−** 22 = 23

Write either + or − in the box to make each problem correct.

85 **−** 35 = 50	63 **+** 23 = 86	66 **−** 25 = 41
50 **+** 12 = 62	28 **−** 16 = 12	27 **+** 35 = 62
14 **+** 61 = 75	43 **−** 10 = 33	72 **+** 11 = 83
97 **−** 53 = 44	14 **+** 23 = 37	50 **−** 36 = 14

Write either + or − in the box to make each problem correct.

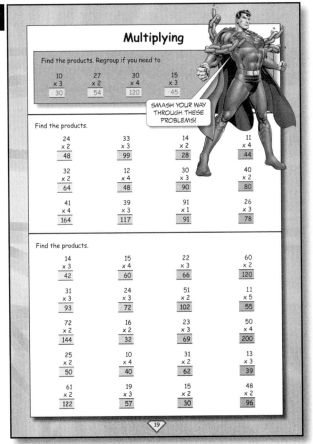

28 m **+** 21 m = 49 m	70 km **−** 39 km = 31 km
37 km **−** 14 km = 23 km	15 cm **−** 11 cm = 4 cm
78 mm **−** 48 mm = 30 mm	41 km **+** 42 km = 83 km
18 m **+** 33 m = 51 m	90 mm **−** 78 mm = 12 mm
71 cm **−** 10 cm = 61 cm	28 m **+** 21 m = 49 m
40 m **+** 51 m = 91 m	86 km **−** 54 km = 32 km

Write the answer in the box.

YOU CHOOSE.

Superman starts with 8 capes and ends up with 10. How many has he added or subtracted? **added 2**

A number is added to 12 and the result is 20. What number has been added? **8**

Steel starts with 5 suits. He finishes up with 3. How many suits has he lost or gained? **lost 2**

I take a number away from 30 and have 12 left. What number did I take away? **18**

Children should realize that if the answer is greater than the first number, they should add, and if the answer is smaller than the first number, they should subtract. They should check some of their answers to make sure that they are correct.

Multiplying

Find the products. Regroup if you need to.

10	27	30	15
x 3	x 2	x 4	x 3
30	**54**	**120**	**45**

SMASH YOUR WAY THROUGH THESE PROBLEMS!

Find the products.

24	33	14	11
x 2	x 3	x 2	x 4
48	**99**	**28**	**44**

32	12	30	40
x 2	x 4	x 3	x 2
64	**48**	**90**	**80**

41	39	91	26
x 4	x 3	x 1	x 3
164	**117**	**91**	**78**

Find the products.

14	15	22	60
x 3	x 4	x 3	x 2
42	**60**	**66**	**120**

31	24	51	11
x 3	x 3	x 2	x 5
93	**72**	**102**	**55**

72	16	23	50
x 2	x 2	x 3	x 4
144	**32**	**69**	**200**

25	10	31	13
x 2	x 4	x 2	x 3
50	**40**	**62**	**39**

61	19	15	48
x 2	x 3	x 2	x 2
122	**57**	**30**	**96**

Make sure that children multiply the ones first and then the tens.

Multiplying

Solve each problem.

14 x 3 = (10 x 3) + (4 x 3)
= 30 + 12
= 42

10	4
x 3	x 3
30	**12**

30 + 12 = 42

UP, UP, AND AWAY!

Solve each problem.

16 x 4	**64**	11 x 6	**66**
15 x 5	**75**	31 x 3	**93**
19 x 3	**57**	12 x 4	**48**
21 x 4	**84**	22 x 5	**110**
32 x 7	**224**	14 x 6	**84**
34 x 4	**136**	27 x 3	**81**

Some children may use distributive property, as shown in the example, to multiply. Others may set up the problems in vertical format, and multiply with regrouping. Both methods are acceptable.

Dividing

BREAKING ROCKS OR DIVIDING NUMBERS, IT'S ALL THE SAME TO ME.

Write the answer to each division problem; "r" means remainder.

$17 \div 4 =$ 4 r 1 $58 \div 10 =$ 5 r 8

$$3\overline{)23} \quad 7\ r\ 2$$
$$\underline{-21}$$
$$2$$

Write the answer to each division problem.

$31 \div 4 =$ 7 r 3	$55 \div 5 =$ 11 r 0	$29 \div 10 =$ 2 r 9	$29 \div 2 =$ 14 r 1
$47 \div 4 =$ 11 r 3	$34 \div 5 =$ 6 r 4	$57 \div 10 =$ 5 r 7	$14 \div 2 =$ 7 r 0
$18 \div 4 =$ 4 r 2	$46 \div 5 =$ 9 r 1	$35 \div 10 =$ 3 r 5	$11 \div 2 =$ 5 r 1
$25 \div 4 =$ 6 r 1	$13 \div 5 =$ 2 r 3	$90 \div 10 =$ 9 r 0	$21 \div 2 =$ 10 r 1

Write the answer to each division problem.

6 r 1 $4\overline{)25}$ -24 / 1

4 r 1 $3\overline{)13}$ -12 / 1

7 r 3 $5\overline{)38}$ -35 / 3

7 r 1 $7\overline{)50}$ -49 / 1

2 r 3 $6\overline{)15}$ -12 / 3

5 r 1 $2\overline{)11}$ -10 / 1

2 r 4 $8\overline{)20}$ -16 / 4

1 r 6 $9\overline{)15}$ -9 / 6

4 r 5 $6\overline{)29}$ -24 / 5

3 r 7 $8\overline{)31}$ -24 / 7

Write the answer in the box.

What is the remainder when 15 is divided by 2? — 1

How many groups of 5 are there in 55? — 11

How many groups of 4 are there in 24 and what is the remainder? — 6, none

What is the remainder when 63 is divided by 10? — 3

Divide 27 by 3. — 9

How many groups of 3 are there in 17? — 5

Solving division problems tests children's knowledge of times tables. If they have difficulty with long division, "walk" them through a few examples.

22

Dividing

Write the answer to each division problem.

$15 \div 4 =$ 3 r 3 $19 \div 2 =$ 9 r 1

$$3\overline{)8} \quad 2\ r\ 2$$
$$\underline{-6}$$
$$2$$

I'M BRAINIAC. I CAN DIVIDE. CAN YOU?

Write the answer in the box.

$24 \div 4 =$ 6 r 0	$80 \div 10 =$ 8 r 0	$19 \div 3 =$ 6 r 1	$29 \div 5 =$ 5 r 4
$29 \div 4 =$ 7 r 1	$38 \div 10 =$ 3 r 8	$13 \div 3 =$ 4 r 1	$31 \div 5 =$ 6 r 1
$14 \div 4 =$ 3 r 2	$17 \div 10 =$ 1 r 7	$33 \div 3 =$ 11 r 0	$12 \div 5 =$ 2 r 2
$32 \div 4 =$ 8 r 0	$24 \div 10 =$ 2 r 4	$23 \div 3 =$ 7 r 2	$38 \div 5 =$ 7 r 3

Write the answer in the box.

7 r 2 $3\overline{)23}$ -21 / 2

7 r 3 $4\overline{)31}$ -28 / 3

4 r 2 $5\overline{)22}$ -20 / 2

14 r 1 $2\overline{)29}$ -28 / 1

3 r 3 $4\overline{)15}$ -12 / 3

11 r 1 $4\overline{)45}$ -44 / 1

8 r 2 $3\overline{)26}$ -24 / 2

29 r 1 $2\overline{)59}$ -58 / 1

11 r 4 $5\overline{)59}$ -55 / 4

5 r 2 $3\overline{)17}$ -15 / 2

Write the answer in the box.

What is the remainder when 36 is divided by 10? — 6

How many whole sets of 5 are there in 16? — 3

How many sets of 3 are there in 20 and what is the remainder? — 6 r 2

What is the remainder when 44 is divided by 40? — 4

As with the previous page, most of the questions involve remainders. Make sure children do not feel the have to include a remainder if there is none. In the final section, the question that asks how many whole sets there are does not require a remainder.

23

Choosing the operation

Write either x or ÷ in the box to make each problem correct.

11 x $3 = 33$ 14 ÷ $2 = 7$

THIS IS HOW I OPERATE.

Write either x or ÷ in the box to make the product correct.

15 x $2 = 30$	12 ÷ $4 = 3$	2 x $7 = 14$
25 ÷ $5 = 5$	3 x $12 = 36$	8 ÷ $4 = 2$
13 x $10 = 130$	5 x $5 = 25$	3 x $3 = 9$
18 ÷ $6 = 3$	40 ÷ $4 = 10$	6 x $10 = 60$

Write either x or ÷ in the box to make the product correct.

$27cm$ ÷ $3 = 9\,cm$	$50\,mm$ ÷ $10 = 5\,mm$	$4\,m$ x $3 = 12\,m$
$16\,mm$ ÷ $2 = 8\,mm$	$4\,m$ x $5 = 20\,m$	$40\,m$ ÷ $4 = 10\,m$
$40\,cm$ ÷ $10 = 4\,cm$	$50\,m$ ÷ $5 = 10\,m$	$60\,cm$ ÷ $3 = 20\,cm$
$6\,m$ x $4 = 24\,m$	$4\,cm$ x $4 = 16\,cm$	$15\,cm$ x $2 = 30\,cm$
$30\,cm$ ÷ $10 = 3\,cm$	$20\,mm$ ÷ $5 = 4\,mm$	$30\,m$ ÷ $3 = 10\,m$
$12\,m$ ÷ $2 = 6\,m$	$1\,mm$ x $10 = 10\,mm$	$3\,cm$ x $2 = 6\,cm$

Write the answer in the box.

Which number multiplied by 3 equals 24? — 8

Which number divided by 10 equals 7? — 70

Which number divided by 8 equals 5? — 40

Which number multiplied by 6 equals 6? — 1

Which number multiplied by 9 equals 36? — 4

Which number multiplied by 5 equals 30? — 6

Children will probably realize that if the answer is greater than the first number, they should multiply, and if the answer is smaller than the first number they should divide. They should check some of the answers to make sure they are correct.

Word problems

Write the answer in the box.

I multiply a number by 4 and the answer is 20. What number did I begin with? — 5

FOR TRUTH AND JUSTICE!

Write the answer in the box.

A number multiplied by 6 equals 24. What is the number? — 4

I divide a number by 10 and the answer is 2. What number did I divide? — 20

I multiply a number by 6 and the answer is 30. What is the number I multiplied? — 5

After dividing a piece of wood into three equal sections, each section is 4 m long. How long was the piece of wood I started with? — 12 m

A number multiplied by 6 gives the answer 36. What is the number? — 6

Some money is divided into four equal amounts. Each amount is 10 cents. How much money was there before it was divided? — 40 cents

I multiply a number by 9 and the result is 45. What number was multiplied? — 5

A number divided by 3 equals 5. What number was divided? — 15

Three children share 18 peanuts equally among themselves. How many peanuts does each child receive? — 6

A number divided by 4 is 8. What is the number? — 32

I multiply a number by 6 and the answer is 36. What is the number? — 6

Four sets of a number equal 16. What is the number? — 4

A number divided by 5 is 5. What is the number? — 25

A child divides a number by 8 and gets 2. What number was divided? — 16

Three groups of a number equal 27. What is the number? — 9

I multiply a number by 10 and the result is 100. What is the number? — 10

Some children find these sorts of problems difficult even if they are good with times tables and division. Many of the problems require children to perform the inverse operation to the one named. Ask them to check their answers to make sure that are correct.

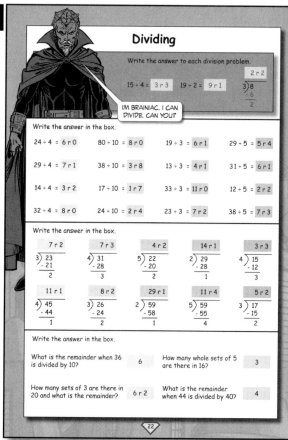

Word problems

THIS IS THE MOMENT OF MY GREATEST TRIUMPH!

Write the answer in the box.
Lex Luthor is given 3 dimes. How much money does he have altogether? **30¢**

Write the answer in the box.

Superman saves Jimmy Olsen 30 times in March, 40 times in April, and 20 times in May. How many times has Jimmy Olsen been saved altogether? **90**

Four lifeboats carry a total of 100 people. How many people are in each boat? **25**

Three women win the lottery and share $900 equally among themselves. How much does each woman receive? **$300**

Wayne has a collection of 120 Superman figures. He gives 40 of them to his friends. How many figures does he have now? **80**

When Peter multiplies his apartment number by 3, the result is 75. What is his apartment number? **25**

A copy of the *Daily Planet* costs $1.40. How much will two copies cost? **$2.80**

DAILY PLANET

Superman has captured some escaped animals. He has three cages. There are 12 animals in each cage. How many animals has Superman captured? **36**

Lois Lane's car trip is supposed to be 70 kilometres long but the car breaks down half-way. How far has the car gone when it breaks down? **35 km**

A teacher has 32 children in her class. 13 children are out with the flu. How many children are left in class? **19**

A safe contains 40 bars of gold. Lex Luthor steals 27 bars. How many bars are left in the safe? **13**

Perry White employs 17 reporters at the *Daily Planet*. He fires 9 of them. How many reporters are left? **8**

Children will need to think carefully about how they will solve each question. If they have difficulty, talk each problem through with them.

26

Problems with measures

Which would be the best unit to use for the length of this girder?
metre

USE YOUR MENTAL POWERS TO FIGURE THESE OUT.

Choose the most appropriate unit for the measurements below.

metre   litre   kilometre   gram   kilogram   centimetre

Write the best unit for each of the following.

The length of Lois Lane's car. **metre**

The weight of a flyer pod. **kilogram**

The weight of Clark Kent's glasses. **gram**

The distance from Koron to Xenon. **kilometre**

Xenon   Koron

The length of Superman's cape. **metre**

The capacity of a soda can. **litre**

Most children are familiar with the units of measurement given. If necessary, give other examples of items that would be meaured using these units.

27

Telling time

What time is shown by these clocks?

18 minutes to 8   **11 minutes after 4**

What is the time shown by these clocks?

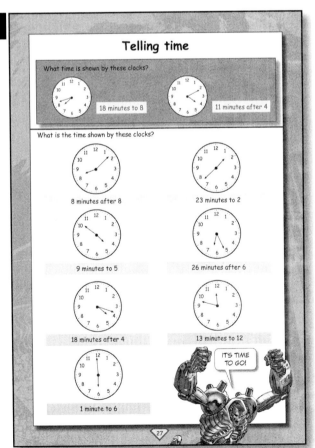

8 minutes after 8   23 minutes to 2

9 minutes to 5   26 minutes after 6

18 minutes after 4   13 minutes to 12

1 minute to 6

IT'S TIME TO GO!

Because of the popularity of digital watches children could write 7:47 for the first answer and be correct, although the convention is to say the minutes to an hour or after an hour. Children should know both ways of saying the time.

28

Telling time

Draw the time on each clock face.

Twenty-six minutes after four. **04:26**

Choose the most appropriate unit for the measurements below.

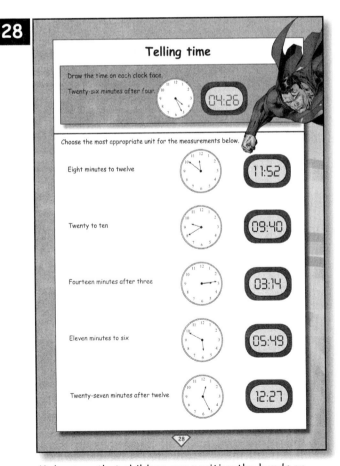

Eight minutes to twelve   **11:52**

Twenty to ten   **09:40**

Fourteen minutes after three   **03:14**

Eleven minutes to six   **05:49**

Twenty-seven minutes after twelve   **12:27**

Make sure that children can position the hands or numbers on the clocks. Show them that the space between numbers on an analog clock is divided into five minutes. The hour hand can be drawn in an approximate position between the correct numbers.

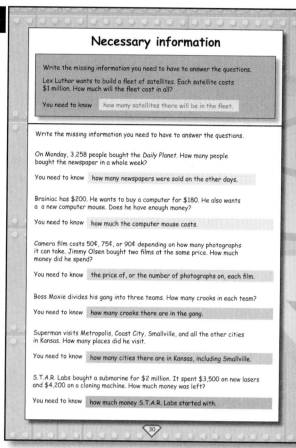

29 — Tables and graphs

Look at this bar graph.

SUPERMAN'S POWERS

Powers: superpowers, superweaknesses
Number: 2 4 6 8 10

How many superpowers does Superman have? **10**

Look at this bar graph.

LEX LUTHOR'S SUITS

Color of suits: green, blue, red, black
Number of suits: 2 4 6 8 10

How many green suits does Luthor have? **2**

Luthor has 1 suit of which color? **red**

How many blue suits does Luthor have? **8**

Of which color does Luthor have the most suits? **black**

How many suits does Luthor have altogether? **21**

Complete the table.

FAVORITE SUPER HERO

Super heroes	tally marks	total
Superman	ЖЖ |||	8
Supergirl	||||	4
Steel	|||	3

Number of children

How many more children prefer Superman to Steel? **5**

Which super hero is prefered by 4 children **Supergirl**

WHOM DO YOU LIKE THE BEST?

The first section requires children to notice that divisions on the scale are in twos rather than ones. To answer some of the questions about the bar graph, children will have to add and compare data.

30 — Necessary information

Write the missing information you need to have to answer the questions.

Lex Luthor wants to build a fleet of satellites. Each satellite costs $1 million. How much will the fleet cost in all?

You need to know **how many satellites there will be in the fleet.**

Write the missing information you need to have to answer the questions.

On Monday, 3,258 people bought the *Daily Planet*. How many people bought the newspaper in a whole week?

You need to know **how many newspapers were sold on the other days.**

Brainiac has $200. He wants to buy a computer for $180. He also wants a a new computer mouse. Does he have enough money?

You need to know **how much the computer mouse costs.**

Camera film costs 50¢, 75¢, or 90¢ depending on how many photographs it can take. Jimmy Olsen bought two films at the same price. How much money did he spend?

You need to know **the price of, or the number of photographs on, each film.**

Boss Moxie divides his gang into three teams. How many crooks in each team?

You need to know **how many crooks there are in the gang.**

Superman visits Metropolis, Coast City, Smallville, and all the other cities in Kansas. How many places did he visit.

You need to know **how many cities there are in Kansas, including Smallville.**

S.T.A.R. Labs bought a submarine for $2 million. It spent $3,500 on new lasers and $4,200 on a cloning machine. How much money was left?

You need to know **how much money S.T.A.R. Labs started with.**

Some children may read a problem and not know how to proceed. Suggest several pieces of information, one of which needs to be found to solve the problem. Help them understand how to identify the missing information.

31 — Number pairs

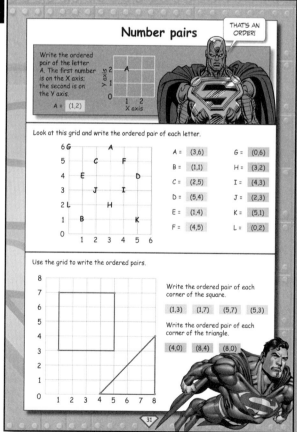

THAT'S AN ORDER!

Write the ordered pair of the letter A. The first number is on the X axis; the second is on the Y axis.

A = **(1,2)**

Look at this grid and write the ordered pair of each letter.

A = (3,6)	G = (0,6)
B = (1,1)	H = (3,2)
C = (2,5)	I = (4,3)
D = (5,4)	J = (2,3)
E = (1,4)	K = (5,1)
F = (4,5)	L = (0,2)

Use the grid to write the ordered pairs.

Write the ordered pair of each corner of the square.
(1,3) (1,7) (5,7) (5,3)

Write the ordered pair of each corner of the triangle.
(4,0) (8,4) (8,0)

Make sure that children understand that the order of the numbers within ordered pairs is important. The first number is from the horizontal or x axis, and the second number is from the vertical or y axis. Ordered pairs are written in parentheses, like this A = (1,2).

32 — 2 times table

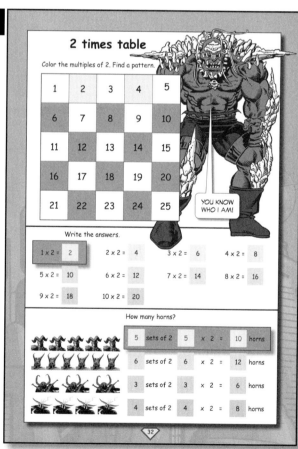

Color the multiples of 2. Find a pattern.

1	2	3	4	5
6	7	8	9	10
11	12	13	14	15
16	17	18	19	20
21	22	23	24	25

YOU KNOW WHO I AM!

Write the answers.

1 x 2 = 2	2 x 2 = 4	3 x 2 = 6	4 x 2 = 8
5 x 2 = 10	6 x 2 = 12	7 x 2 = 14	8 x 2 = 16
9 x 2 = 18	10 x 2 = 20		

How many horns?

5 sets of 2   5 x 2 = 10 horns
6 sets of 2   6 x 2 = 12 horns
3 sets of 2   3 x 2 = 6 horns
4 sets of 2   4 x 2 = 8 horns

33

Multiplying by 2

Write the problems.

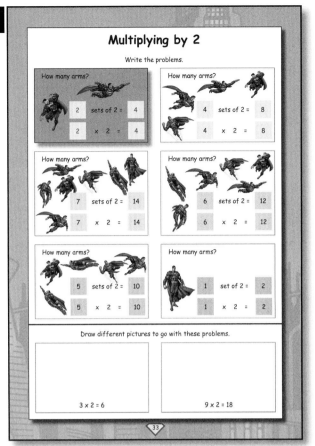

How many arms?	How many arms?
2 sets of 2 = 4	4 sets of 2 = 8
2 × 2 = 4	4 × 2 = 8
How many arms?	How many arms?
7 sets of 2 = 14	6 sets of 2 = 12
7 × 2 = 14	6 × 2 = 12
How many arms?	How many arms?
5 sets of 2 = 10	1 set of 2 = 2
5 × 2 = 10	1 × 2 = 2

Draw different pictures to go with these problems.

3 × 2 = 6	9 × 2 = 18

33

34

Dividing by 2

Share the kryptonite equally between the boxes.

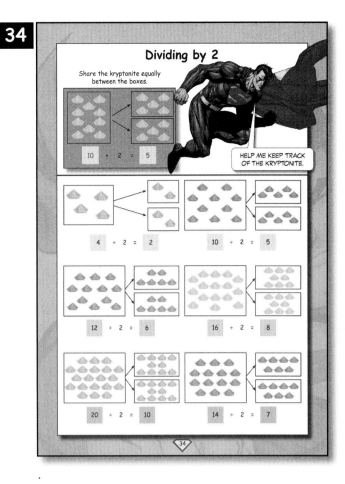

10 ÷ 2 = 5

HELP ME KEEP TRACK OF THE KRYPTONITE.

4 ÷ 2 = 2   10 ÷ 2 = 5

12 ÷ 2 = 6   16 ÷ 2 = 8

20 ÷ 2 = 10   14 ÷ 2 = 7

34

35

Using the 2 times table

Write the problems to match Superman's shields.

4 rows of 2	8 rows of 2
4 × 2 = 8	8 × 2 = 16
3 rows of 2	5 rows of 2
3 × 2 = 6	5 × 2 = 10
9 rows of 2	1 row of 2
9 × 2 = 18	1 × 2 = 2

Draw shields to match these problems.

3 × 2	4 × 2
2 × 2	7 × 2

35

36

Using the 2 times table

Each cape stands for 2. Join each set of capes to the correct number.

COUNT IN TWOS!

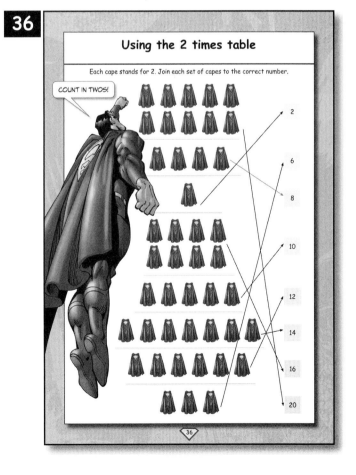

2

6

8

10

12

14

16

20

36

37

Using the 2 times table

How many eyes?

3 × 2 = 6 eyes

5 × 2 = 10 eyes

9 × 2 = 18 eyes

2 × 2 = 4 eyes

8 × 2 = 16 eyes

4 × 2 = 8 eyes

Draw your own pictures to match these number sentences.

2 × 2 = 4

6 × 2 = 12

7 × 2 = 14

10 × 2 = 20

37

38

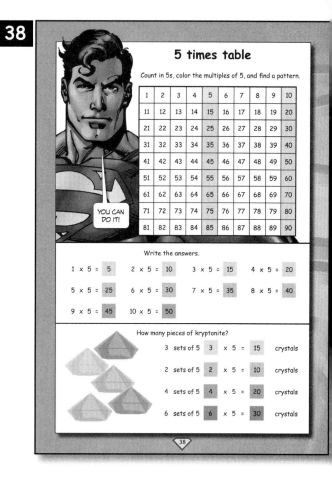

5 times table

Count in 5s, color the multiples of 5, and find a pattern.

1	2	3	4	5	6	7	8	9	10
11	12	13	14	15	16	17	18	19	20
21	22	23	24	25	26	27	28	29	30
31	32	33	34	35	36	37	38	39	40
41	42	43	44	45	46	47	48	49	50
51	52	53	54	55	56	57	58	59	60
61	62	63	64	65	66	67	68	69	70
71	72	73	74	75	76	77	78	79	80
81	82	83	84	85	86	87	88	89	90

YOU CAN DO IT!

Write the answers.

1 × 5 = 5   2 × 5 = 10   3 × 5 = 15   4 × 5 = 20

5 × 5 = 25   6 × 5 = 30   7 × 5 = 35   8 × 5 = 40

9 × 5 = 45   10 × 5 = 50

How many pieces of kryptonite?

3 sets of 5   3 × 5 = 15   crystals

2 sets of 5   2 × 5 = 10   crystals

4 sets of 5   4 × 5 = 20   crystals

6 sets of 5   6 × 5 = 30   crystals

38

39

Multiplying by 5

Draw a ring around rows of 5. Complete the problem.

3 × 5 = 15

PUNCH YOUR WAY THROUGH THESE!

Draw a ring around rows of 5.

5 rings of 5   5 × 5 = 25

2 rings of 5   2 × 5 = 10

1 ring of 5   1 × 5 = 5

6 rings of 5   6 × 5 = 30

4 rings of 5   4 × 5 = 20

3 rings of 5   3 × 5 = 15

39

40

Dividing by 5

Write a number sentence to show how many cubes are in each stack.

15 cubes altogether

5 stacks

15 ÷ 5 = 3

EVERY SECOND COUNTS!

Write a number sentence to show how many cubes are in each stack.

20 cubes
5 stacks
20 ÷ 5 = 4

30 cubes
5 stacks
30 ÷ 5 = 6

25 cubes
5 stacks
25 ÷ 5 = 5

10 cubes
5 stacks
10 ÷ 5 = 2

35 cubes
5 stacks
35 ÷ 5 = 7

40 cubes
5 stacks
40 ÷ 5 = 8

40

41

Using the 5 times table

I'LL USE MY POWERS TO SOLVE THESE PROBLEMS!

Write the number that is hiding under the star.

8 × 5 = 40

Write the number that is hiding under the star.

5 × 5 = 25   6 × 5 = 30

1 × 5 = 5   10 × 5 = 50

7 × 5 = 35   4 × 5 = 20

9 × 5 = 45   3 × 5 = 15

2 × 5 = 10   0 × 5 = 0

42

Using the 5 times table

Each shape stands for 5. Join each set of items to the correct number.

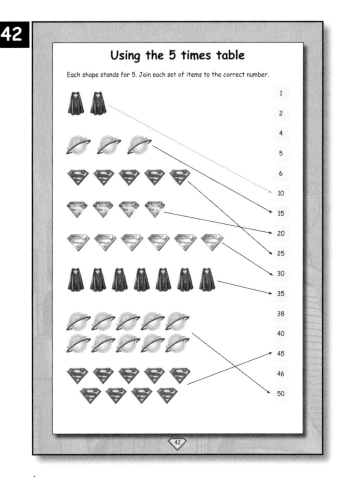

1
2
4
5
6
10
15
20
25
30
35
38
40
45
46
50

43

Using the 5 times table

How many altogether?

Lex Luthor has 7 jet airplanes. Each airplane has 5 seats. How many seats are there altogether?

7 × 5 = 35 seats

How many altogether?

Superman has 3 capes. Each cape has 5 pockets. How many pockets are there altogether?

3 × 5 = 15 pockets

Doomsday destroys 8 stars. Each star had 5 planets. How many planets are there altogether?

8 × 5 = 40 planets

Supergirl catches 6 gangs. Each gang contains 5 crooks. How many crooks are there altogether?

6 × 5 = 30 crooks

How many in each?

Lois Lane had 50 pens in 5 cases. How many pens were in each case?

50 ÷ 5 = 10 pens

How many in each?

Superman has 60 oxygen cartridges on 5 belts. How many cartidges are there on each belt?

60 ÷ 5 = 12 cartridges

Jimmy Olsen has 35 photographs on 5 films. How many photos are there on each film?

35 ÷ 5 = 7 photos

S.T.A.R. Labs has 25 clones in 5 buildings. How many clones are there in each building?

25 ÷ 5 = 5 clones

44

10 times table

I'M BRAINIAC. I CAN COUNT IN 10S. CAN YOU?

Count in 10s, color the multiples of 10, and find a pattern.

1	2	3	4	5	6	7	8	9	10
11	12	13	14	15	16	17	18	19	20
21	22	23	24	25	26	27	28	29	30
31	32	33	34	35	36	37	38	39	40
41	42	43	44	45	46	47	48	49	50
51	52	53	54	55	56	57	58	59	60
61	62	63	64	65	66	67	68	69	70
71	72	73	74	75	76	77	78	79	80
81	82	83	84	85	86	87	88	89	90

Find the products.

1 × 10 = 10   2 × 10 = 20   3 × 10 = 30   4 × 10 = 40

5 × 10 = 50   6 × 10 = 60   7 × 10 = 70   8 × 10 = 80

10 × 10 = 100   9 × 10 = 90

Each stack contains 10 cards. How many cards are there altogether?

2 sets of 10   2 × 10 = 20 cards

4 sets of 10   4 × 10 = 40 cards

6 sets of 10   6 × 10 = 60 cards

9 sets of 10   9 × 10 = 90 cards

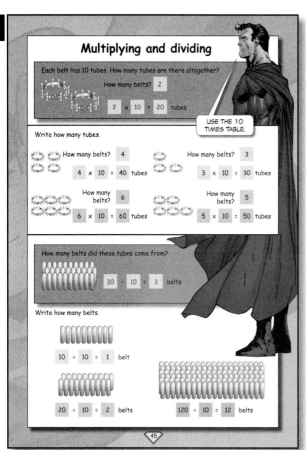

45

Multiplying and dividing

Each belt has 10 tubes. How many tubes are there altogether?

How many belts? `2`

`2` × `10` = `20` tubes

USE THE 10 TIMES TABLE.

Write how many tubes.

How many belts? `4`

`4` × `10` = `40` tubes

How many belts? `3`

`3` × `10` = `30` tubes

How many belts? `6`

`6` × `10` = `60` tubes

How many belts? `5`

`5` × `10` = `50` tubes

How many belts did these tubes come from?

`30` ÷ `10` = `3` belts

Write how many belts.

`10` ÷ `10` = `1` belt

`20` ÷ `10` = `2` belts

`120` ÷ `10` = `12` belts

46

Dividing by 10

HOW MANY DIMES DO I HAVE?

$1

One dollar is worth the same as 10 dimes.

One dime (×10)

30 dimes
`30` ÷ 10 = $ `3`

60 dimes
`60` ÷ 10 = $ `6`

40 dimes
`40` ÷ 10 = $ `4`

50 dimes
`50` ÷ 10 = $ `5`

90 dimes
`90` ÷ 10 = $ `9`

100 dimes
`100` ÷ 10 = $ `10`

10 dimes
`10` ÷ 10 = $ `1`

20 dimes
`20` ÷ 10 = $ `2`

47

Using the 10 times table

How many altogether?

Steel has 3 tool boxes. Each box has 10 hammers. How many hammers are there altogether?

`3` × `10` = `30` hammers

THIS MATH ISN'T AS TOUGH AS I AM!

How many altogether?

Clark Kent had 6 notebooks. There were 10 pages in each book. How many pages were there altogether?

`6` × `10` = `60` pages

LexCorp had 2 offices. Each office had 10 desks. How many desks were there altogether?

`2` × `10` = `20` desks

Project Cadmus had 5 tanks. Each tank had 10 guns on it. How many guns were there altogether?

`5` × `10` = `50` guns

S.T.A.R. Labs built 7 rockets. Each rocket had 10 engines. How many engines were there altogether?

`7` × `10` = `70` engines

How many in each?

Lois Lane had 20 lipsticks in 10 handbags. How many lipsticks were in each bag?

`20` ÷ `10` = `2` lipsticks

How many in each?

There were 80 jewels in 10 safes. How many jewels were in each safe?

`80` ÷ `10` = `8` jewels

There were 60 villains in 10 spaceships. How many villians in each spaceship?

`60` ÷ `10` = `6` villains

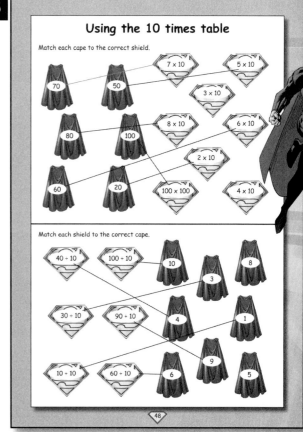

48

Using the 10 times table

Match each cape to the correct shield.

7 × 10   5 × 10   3 × 10   8 × 10   6 × 10   2 × 10   100 × 100   4 × 10

70   50   80   100   60   20

Match each shield to the correct cape.

40 ÷ 10   100 ÷ 10   30 ÷ 10   90 ÷ 10   10 ÷ 10   60 ÷ 10

10   8   3   4   1   9   6   5

HELP ME FIND WHAT'S MISSING.

Using the 10 times table

Write in the missing numbers.

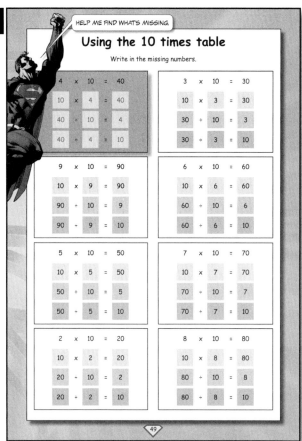

4	x	10	=	40
10	x	4	=	40
40	÷	10	=	4
40	÷	4	=	10

3	x	10	=	30
10	x	3	=	30
30	÷	10	=	3
30	÷	3	=	10

9	x	10	=	90
10	x	9	=	90
90	÷	10	=	9
90	÷	9	=	10

6	x	10	=	60
10	x	6	=	60
60	÷	10	=	6
60	÷	6	=	10

5	x	10	=	50
10	x	5	=	50
50	÷	10	=	5
50	÷	5	=	10

7	x	10	=	70
10	x	7	=	70
70	÷	10	=	7
70	÷	7	=	10

2	x	10	=	20
10	x	2	=	20
20	÷	10	=	2
20	÷	2	=	10

8	x	10	=	80
10	x	8	=	80
80	÷	10	=	8
80	÷	8	=	10

---

3 times table

Count in 3s, color the multiples of 3, and find a pattern.

1	2	3	4	5
6	7	8	9	10
11	12	13	14	15
16	17	18	19	20
21	22	23	24	25

RUN THROUGH THESE SUMS AS FAST AS YOU CAN!

Find the products.

1 x 3 = 3   2 x 3 = 6   3 x 3 = 9   4 x 3 = 12

Count each star as 3.

2 sets of 3   2 x 3 = 6

3 sets of 3   3 x 3 = 9

4 sets of 3   4 x 3 = 12

5 sets of 3   5 x 3 = 15

Multiplying by 3

Write the number sentences to match the pictures.

2 sets of 3 = 6
2 x 3 = 6

4 sets of 3 = 12
4 x 3 = 12

2 sets of 3 = 6
2 x 3 = 6

5 sets of 3 = 15
5 x 3 = 15

3 sets of 3 = 9
3 x 3 = 9

1 set of 3 = 3
1 x 3 = 3

Draw you own pictures to match these number sentences.

5 x 3 = 15

2 x 3 = 6

3 x 3 = 9

4 x 3 = 12

I ALWAYS SHARE THE SPOILS EQUALLY!

Dividing by 3

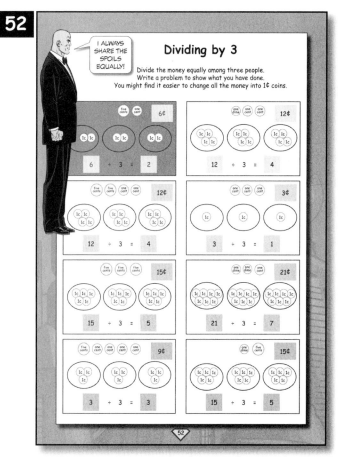

Divide the money equally among three people.
Write a problem to show what you have done.
You might find it easier to change all the money into 1¢ coins.

6¢   6 ÷ 3 = 2

12¢   12 ÷ 3 = 4

12¢   12 ÷ 3 = 4

3¢   3 ÷ 3 = 1

15¢   15 ÷ 3 = 5

21¢   21 ÷ 3 = 7

9¢   3 ÷ 3 = 3

15¢   15 ÷ 3 = 5

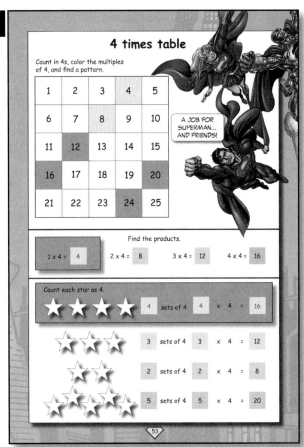

4 times table

Count in 4s, color the multiples of 4, and find a pattern.

1	2	3	4	5
6	7	8	9	10
11	12	13	14	15
16	17	18	19	20
21	22	23	24	25

A JOB FOR SUPERMAN... AND FRIENDS!

Find the products.

1 x 4 = 4   2 x 4 = 8   3 x 4 = 12   4 x 4 = 16

Count each star as 4.

★ ★ ★ ★   4 sets of 4   4 x 4 = 16

3 sets of 4   3 x 4 = 12

2 sets of 4   2 x 4 = 8

5 sets of 4   5 x 4 = 20

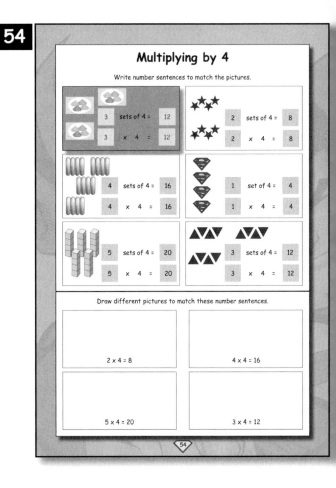

Multiplying by 4

Write number sentences to match the pictures.

3 sets of 4 = 12
3 x 4 = 12

2 sets of 4 = 8
2 x 4 = 8

4 sets of 4 = 16
4 x 4 = 16

1 set of 4 = 4
1 x 4 = 4

5 sets of 4 = 20
5 x 4 = 20

3 sets of 4 = 12
3 x 4 = 12

Draw different pictures to match these number sentences.

| 2 x 4 = 8 | 4 x 4 = 16 |
| 5 x 4 = 20 | 3 x 4 = 12 |

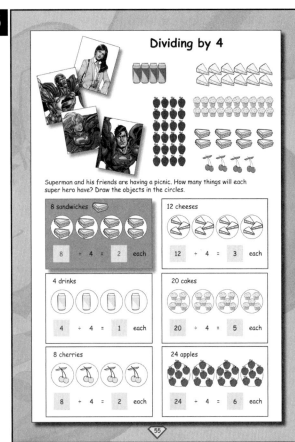

Dividing by 4

Superman and his friends are having a picnic. How many things will each super hero have? Draw the objects in the circles.

8 sandwiches
8 ÷ 4 = 2 each

12 cheeses
12 ÷ 4 = 3 each

4 drinks
4 ÷ 4 = 1 each

20 cakes
20 ÷ 4 = 5 each

8 cherries
8 ÷ 4 = 2 each

24 apples
24 ÷ 4 = 6 each

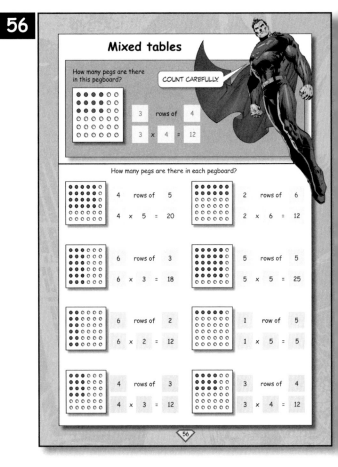

Mixed tables

How many pegs are there in this pegboard?

COUNT CAREFULLY

3 rows of 4
3 x 4 = 12

How many pegs are there in each pegboard?

4 rows of 5
4 x 5 = 20

2 rows of 6
2 x 6 = 12

6 rows of 3
6 x 3 = 18

5 rows of 5
5 x 5 = 25

6 rows of 2
6 x 2 = 12

1 row of 5
1 x 5 = 5

4 rows of 3
4 x 3 = 12

3 rows of 4
3 x 4 = 12

Mixed tables

Divide the 12 pennies equally. Draw the coins
and write the problem to show how many each character gets.

one cent · one cent · one cent · one cent · one cent · one cent · one cent · one cent · one cent · one cent · one cent · one cent

12 ÷ 3 = 4

4 ¢ each

12 ÷ 2 = 6

6 ¢ each

12 ÷ 6 = 2

2 ¢ each

12 ÷ 1 = 12

12 ¢

12 ÷ 12 = 1

1 ¢ each

Mixed tables

How much will Supergirl get paid?

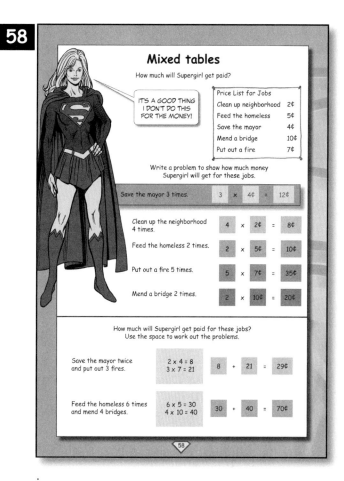

IT'S A GOOD THING I DON'T DO THIS FOR THE MONEY!

Price List for Jobs	
Clean up neighborhood	2¢
Feed the homeless	5¢
Save the mayor	4¢
Mend a bridge	10¢
Put out a fire	7¢

Write a problem to show how much money
Supergirl will get for these jobs.

Save the mayor 3 times.   3 × 4¢ = 12¢

Clean up the neighborhood 4 times.   4 × 2¢ = 8¢

Feed the homeless 2 times.   2 × 5¢ = 10¢

Put out a fire 5 times.   5 × 7¢ = 35¢

Mend a bridge 2 times.   2 × 10¢ = 20¢

How much will Supergirl get paid for these jobs?
Use the space to work out the problems.

Save the mayor twice
and put out 3 fires.
2 × 4 = 8
3 × 7 = 21
8 + 21 = 29¢

Feed the homeless 6 times
and mend 4 bridges.
6 × 5 = 30
4 × 10 = 40
30 + 40 = 70¢

Mixed tables

Write the numbers that the
capes are hiding.

4 × 5 = 20

20 ÷ 4 = 5

2 × 4 = 8

8 ÷ 2 = 4

6 ÷ 3 = 2

2 × 3 = 6

1 × 3 = 3

3 × 3 = 9

5 × 9 = 45

45 ÷ 5 = 9

8 × 2 = 16

16 ÷ 2 = 8

60 ÷ 10 = 6

10 × 6 = 60

3 × 4 = 12

12 ÷ 4 = 3

7 × 5 = 35

35 ÷ 5 = 7

5 × 10 = 50

50 ÷ 10 = 5

Mixed tables

10 → 5   15 → 3

12 → ÷ 2 → 6   30 → ÷ 5 → 6

2 → 1   50 → 10

8 → 4   35 → 7

9 → 3   4 → 1

12 → ÷ 3 → 4   8 → ÷ 4 → 2

15 → 5   12 → 3

6 → 2   16 → 4

70 → 7

30 → ÷ 10 → 3

100 → 10

40 → 4

THIS LOOKS LIKE A JOB FOR SUPERMAN!

Mixed tables

3	→	6
10	→ (× 2) →	20
7	→	14
5	→	10

3	→	9
5	→ (× 3) →	15
4	→	12
1	→	3

3	→	12
5	→ (× 4) →	20
4	→	16
2	→	8

0	→	0
10	→ (× 5) →	50
8	→	40
9	→	45

10	→	100
7	→ (× 10) →	70
5	→	50
2	→	20

Mixed tables

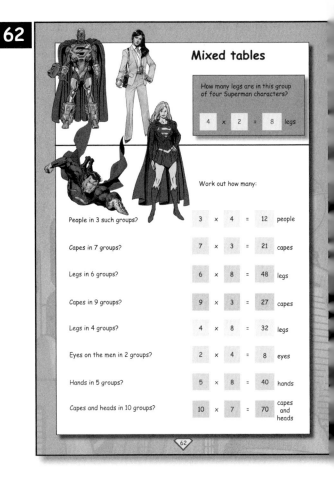

How many legs are in this group of four Superman characters?

4 × 2 = 8 legs

Work out how many:

People in 3 such groups?	3	×	4	=	12	people
Capes in 7 groups?	7	×	3	=	21	capes
Legs in 6 groups?	6	×	8	=	48	legs
Capes in 9 groups?	9	×	3	=	27	capes
Legs in 4 groups?	4	×	8	=	32	legs
Eyes on the men in 2 groups?	2	×	4	=	8	eyes
Hands in 5 groups?	5	×	8	=	40	hands
Capes and heads in 10 groups?	10	×	7	=	70	capes and heads

Number pairs

Put an X at (2,3).

UP, UP, AND AWAY! THIS IS A JOB FOR SUPERMAN.

Put an X on this grid at each of these ordered pairs:
(1,1) (1,9) (3,9) (3,6) (7,6) (7,9) (9,9) (9,1) (7,1) (7,4) (3,4) (3,1) (1,1)

Join the Xs in the same order.
Which capital letter have you drawn?   H

If children complete the ordered pairs so that they form a capital H, they understand the concept. If not, find any errors that they have made and help them see what they did incorrectly.

Logic problems

Read the clues to find the secret number.

2 3 4 5 6 7   (6 4 8 2)   (4 5 9 7)

It is in both the rectangle and the oval.
It is not in the triangle. It is greater than 4.
What number is it?   6

Read the clues to find the secret number.

| Triangle: 15, 11, 13, 18, 20 | 15 12, 11 14, 13 | 23 22 14, 12 16 10 |

It is not in the square. It is an odd number.
It is greater than any number in the triangle.
What number is it?   23

| 11 10, 16 19, 15 14 | (13, 15 11, 12 8) | 14 15 12, 7 21 |

It is in the rectangle and the oval.
It is greater than 10 and less than 17. It is an even number.
What number is it?   12

It is in the triangle.
It is not an even number.
It is in the big rectangle and the small rectangle.
What number is it?   3

4 2, 1 3 9, 5 6 8 7

Children can solve these problems by guess-and-check or they can use a systematic approach by eliminating numbers that do not meet the conditions given.

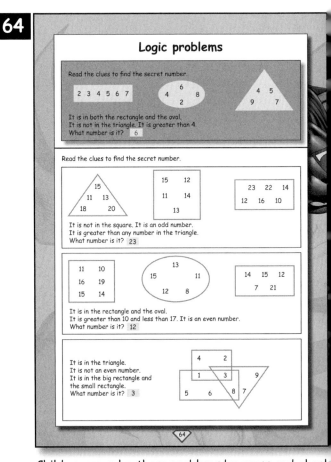

Dividing

SPLIT 'EM UP!

Write the quotient in the box.

$80 \div 10 = 8$ $30 \div 10 = 3$

$$10\overline{)70}$$
-70
0

quotient: 7

Write the quotient in the box.

$40 \div 10 = 4$	$320 \div 10 = 32$	$50 \div 10 = 5$
$130 \div 10 = 13$	$490 \div 10 = 49$	$100 \div 10 = 10$
$210 \div 10 = 21$	$10 \div 10 = 1$	$630 \div 10 = 63$
$20 \div 10 = 2$	$80 \div 10 = 8$	$220 \div 10 = 22$
$90 \div 10 = 9$	$200 \div 10 = 20$	$870 \div 10 = 87$
$60 \div 10 = 6$	$160 \div 10 = 16$	$30 \div 10 = 3$

Write the quotient in the box.

7 — $10\overline{)70}$ -70 0

13 — $10\overline{)130}$ -130 0

4 — $10\overline{)40}$ -40 0

9 — $10\overline{)90}$ -90 0

26 — $10\overline{)260}$ -260 0

1 — $10\overline{)10}$ -10 0

30 — $10\overline{)300}$ -300 0

42 — $10\overline{)420}$ -130 0

Write the quotient in the box.

$1,560 \div 10 = 156$	$6,030 \div 10 = 603$	$4,020 \div 10 = 402$
$3,040 \div 10 = 304$	$8,750 \div 10 = 875$	$6,730 \div 10 = 673$
$4,700 \div 10 = 470$	$2,000 \div 10 = 200$	$1,010 \div 10 = 101$
$5,430 \div 10 = 543$	$3,980 \div 10 = 398$	$9,990 \div 10 = 999$

Children should understand quickly that dividing multiples of 10 by 10 results in the removal of the final zero. Make sure that they remove the commas in any thousands when they divide by 10.

Rounding

Round each amount to the nearest whole unit. If the number to the right of the unit is 5 or more, round up; if 4 or less, round down.

$2.70	$1.10	3.40 m	1.50 m
$3.00	$1.00	3 m	2 m

WHO CARES ABOUT THE CENTS?

Round each amount to the nearest dollar.

$1.35 $1.00	$4.20 $4.00	$15.50 $16.00	$8.55 $9.00
$4.25 $4.00	$6.90 $7.00	$3.75 $4.00	$1.50 $2.00
$5.80 $6.00	$11.35 $11.00	$9.90 $10.00	$6.70 $7.00
$12.55 $13.00	$17.20 $17.00	$2.45 $2.00	$5.15 $5.00
$10.10 $10.00	$6.65 $7.00	$13.40 $13.00	$19.70 $20.00

Round each amount to the nearest metre.

1.65 m 2 m	4.05 m 4 m	6.50 m 7 m	5.65 m 6 m
3.35 m 3 m	6.55 m 7 m	1.30 m 1 m	2.25 m 2 m
2.95 m 3 m	5.80 m 6 m	8.35 m 8 m	2.45 m 2 m
7.40 m 7 m	9.10 m 9 m	7.55 m 8 m	3.80 m 4 m
4.70 m 5 m	1.75 m 2 m	9.25 m 9 m	7.50 m 8 m

Round each amount to the nearest whole unit.

$4.95 $5.00	20.65 m 21 m	2.85 m 3 m	$5.10 $5.00
8.05 m 8 m	$9.15 $9.00	$1.40 $1.00	19.70 m 20 m
$12.40 $12.00	$6.50 $7.00	8.50 m 9 m	$7.10 $7.00

Children should recognize that amounts of 50¢ or 50 m and above are rounded up, and amounts below 50¢ and 50 m are rounded down. Make sure that children increase the whole number by 1 when they round up.

Congruency

Figures that are the same size and shape are congruent. Are these figures congruent?

yes   no   no   yes

Circle the congruent figures.

Point out to children that figures do not have to be oriented in the same way to be congruent; it is size and shape that are important. Make sure they know that there may be more than two congruent figures to identify.

Identifying patterns

Complete each pattern.

88	78	68	58	48	38	28	18
38	35	32	29	26	23	20	17

Complete each pattern.

41	39	37	35	33	31	29	27
67	61	55	49	43	37	31	25
54	49	44	39	34	29	24	19
77	73	69	65	61	57	53	49
98	90	82	74	66	58	50	42
27	25	23	21	19	17	15	13
85	80	75	70	65	60	55	50
64	56	48	40	32	24	16	8
89	80	71	62	53	44	35	26
50	44	38	32	26	20	14	8
31	28	25	22	19	16	13	10
46	41	36	31	26	21	16	11
92	84	76	68	60	52	44	36
19	17	15	13	11	9	7	5
9	8	7	6	5	4	3	2
59	52	45	38	31	24	17	10
83	73	63	53	43	33	23	13

Point out that some of the patterns show an increase and some a decrease. Children should check that the operation that turns the first number into the second also turns the second number into the third. They can then continue the pattern.

Odds and evens

Write the sum in the box.

$4 + 4 =$ 8 $1 + 3 =$ 4 $3 + 3 =$ 6

Add the even number to the even number.

$2 + 4 =$ 6	$12 + 4 =$ 16	$2 + 20 =$ 22	$8 + 18 =$ 26
$8 + 14 =$ 22	$10 + 22 =$ 32	$30 + 40 =$ 70	$12 + 14 =$ 36
$8 + 2 =$ 10	$28 + 4 =$ 32	$6 + 6 =$ 12	$2 + 12 =$ 14

What do you notice about each answer?   All the answers are even numbers.

Add the odd number to the odd number.

$3 + 7 =$ 10	$1 + 15 =$ 16	$9 + 9 =$ 18	$11 + 9 =$ 20
$3 + 3 =$ 6	$5 + 7 =$ 12	$1 + 1 =$ 2	$19 + 13 =$ 32
$9 + 13 =$ 22	$3 + 17 =$ 20	$5 + 33 =$ 38	$11 + 3 =$ 14

What do you notice about each answer?   All the answers are even numbers.

Add the odd number to the even number.

$7 + 6 =$ 13	$5 + 20 =$ 25	$13 + 6 =$ 19	$11 + 12 =$ 23
$17 + 4 =$ 21	$9 + 4 =$ 13	$1 + 10 =$ 11	$19 + 8 =$ 27
$1 + 2 =$ 3	$7 + 10 =$ 17	$3 + 12 =$ 15	$9 + 4 =$ 13

What do you notice about each answer?   All the answers are odd numbers.

Add the even number to the odd number.

$10 + 7 =$ 17	$4 + 1 =$ 5	$12 + 13 =$ 25	$28 + 5 =$ 33
$2 + 3 =$ 5	$2 + 17 =$ 19	$20 + 3 =$ 23	$2 + 11 =$ 13
$8 + 7 =$ 15	$6 + 3 =$ 9	$32 + 7 =$ 39	$14 + 7 =$ 21

What do you notice about each answer?   All the answers are odd numbers.

Children should note that adding two even numbers results in an even number, adding two odd numbers results in an odd number, and adding an odd and an even number results in an odd number. The order in which numbers are added does not matter.

Probability

Look at the crystals in the oval.

This kind of crystal is least likely to be picked from the oval.

This kind of crystal is most likely to be picked from the oval.

Look at this table.

TYPES OF JEWELS IN LEX LUTHOR'S SAFE

diamond	ruby	emerald	sapphire	jade
2	9	12	5	1

Which type of jewel is the least likely to be stolen?   jade

Which type of jewel is the most likely to be stolen?   emerald

Look at the chart.

PENS IN LOIS'S HANDBAG

color	tally
blue	$\cancel{||||}$
green	|||
black	$\cancel{||||}$ ||
red	$\cancel{||||}$

Which color pen is most likely to be picked?   black

Which color pen is least likely to be picked?   green

Which color pen is as likely to be picked as a blue pen?   red

Children should realize that the more of a particular item there is in a set, the more likely it is to be picked.

Place value

WORK IT OUT!

What is the value of each of the numbers in 492?

The value of 4 in 492 is 400 or four hundred

The value of 9 in 492 is 90 or ninety

The value of 2 in 492 is 2 or two

What is the value of 6 in each of these numbers?

26	369	13,697
6	60	600
six	sixty	six hundred

961,782	6,910	8,461	12,946
60,000	6,000	60	6
sixty thousand	six thousand	sixty	six

Circle each number with a 5 having the value of fifty.

(672,459)   896,577   501,813   (575,555)

Circle each number with a 4 having the value of four hundred.

454,689   (330,421)   400,525   (969,410)

Write "increases" or "decreases" and by how much.

Change the 3 in 31 to 4. The value of the number increases by 10

Change the 7 in 87 to 3. The value of the number decreases by 4

Change the 1 in 19 to 4. The value of the number increases by 30

Change the 2 in 24 to 9. The value of the number increases by 70

Change the 7 in 372 to 5. The value of the number decreases by 20

Change the 4 in 4,320 to 6. The value of the number increases by 2,000

If children have difficulty, suggest that they read the numbers aloud, so that they can more easily identify the place value of each digit.

Fractions

Write the answer in the box.

$\frac{1}{4} + \frac{1}{4} = \frac{2}{4} = \frac{1}{2}$ $\frac{1}{2} + \frac{1}{2} =$ 1

DON'T WASTE A SECOND!

Write the answer in the box.

$\frac{3}{9} + \frac{3}{9} = \frac{6}{9} = \frac{2}{3}$	$\frac{1}{8} + \frac{5}{8} = \frac{6}{8} = \frac{3}{4}$	$\frac{3}{16} + \frac{5}{16} = \frac{8}{16} = \frac{1}{2}$
$\frac{1}{5} + \frac{2}{5} = \frac{3}{5}$	$\frac{4}{5} + \frac{1}{5} = 1$	$\frac{4}{8} + \frac{4}{8} = 1$
$\frac{2}{10} + \frac{3}{10} = \frac{5}{10} = \frac{1}{2}$	$\frac{1}{15} + \frac{3}{15} = \frac{4}{15}$	$\frac{4}{16} + \frac{8}{16} = \frac{12}{16} = \frac{3}{4}$
$\frac{3}{12} + \frac{6}{12} = \frac{9}{12} = \frac{3}{4}$	$\frac{1}{9} + \frac{8}{9} = 1$	$\frac{2}{9} + \frac{1}{9} = \frac{3}{9} = \frac{1}{3}$
$\frac{2}{6} + \frac{1}{6} = \frac{3}{6} = \frac{1}{2}$	$\frac{1}{15} + \frac{4}{15} = \frac{5}{15} = \frac{1}{3}$	$\frac{1}{9} + \frac{3}{9} = \frac{4}{9}$

Write the answer in the box.

$\frac{2}{6} + \frac{2}{6} = \frac{4}{6} = \frac{2}{3}$	$\frac{1}{7} + \frac{5}{7} = \frac{6}{7}$	$\frac{4}{16} + \frac{8}{16} = \frac{12}{16} = \frac{3}{4}$
$\frac{1}{5} + \frac{3}{5} = \frac{4}{5}$	$\frac{2}{4} + \frac{2}{4} = 1$	$\frac{2}{3} + \frac{1}{3} = 1$
$\frac{2}{12} + \frac{4}{12} = \frac{6}{12} = \frac{1}{2}$	$\frac{3}{15} + \frac{5}{15} = \frac{8}{15}$	$\frac{4}{19} + \frac{10}{19} = \frac{14}{19}$
$\frac{1}{10} + \frac{8}{10} = \frac{9}{10}$	$\frac{4}{4} + \frac{4}{4} = 2$	$\frac{4}{21} + \frac{3}{21} = \frac{7}{21} = \frac{1}{3}$
$\frac{2}{15} + \frac{4}{15} = \frac{6}{15} = \frac{2}{5}$	$\frac{2}{14} + \frac{5}{14} = \frac{7}{14} = \frac{1}{2}$	$\frac{1}{10} + \frac{3}{10} = \frac{4}{10}$

Write the answer in the box.

$2\frac{2}{5} + 1\frac{1}{5} = 3\frac{3}{5}$	$3\frac{2}{5} + 3\frac{2}{5} = 6\frac{4}{5}$	$3\frac{1}{5} + 1 = 4\frac{1}{5}$
$3\frac{3}{5} + 2\frac{2}{5} = 6$	$1\frac{2}{5} + \frac{1}{5} = 1\frac{3}{5}$	$4\frac{2}{5} + 1\frac{1}{5} = 5\frac{4}{5}$
$\frac{3}{5} + \frac{3}{5} = 1\frac{1}{5}$	$5\frac{1}{5} + 2\frac{2}{5} = 7\frac{3}{5}$	$1\frac{1}{5} + \frac{4}{5} = 2$

It is technically correct if children add $\frac{1}{4}$ and $\frac{1}{4}$ to get $\frac{2}{4}$, but they should be encouraged to simplify this as $\frac{1}{2}$. Some children may not simplify improper fractions that are part of a mixed number (such as $3\frac{6}{5}$). Show them how to do this.

Part of a whole

SHADY STUFF

Write the fraction that shows the shaded part.

How many parts are shaded? **3 parts**

How many parts in all? **4 parts**

The shade part is **$\frac{3}{4}$**

Circle the fraction that shows the shaded part.

$\frac{1}{3}$ $\boxed{\frac{1}{2}}$ $\frac{1}{4}$ $\frac{3}{4}$ $\frac{2}{3}$ $\boxed{\frac{3}{5}}$ $\frac{7}{9}$ $\boxed{\frac{7}{8}}$ $\frac{4}{5}$

Write the fraction that shows the shaded part.

$\frac{1}{6}$ $\frac{3}{8}$ $\frac{3}{5}$

$\frac{5}{8}$ $\frac{4}{12}$ $\frac{4}{8}$

$\frac{3}{10}$ $\frac{4}{9}$ $\frac{5}{6}$

$\frac{2}{6}$ $\frac{5}{16}$ $\frac{5}{8}$

If children have difficulty, point out that the denominator (the bottom number of the fraction) is the total number of parts. The numerator (the top number of the fraction) is the number of shaded parts.

Decimals

ARE YOU GETTING THE POINT?

Write these decimals in order, from least to greatest.

0.3 0.45 0.25 0.1 0.2 | 0.1 | 0.2 | 0.25 | 0.3 | 0.45 |

Write each row of decimals in order, from least to greatest.

0.42	0.48	0.41	0.49	0.45	0.41	0.42	0.45	0.48	0.49
1.75	1.45	1.9	1.25	1.65	1.25	1.45	1.65	1.75	1.9
4.73	4.83	4.23	4.13	4.33	4.13	4.23	4.33	4.73	4.83
6.37	6.77	6.27	6.07	6.97	6.07	6.27	6.37	6.77	6.97
8.31	6.31	1.31	9.31	4.31	1.31	4.31	6.31	8.31	9.31
4.63	3.91	8.32	7.02	2.9	2.9	3.91	4.63	7.02	8.32
3.25	8.2	5.9	1.33	4.32	1.33	3.25	4.32	5.9	8.2
1.56	6.22	9.34	8.75	4.65	1.56	4.65	6.22	8.75	9.34
4.6	2.38	6.32	8.2	7.32	2.38	4.6	6.32	7.32	8.2

Write each row of decimals in order, from least to greatest.

2.67	5.28	1.73	4.92	2.56	1.73	2.56	2.67	4.92	5.28
7.27	4.94	2.91	4.38	5.68	2.91	4.38	4.94	5.68	7.27
8.27	4.56	8.42	9.28	8.44	4.56	8.27	8.42	8.44	9.28
1.37	1.94	2.36	3.16	4.21	1.37	1.94	2.36	3.16	4.21
4.36	7.27	5.25	6.28	5.29	4.36	5.25	5.29	6.28	7.27
3.34	2.63	4.13	3.21	4.28	2.63	3.21	3.34	4.13	4.28
7.35	6.48	7.21	6.22	4.46	4.46	6.22	6.48	7.21	7.35
5.45	4.97	5.21	4.89	5.03	4.89	4.97	5.03	5.21	5.45

Children should understand that place value with decimals is just as important as it is with whole numbers. Make sure they compare the numbers in order—the whole number first, then the first decimal place, and then the second decimal place.

Fractions and decimals

Write each fraction as a decimal.

$1\frac{1}{10}$ = **1.1** $1\frac{2}{10}$ = **1.2** $1\frac{7}{10}$ = **1.7**

Write each decimal as a fraction.

2.5 $2\frac{1}{2}$ 1.7 $1\frac{7}{10}$ 3.3 $3\frac{3}{10}$

Write each fraction as a decimal.

$3\frac{1}{2}$ = **3.5** $2\frac{1}{10}$ = **2.1** $5\frac{4}{10}$ = **5.4** $4\frac{1}{2}$ = **4.5**

$5\frac{2}{10}$ = **5.2** $3\frac{6}{10}$ = **3.6** $8\frac{1}{10}$ = **8.1** $8\frac{1}{2}$ = **8.5**

$7\frac{1}{10}$ = **7.1** $1\frac{3}{10}$ = **1.3** $6\frac{8}{10}$ = **6.8** $10\frac{9}{10}$ = **10.9**

$9\frac{6}{10}$ = **9.6** $4\frac{5}{10}$ = **4.5** $9\frac{1}{2}$ = **9.5** $10\frac{1}{2}$ = **10.5**

Write each decimal as a fraction.

3.4 $3\frac{4}{10}$ 4.5 $4\frac{1}{2}$ 1.3 $1\frac{3}{10}$ 2.2 $2\frac{2}{10}$

5.5 $5\frac{1}{2}$ 2.6 $2\frac{6}{10}$ 5.2 $5\frac{2}{10}$ 1.7 $1\frac{7}{10}$

7.2 $7\frac{2}{10}$ 8.5 $8\frac{1}{2}$ 9.8 $9\frac{8}{10}$ 10.2 $10\frac{2}{10}$

11.5 $11\frac{1}{2}$ 12.7 $12\frac{7}{10}$ 18.4 $18\frac{4}{10}$ 14.5 $14\frac{1}{2}$

16.9 $16\frac{9}{10}$ 11.3 $11\frac{3}{10}$ 17.6 $17\frac{6}{10}$ 17.5 $17\frac{1}{2}$

Write each fraction as a decimal.

$\frac{1}{2}$ = **0.5** $\frac{2}{10}$ = **0.2** $\frac{3}{10}$ = **0.3**

Write each decimal as a fraction.

0.5 $\frac{1}{2}$ 0.1 $\frac{2}{10}$ 0.8 $\frac{8}{10}$

If children have difficulty, you may want to use a number line showing tenths and decimals.

Adding

Write the sum between the lines. First, add the ones, then add the tens. Regroup if needed.

ADD 'EM UP OR ELSE!

38	55	27
+ 13	+ 26	+ 25
51	81	52

Write the sum between the lines.

56	18	28	47	58
+ 17	+ 14	+ 14	+ 26	+ 15
73	32	42	73	73

16	47	56	34	57
+ 16	+ 34	+ 38	+ 19	+ 37
32	81	94	53	94

29	19	33	48	33
+ 16	+ 14	+ 19	+ 27	+ 18
45	33	52	75	51

27	19	23	57	68
+ 14	+ 14	+ 16	+ 15	+ 13
41	33	39	72	81

26	34	13	18	25
+ 35	+ 48	+ 27	+ 32	+ 45
61	82	40	50	70

17	33	29	32	23
+ 44	+ 58	+ 53	+ 53	+ 48
61	91	82	85	71

Children must regroup to answer these addition problems. If they get confused when the lower number is larger than the upper, point out that the order of addition does not change the sum.

Adding

Write the sum between the lines. First, add the ones, then add the tens. Regroup if needed.

35 + 15 **50**	56 + 33 **89**	54 + 18 **72**

GET ADDING!

Write the sum between the lines.

17 + 13 **30**	23 + 17 **40**	45 + 35 **80**	52 + 18 **70**	38 + 22 **60**
25 + 25 **50**	47 + 43 **90**	32 + 18 **50**	40 + 17 **57**	32 + 46 **78**
46 + 34 **80**	74 + 16 **90**	42 + 38 **80**	67 + 23 **90**	37 + 43 **80**
54 + 46 **100**	35 + 45 **80**	47 + 33 **80**	83 + 17 **100**	31 + 39 **70**
76 + 24 **100**	67 + 33 **100**	73 + 27 **100**	55 + 45 **100**	74 + 26 **100**
73 + 16 **89**	48 + 33 **81**	49 + 42 **91**	28 + 26 **54**	65 + 45 **110**

Many of these questions result in sums with a zero in the ones place. Make sure that children do not neglect to add the addititional 10 when they regroup.

Subtracting

Write the difference between the lines. First, subtract the ones, then the tens. Regroup if needed.

45 - 15 **30**	66 - 23 **43**	43 - 18 **25**

YOU SHOULD FIND THESE EASY.

Write the difference between the lines.

45 - 23 **22**	27 - 14 **13**	53 - 20 **33**	85 - 41 **44**	47 - 25 **22**
29 - 16 **13**	53 - 12 **41**	82 - 40 **42**	37 - 26 **11**	44 - 31 **13**
63 - 21 **42**	74 - 32 **42**	47 - 36 **11**	63 - 42 **21**	76 - 35 **41**
85 - 42 **43**	83 - 41 **42**	95 - 35 **60**	67 - 53 **14**	86 - 45 **41**
65 - 35 **30**	74 - 54 **20**	86 - 66 **20**	96 - 86 **10**	67 - 17 **50**
59 - 39 **20**	48 - 27 **21**	46 - 32 **14**	78 - 47 **31**	67 - 56 **11**

Children must regroup to answer these subtraction questions. Check any errors and make sure children understand what they did incorrectly.

Subtracting

Write the difference between the lines. First, subtract the ones, then the tens. Regroup if needed.

54 - 28 **26**	68 - 39 **29**	72 - 24 **48**

TAKE IT AWAY, LOIS!

Write the difference between the lines.

45 - 28 **17**	42 - 17 **25**	50 - 45 **5**	62 - 17 **45**	36 - 18 **18**
57 - 39 **18**	36 - 27 **9**	64 - 48 **16**	62 - 34 **28**	78 - 69 **9**
63 - 49 **14**	65 - 48 **17**	90 - 37 **53**	74 - 47 **27**	43 - 29 **14**
54 - 26 **28**	68 - 39 **29**	50 - 27 **23**	38 - 28 **10**	44 - 36 **8**
31 - 16 **15**	43 - 28 **15**	70 - 36 **34**	53 - 37 **16**	46 - 28 **18**
90 - 46 **44**	50 - 26 **24**	54 - 35 **19**	66 - 48 **18**	90 - 44 **46**

Children must regroup to answer these subtraction questions.

Real-life problems

Write the sum in the box.
Steel has two suits and makes four spares.
How many suits does he have now?

2 + 4 = 6

Write the answer in the box.

Superman has 14 oxygen cartridges but uses 8 in a fight with Parasite. How many oxygen cartridges does Superman have left?
$14 - 8 = 6$

After buying some candies for 50¢, Chris still has 45¢ left. How much did he have to begin with?
$50¢ + 45¢ = 95¢$

Supergirl saves 5 children from a runaway bus. There are 20 children still in the bus. How many children are there altogether?
$20 + 5 = 25$

Harry counts 150 stamps and his father counts 60 more. How many stamps does Harry have altogether?
$150 + 60 = 210$

Tom puts 15 toys in a box that already has 20 toys in it. How many toys are in the box now?
$15 + 20 = 35$

Lorna leaves 40¢ at home and takes 50¢ with her. How much money does Lorna have altogether?
$40¢ + 50¢ = 90¢$

Faruk gives some of his allowance to his brother. He gives his brother 85¢ and has 65¢ left. How much allowance did Faruk have in the first place?
$85¢ + 65¢ = \$1.50$

Five letters of the alphabet are vowels. How many letters of the alphabet are not vowels?
$26 - 5 = 21$

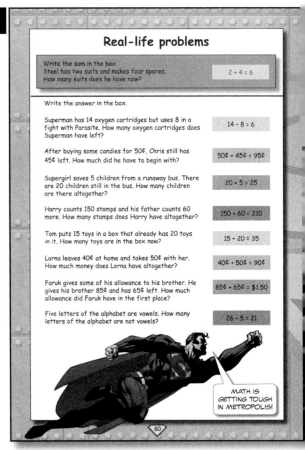

MATH IS GETTING TOUGH IN METROPOLIS!

These problems test whether children know when to add and when to subtract. Some words such as "altogether" may need to be explained.

Multiplying

TIMES AND TIMES AGAIN.

Write the product between the lines. Multiply the ones, then multiply the tens and add any extra tens (regroup as needed).

34 × 3 = 102	71 × 6 = 426	26 × 3 = 78

Write the answers between the lines.

66 × 2 = 132	85 × 2 = 170	72 × 2 = 144	28 × 2 = 56	46 × 2 = 92
55 × 3 = 165	39 × 3 = 117	53 × 3 = 159	75 × 3 = 225	43 × 3 = 129
36 × 4 = 144	17 × 4 = 68	75 × 4 = 300	44 × 4 = 176	62 × 4 = 248
75 × 5 = 375	72 × 5 = 360	94 × 5 = 470	38 × 5 = 190	64 × 5 = 320
94 × 6 = 564	88 × 6 = 528	72 × 6 = 432	63 × 6 = 378	46 × 6 = 276
85 × 7 = 595	48 × 7 = 336	93 × 7 = 651	37 × 7 = 259	55 × 7 = 385

Some of the multiplication will require children to regroup. Go through any incorrect answers with them to find out whether the problem results from incorrect regrouping or poor knowledge of times tables.

Multiplying

I HAVE TO DO THESE BEFORE BRAINIAC.

Write the product between the lines.

35 × 3 = 105	18 × 4 = 72	62 × 5 = 310

Write the product between the lines.

42 × 9 = 378	64 × 9 = 576	53 × 9 = 477	22 × 9 = 198	38 × 9 = 342
33 × 4 = 132	26 × 4 = 104	84 × 4 = 336	65 × 4 = 260	27 × 4 = 108
35 × 8 = 280	92 × 8 = 736	52 × 8 = 416	98 × 8 = 784	43 × 8 = 344
47 × 5 = 235	36 × 5 = 180	23 × 5 = 115	58 × 5 = 290	29 × 5 = 145
84 × 4 = 336	39 × 5 = 195	96 × 6 = 576	26 × 7 = 182	56 × 8 = 448
29 × 4 = 116	59 × 5 = 295	39 × 6 = 234	69 × 7 = 483	79 × 8 = 632

See the comments for the previous page.

Dividing

Write the quotient in the box.

37 ÷ 6 = 6 r 1	27 ÷ 4 = 6 r 3	74 ÷ 8 = 9 r 2
6)37 −36 = 1	4)27 −24 = 3	8)74 −72 = 2

Write the quotient between the lines.

45 ÷ 6 = 7 r 3	35 ÷ 6 = 5 r 5	62 ÷ 6 = 10 r 2
22 ÷ 6 = 3 r 4	43 ÷ 6 = 7 r 1	66 ÷ 6 = 11 r 0
17 ÷ 6 = 2 r 5	25 ÷ 6 = 4 r 1	30 ÷ 6 = 5 r 0
31 ÷ 6 = 5 r 1	33 ÷ 6 = 5 r 3	49 ÷ 6 = 8 r 1
58 ÷ 7 = 8 r 2	15 ÷ 7 = 2 r 1	68 ÷ 7 = 9 r 5
29 ÷ 7 = 4 r 1	61 ÷ 7 = 8 r 5	77 ÷ 7 = 11 r 0
39 ÷ 7 = 5 r 4	35 ÷ 7 = 5 r 0	24 ÷ 7 = 3 r 3
76 ÷ 7 = 10 r 6	82 ÷ 7 = 11 r 5	64 ÷ 7 = 9 r 1
33 ÷ 8 = 4 r 1	57 ÷ 8 = 7 r 1	73 ÷ 8 = 9 r 1
42 ÷ 8 = 5 r 2	21 ÷ 8 = 2 r 5	46 ÷ 8 = 5 r 6
67 ÷ 8 = 8 r 3	38 ÷ 8 = 4 r 6	51 ÷ 8 = 6 r 3
49 ÷ 8 = 6 r 1	13 ÷ 8 = 1 r 5	64 ÷ 8 = 8 r 0
37 ÷ 9 = 4 r 1	59 ÷ 9 = 6 r 5	92 ÷ 9 = 10 r 2
24 ÷ 9 = 2 r 6	73 ÷ 9 = 8 r 1	100 ÷ 9 = 11 r 1
46 ÷ 9 = 5 r 1	35 ÷ 9 = 3 r 8	65 ÷ 9 = 7 r 2
22 ÷ 9 = 2 r 4	81 ÷ 9 = 9 r 0	50 ÷ 9 = 5 r 5

These division problems test children's knowledge of times tables. Children should be able to calculate the remainders easily.

Dividing

CLARK CAN'T DO THESE DIVISIONS, SO CAN YOU HELP HIM?

Write the answer in the box above the line.

4 r 3	6 r 2	8 r 1
8)35 −32 = 3	4)26 −24 = 2	7)57 −56 = 1

Write the answer in the box above the line.

7 r 3	4 r 3	6 r 1	6 r 2	6 r 5
6)45 42 = 3	6)27 24 = 3	6)37 36 = 1	6)38 36 = 2	6)41 36 = 5
5 r 6	4 r 1	9 r 5	7 r 2	6 r 4
7)41 35 = 6	7)29 28 = 1	7)68 63 = 5	7)51 49 = 2	7)46 42 = 4
6 r 4	2 r 7	8 r 5	5 r 2	3 r 7
8)52 48 = 4	8)23 16 = 7	8)69 64 = 5	8)42 40 = 2	8)31 24 = 7
5 r 1	2 r 3	4 r 8	8 r 2	4 r 2
9)46 45 = 1	9)21 18 = 3	9)44 36 = 8	9)74 72 = 2	9)38 36 = 2

These problems are similar to those on the previous pages, but are presented using a division housing or box. Look for errors that highlight particular times tables that children need to work on.

Choosing the operation

Write either x or ÷ in the box.

5 **x** 7 = 35   70 **÷** 7 = 10   6 **x** 7 = 42

MAKE YOUR MIND UP!

Write either x or ÷ in the box.

84 ÷ 7 = 12	8 ÷ 8 = 1	5 x 9 = 45
27 ÷ 9 = 3	8 x 7 = 56	4 x 9 = 36
80 ÷ 10 = 8	70 ÷ 7 = 10	28 ÷ 4 = 7
21 ÷ 7 = 3	16 ÷ 4 = 4	54 ÷ 6 = 9
18 ÷ 3 = 6	64 ÷ 8 = 8	56 ÷ 7 = 8
40 ÷ 8 = 5	6 x 8 = 48	3 x 8 = 24
30 ÷ 5 = 6	63 ÷ 7 = 9	48 ÷ 8 = 6
28 ÷ 7 = 4	8 x 8 = 64	81 ÷ 9 = 9
24 ÷ 8 = 3	4 x 6 = 24	27 ÷ 3 = 9
7 x 9 = 63	48 ÷ 6 = 8	7 x 8 = 56
45 ÷ 9 = 5	36 ÷ 4 = 9	49 ÷ 7 = 7
30 ÷ 6 = 5	5 x 8 = 40	54 ÷ 9 = 6
8 x 6 = 48	9 x 7 = 63	20 x 6 = 120
700 ÷ 7 = 100	8 ÷ 8 = 1	84 ÷ 7 = 12
100 ÷ 5 = 20	400 ÷ 8 = 50	42 ÷ 6 = 7
5 x 5 = 25	100 ÷ 10 = 10	6 ÷ 6 = 1

Children will probably realize that if the answer is larger than the first number, they should multiply, and if the answer is smaller than the first number they should divide. They can check some of their answers to make sure that they are correct.

Real-life problems

Write the answer in the box.

A number multiplied by 7 is 56. What is the number? — 8

I divide a number by 9 and the result is 6. What is the number? — 54

Write the answer in the box.

A number multiplied by 8 is 48. What is the number? — 6

I divide a number by 4 and the result is 9. What is the number? — 36

I divide a number by 7 and the result is 6. What number did I begin with? — 42

A number multiplied by itself gives the answer 16. What is the number? — 4

I divide a number by 7 and the result is 7. What number did I begin with? — 49

A number multiplied by itself gives the answer 49. What is the number? — 7

I multiply a number by 7 and I end up with 63. What number did I begin with? — 9

Nine times a number is 72. What is the number? — 8

What do I have to multiply 7 by to get the result 63? — 9

Nine times a number is 63. What is the number? — 7

When 6 is multiplied by a number the result is 42. What number was 6 multiplied by? — 7

A number divided by 7 gives the answer 10. What was the starting number? — 70

I multiply a number by 9 and end up with 45. What number did I multiply? — 5

I multiply a number by 9 and the result is 81. What number did I begin with? — 9

I MUST BREAK FREE AND STOP DOOMSDAY!

Some children find these problems difficult even if they are good with times tables and division. Many of the problems require children to perform the operati inverse to the one named. Have children check their answers to make sure they are correct.

Real-life problems

A chain is 1.60 m long but Superman breaks 45 cm off. How much of the chain is left?

$$\begin{array}{r} {}^{5\ 10}\\ 1\cancel{6}\cancel{0}\\ -\ 45\\ \hline 115 \end{array}$$ (1.60 m = 160 cm)

1.15 m

I HAVE ALL OF SUPERMAN'S POWERS!

Solve the problem. Write the answer in the box.

Mario is given 4 cans of juice. Each can contains 425 ml. How much does Mario have altogether?

$$\begin{array}{r} {}^{1\ 2}\\ 425\\ \times\ 4\\ \hline 1,700 \end{array}$$

1,700 ml or 1 litre and 700 ml

A tower at Steel's SteelWorks is 145 m tall. Doomsday destroys 68 m of the tower. How much of the tower is left?

$$\begin{array}{r} {}^{13\ 15}\\ 1\cancel{4}\cancel{5}\\ -\ 68\\ \hline 77 \end{array}$$

77 m of tower

Lois's swimming pool is 947 cm deep at one end and 119 cm deep at the other. How much deeper is the deep end of the pool?

$$\begin{array}{r} {}^{3\ 1}\\ 947\\ -\ 119\\ \hline 828 \end{array}$$

828 cm deeper

Lex Luthor's suits cost $8.30 to be cleaned. He pays with a $10.00 bill. How much change will he receive?

$$\begin{array}{r} {}^{9\ 10}\\ 1\cancel{0}\cancel{0}0\\ -\ 830\\ \hline 170 \end{array}$$

$1.70

A galaxy has 472 planets. Doomsday destroys half the planets in the galaxy. How many planets are left?

$$\begin{array}{r} 236\\ 2)\overline{472}\\ -\ 4\\ \hline 07\\ -\ 6\\ \hline 12\\ -\ 12\\ \hline 00 \end{array}$$

236 planets

These problems involve fairly large or awkward numbers and may be a challenge. Answers in metric units can be given as whole numbers (for example, 1,700 millilitres) or as decimals (1.7 litres).

Real-life problems

Superman weighs 40 kg more than Supergirl. Supergirl weighs 59 kg. How much does Superman weigh?

$$\begin{array}{r} 59\\ +\ 40\\ \hline 99 \end{array}$$

99 kg

Solve the problem. Write the answer in the box.

Two bags of money weigh a total of 70 kg. One bag weighs 40 kg. How much does the other bag weigh?

$$\begin{array}{r} 70\\ -\ 40\\ \hline 30 \end{array}$$

30 kg

Encantadora has 34 lumps of kryptonite in each box. How many lumps will there be in 6 boxes?

$$\begin{array}{r} {}^{2}\\ 34\\ \times\ 6\\ \hline 204 \end{array}$$

204

Lex Luthor has $290, which is $140 more than his daughter. How much money does his daughter have?

$$\begin{array}{r} 290\\ -\ 140\\ \hline 150 \end{array}$$

$150

Supergirl has a bottle of lemonade that contains 2 litres. She drinks 425 ml. How much drink is left?

$$\begin{array}{r} {}^{1\ 9\ 9\ 10}\\ 2\cancel{,}\cancel{0}\cancel{0}0\\ -\ 425\\ \hline 1,575 \end{array}$$

1 litre 575 ml or 1,575 millilitres

Superman's capes can be measured in millimetres. How long is 1.80 m in mm?

1.80 x 1,000 = 1,800

1,800 mm

Metropolis has 132 buildings in each precinct. How many buildings are there in 8 precincts?

$$\begin{array}{r} {}^{2\ 1}\\ 132\\ \times\ 8\\ \hline 1,056 \end{array}$$

1,056

Two problems require children to convert between units. Make sure that children understand how to convert metric units.

89

Problems using time

Write the answer in the box.

6:20 What time will it be in 10 minutes?
6.30

TIME TO FLY!

Write the answer in the box.

7:10 What time will it be in 15 minutes?
7.25

What time will it be in 45 minutes?
7.55

What time was it 6 minutes ago?
7.04

Write the answer in the box.

9:45 What time was it 1 hour ago?
8:45

What time will it be in 40 minutes?
10:25

What time will it be in half an hour?
10:15

Write the answer in the box.

3:30 How many hours until 6.30?
3 hours

What time was it 35 minutes ago?
2.55

What time will it be in 50 minutes?
4:20

When regrouping in addition problems involving time, children should avoid using decimal regrouping and must understand that 60 minutes (not 100 minutes) is added to 1 hour.

90

Charts

	Period 1	Period 2	Period 3	Period 4
Monday	Math	Krypton	Spanish	Hypnotism
Tuesday	Math	English	Krypton	Flying practice
Wednesday	Math	Krypton	Laser-beam practice	Laser-beam practice
Thursday	Math	English	Science	Science
Friday	Krypton	Flying practice	Hypnotism	X-ray vision test

A.M   P.M

Write the answer in the box.

What subject does Supergirl have last period on Tuesday? — Flying practice

How many periods of Krypton does Supergirl have? — 4

When does Supergirl have an afternoon of Science? — Thursday

How many periods of Laser-beam practice does she have? — 2

What subject comes before Spanish? — Krypton

Which subject is taught third period on Friday? — Hypnotism

Which day is the X-ray vision test? — Friday

What is the first period on Thursday? — Math

When is Spanish? — Monday

What subject is taught second period on Tuesday? — English

If children have difficulty reading the information on the chart, help them answer one question, reading across the appropriate row and down the appropriate column, to show them the intersection of the two.

91

Symmetry

The dotted line is the line of symmetry. Complete each shape.

I USE MY X-RAY VISION TO SEE THE SHAPES.

Complete each shape.

If children have difficulty with these shapes, let them use a mirror. Even if they are confident, let them check the shapes with a mirror when they finish.

92

3-dimensional shapes

Draw a small circle around each vertex in this shape.

Draw a small circle around each vertex in this shape.

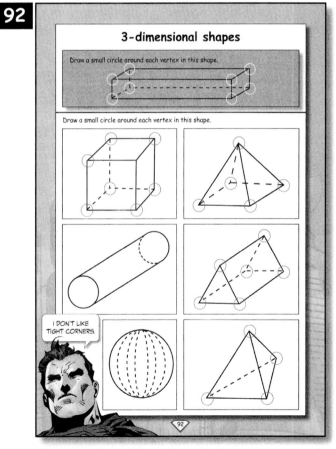

I DON'T LIKE TIGHT CORNERS.

Make sure that children know that a vertex is a single point and that a cylinder and a sphere have no vertices.

Number pairs

(graph with x-marks labeled A–L on an 8×8 grid)

Write the coordinates of the x by each letter.

A =	4, 1	D =	3, 7	G =	7, 3	J =	5, 6
B =	7, 5	E =	4, 5	H =	7, 2	K =	4, 3
C =	2, 3	F =	6, 7	I =	5, 4	L =	8, 4

Make sure that children understand that the order of the numbers within ordered pairs is important. The first number is from the horizontal or x axis, and the second number is from the vertical or y axis. Ordered pairs are written in parentheses, like this A = (1,2).

Adding and subtracting

Add 100 to 286.
386

Add 100 to 3,156.
3,256

Subtract 100 from 7,934.
7,834

Subtract 100 from 1,755.
1,655

Add 100 to each number.

824	924	318	418	529	629	224	324
43	143	974	1,074	634	734	7,325	7,425
3,890	3,990	25	125	827	927	4,236	4,336

Add 100 to each number.

707	807	523	623	76	176	443	543
34	134	6,021	6,121	5,897	5,997	2,890	2,990
6,132	6,232	9,873	9,973	5,499	5,599	8,003	8,103

Subtract 100 from each number.

672	572	189	89	343	243	682	582
100	0	5,900	5,800	7,273	7,173	399	299
106	6	1,378	1,278	201	101	9,546	9,446

Subtract 100 from each number.

1,400	1,300	8,610	8,510	5,307	5,207	9,362	9,262
2,834	2,734	1,452	1,352	8,445	8,345	1,423	1,323
1,300	1,200	529	429	7,982	7,882	4,256	4,156

There is no regrouping on this page, so children should realize that they need only change the digit in the hundreds place for each number.

Dividing by 10

Divide 30 by 10.
3

Divide 2,700 by 10.
270

I BET SUPERMAN CAN'T DO THESE. CAN YOU?

Divide each number by 10.

90	9	860	86	270	27	70	7
200	20	330	33	10	1	300	30
540	54	490	49	130	13	660	66
60	6	170	17	20	2	110	11
680	68	50	5	980	98	730	73

Multiply each number by 10.

40	400	60	600	900	9,000	750	7,500
50	500	10	100	560	5,600	840	8,400
160	1,600	350	3,500	670	6,700	600	6,000
420	4,200	70	700	20	200	100	1,000
730	7,300	11	110	310	3,100	390	3,900

Divide each number by 10.

700	70	2,300	230	4,100	410	3,650	365
6,480	648	7,080	708	3,540	354	2,030	203
1,030	103	9,670	967	6,320	632	1,400	140
300	30	900	90	1,020	102	3,660	366
20	20	18,000	1,800	13,600	1,360	17,890	1,789

Children should understand quickly that dividing multiples of 10 by 10 results in the removal of the final zero. Make sure that they remove the commas in any thousands when they divide by 10.

Length

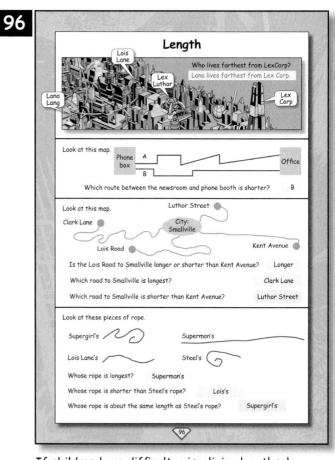

Who lives farthest from LexCorp?
Lana lives farthest from Lex Corp.

Look at this map.

Which route between the newsroom and phone booth is shorter?   B

Look at this map.

Is the Lois Road to Smallville longer or shorter than Kent Avenue?   Longer

Which road to Smallville is longest?   Clark Lane

Which road to Smallville is shorter than Kent Avenue?   Luthor Street

Look at these pieces of rope.

Whose rope is longest?   Superman's

Whose rope is shorter than Steel's rope?   Lois's

Whose rope is about the same length as Steel's rope?   Supergirl's

If children have difficulty visualizing lengths, have them use a ruler or a piece of string for making comparisons.

97

Identifying patterns

Continue each pattern.

| 11 | 22 | 33 | 44 | 55 | 66 | 77 | 88 |
| 12 | 24 | 36 | 48 | 60 | 72 | 84 | 96 |

Continue each pattern.

8	20	32	44	56	68	80	92
7	18	29	40	51	62	73	84
25	36	47	58	69	80	91	102
3	15	27	39	51	63	75	87
1	12	23	34	45	56	67	78
34	46	58	70	82	94	106	118
5	16	27	38	49	60	71	82
11	23	35	47	59	71	83	95

Continue each pattern.

96	84	72	60	48	36	24	12
99	88	77	66	55	44	33	22
100	88	76	64	52	40	28	16
78	67	56	45	34	23	12	1
9	20	31	42	53	64	75	86
7	19	31	43	55	67	79	91
95	84	73	62	51	40	29	18
10	22	34	46	58	70	82	94

Point out that some of the patterns show an increase and some a decrease. Children should check that the operation that turns the first number into the second also turns the second into the third. They can then continue the pattern.

98

Properties of polygons

LET'S GET INTO SHAPE!

Circle the polygon that has 4 sides of the same length.

Circle the polygon described.

The 3 sides are all the same length.

Exactly 2 pairs of sides are parallel.

Exactly 1 pair of sides is parallel.

All the sides are of equal length and each side is parallel to one other side.

Each of the sides is a different length.

Has 6 sides of equal length.

Make sure children understand the term parallel.

99

Square numbers

This square has two rows and two columns. It is 2 x 2. How many dots are there? **4**

Draw a picture like the one above to show each of these numbers.

3 x 3

4 x 4

5 x 5

How many dots are there? **9**

How many dots are there? **16**

How many dots are there? **25**

6 x 6

7 x 7

8 x 8

How many dots are there? **36**

How many dots are there? **49**

How many dots are there? **64**

9 x 9

10 x 10

How many dots are there? **81**

How many dots are there? **100**

This page introduces the concept of square numbers, and is a precursor to understanding area.

100

Fractions and decimals

Write the fraction as a decimal.
$\frac{1}{2}$ 0.5 $\frac{1}{10}$ 0.1

Write the decimal as a fraction.
$0.25 = \frac{25}{100} = \frac{1}{4}$

WHAT FRACTION SHALL I BREAK DOOMSDAY INTO? YOU DECIDE!

Write each fraction as a decimal.

$\frac{1}{10}$ 0.1	$\frac{1}{2}$ 0.5	$\frac{7}{10}$ 0.7	$\frac{2}{10}$ 0.2
$\frac{8}{10}$ 0.8	$\frac{3}{10}$ 0.3	$\frac{9}{10}$ 0.9	$\frac{3}{10}$ 0.3
$\frac{6}{10}$ 0.6	$\frac{4}{10}$ 0.4	$\frac{1}{10}$ 0.1	$\frac{5}{10}$ 0.5
$\frac{2}{10}$ 0.2	$\frac{5}{10}$ 0.5	$\frac{6}{10}$ 0.6	$\frac{4}{10}$ 0.4

Write each decimal as a fraction.

0.2 $\frac{2}{10}$	0.7 $\frac{7}{10}$	0.3 $\frac{3}{10}$	0.4 $\frac{2}{5}$
0.1 $\frac{1}{10}$	0.6 $\frac{6}{10}$	0.2 $\frac{1}{5}$	0.75 $\frac{3}{4}$
0.5 $\frac{5}{10}$	0.4 $\frac{4}{10}$	0.5 $\frac{1}{2}$	0.9 $\frac{9}{10}$
0.25 $\frac{1}{4}$	0.8 $\frac{8}{10}$	0.6 $\frac{3}{5}$	0.8 $\frac{4}{5}$

Write the answer in the box.

Which of the two fractions above are the same as 0.5? $\frac{5}{10}$ $\frac{1}{2}$

Which of the two fractions above are the same as 0.8? $\frac{8}{10}$ $\frac{4}{5}$

Which of the two fractions above are the same as 0.2? $\frac{2}{10}$ $\frac{1}{5}$

Which of the two fractions above are the same as 0.4? $\frac{4}{10}$ $\frac{2}{5}$

Which of the two fractions above are the same as 0.6? $\frac{6}{10}$ $\frac{3}{5}$

Children should realize that $\frac{1}{10}$ is equivalent to 0.1. If necessary, help them understand that $\frac{2}{10}$ is equivalent to 0.2, and so on. Children also need to know the decimal equivalents of $\frac{1}{4}$ and $\frac{3}{4}$.

Fractions of shapes

Shade $\frac{3}{5}$ of each shape

Shade $\frac{4}{5}$ of each shape

YOU'LL NEVER BREAK ME!

Shade $\frac{8}{10}$ of each shape

Shade the fraction of each shape.

$\frac{4}{10}$ $\frac{8}{10}$ $\frac{3}{10}$

$\frac{7}{10}$ $\frac{6}{10}$ $\frac{9}{10}$

101

Children may shade in any combination of the sections as long as the shaded area represents the fraction.

Comparing fractions

In each pair, circle the fraction with the greater value.

$\frac{1}{3}$ or $\frac{1}{5}$

In each pair, circle the fraction with the greater value.

$\frac{1}{4}$ or $\left(\frac{1}{3}\right)$ $\left(\frac{1}{5}\right)$ or $\frac{1}{7}$ $\frac{1}{6}$ or $\left(\frac{1}{3}\right)$ $\left(\frac{1}{4}\right)$ or $\frac{1}{5}$

$\left(\frac{1}{2}\right)$ or $\frac{1}{4}$ $\frac{1}{12}$ or $\left(\frac{1}{4}\right)$ $\left(\frac{1}{4}\right)$ or $\frac{1}{9}$ $\left(\frac{1}{10}\right)$ or $\frac{1}{100}$

$\frac{1}{3}$ or $\left(\frac{2}{3}\right)$ $\frac{3}{5}$ or $\left(\frac{4}{5}\right)$ $\left(\frac{2}{5}\right)$ or $\frac{1}{5}$ $\frac{1}{4}$ or $\left(\frac{3}{4}\right)$

$\left(\frac{5}{8}\right)$ or $\frac{3}{8}$ $\frac{1}{12}$ or $\left(\frac{3}{12}\right)$ $\left(\frac{5}{8}\right)$ or $\frac{3}{8}$ $\frac{1}{6}$ or $\left(\frac{5}{6}\right)$

In each pair, circle the fraction with the greater value.

$\left(1\frac{2}{3}\right)$ or $1\frac{1}{3}$ $1\frac{1}{4}$ or $\left(1\frac{1}{2}\right)$ $\left(2\frac{2}{5}\right)$ or $1\frac{3}{5}$ $\left(2\frac{3}{4}\right)$ or $2\frac{1}{4}$

$3\frac{1}{2}$ or $\left(4\frac{1}{4}\right)$ $\left(1\frac{3}{4}\right)$ or $1\frac{1}{2}$ $\left(5\frac{2}{3}\right)$ or $4\frac{2}{3}$ $\left(6\frac{5}{8}\right)$ or $6\frac{3}{8}$

$\left(\frac{3}{4}\right)$ or $\frac{1}{3}$ $\frac{3}{5}$ or $\left(\frac{2}{3}\right)$ $\left(\frac{5}{6}\right)$ or $\frac{3}{4}$

$3\frac{1}{2}$ or $\left(3\frac{2}{3}\right)$ $4\frac{3}{5}$ or $\left(4\frac{5}{6}\right)$

LITTLE PIECES!

$2\frac{6}{10}$ or $\left(2\frac{4}{5}\right)$ $\left(1\frac{4}{5}\right)$ or $1\frac{4}{6}$

102

If children have difficulty comparing fractions, you may want to model the fractions with a cut-up paper plate or sheet of paper.

Rounding decimals

Write each amount to the nearest dollar.

$1.76	$3.56	$1.23	$2.43
$2.00	$4.00	$1.00	$2.00

ROUND 'EM UP!

Write each amount to the nearest dollar.

$2.86	$3.00	$3.29	$3.00	$6.82	$7.00	$7.12	$7.00
$8.63	$9.00	$4.96	$5.00	$8.32	$8.00	$2.78	$3.00
$4.33	$4.00	$8.70	$9.00	$6.65	$7.00	$5.30	$5.00
$7.02	$7.00	$6.74	$7.00	$7.89	$8.00	$12.89	$13.00
$11.64	$12.00	$10.64	$11.00	$15.67	$16.00	$21.37	$21.00

Write each amount to the nearest metre.

1.65 m	2 m	4.42 m	4 m	6.80 m	7 m	4.84 m	5 m
7.5 m	8 m	3.18 m	3 m	7.92 m	8 m	9.63 m	10 m
5.42 m	5 m	12.82 m	13 m	18.09 m	18 m	16.45 m	16 m
10.53 m	11 m	20.65 m	21 m	17.45 m	17 m	14.95 m	15 m
12.46 m	12 m	19.05 m	19 m	15.51 m	16 m	27.47 m	27 m

Write each amount to the nearest dollar or metre.

6.34 m	6 m	$3.50	$4.00	$5.01	$5.00	6.50 m	7 m
12.50 m	13 m	18.99 m	19 m	$12.50	$13.00	23.50 m	24 m
$61.67	$62	$45.52	$46	50.50 m	51 m	67.50 m	68 m
$15.11	$15.00	$21.56	$22.00	$98.59	$99.00	$14.99	$15
$91.50	$92.00	$78.03	$78.00	$63.56	$64.00	$95.50	$96.00

103

Children should recognize that amounts of 50 cents or 50 m and above are rounded up, and amounts below 50 cents and 50 m are rounded down. Make sure that children increase the whole number by 1 when they round up.

Adding

Write the sum between the lines.

SUPERMAN DID IT AND SO CAN YOU.

77	39	46
+ 22	+ 34	+ 36
99	73	82

Write the sum between the lines.

47	28	56	78	45
+ 13	+ 13	+ 14	+ 16	+ 13
60	41	70	94	58

54	47	84	54	36
+ 19	+ 16	+ 13	+ 17	+ 25
73	63	97	71	61

45	70	64	28	45
+ 27	+ 14	+ 29	+ 14	+ 35
72	84	93	42	80

14	18	14	17	18
+ 54	+ 44	+ 56	+ 54	+ 43
68	62	70	71	61

82	46	74	45	26
+ 9	+ 27	+ 18	+ 34	+ 36
91	73	92	79	62

45	43	57	59	57
+ 35	+ 28	+ 44	+ 37	+ 36
80	71	101	96	93

32	28	34	71	39
+ 45	+ 46	+ 19	+ 19	+ 38
77	74	53	90	77

104

Most of the sums require regrouping. Make sure that children do not neglect to add 10 to the tens column when they regroup.

Adding

Write the sum between the lines.

45 cm + 35 cm = 80 cm	34 cm + 28 cm = 62 cm	35 cm + 48 cm = 83 cm

Write the sum between the lines.

28 cm + 36 cm = 64 cm	56 cm + 36 cm = 92 cm	68 cm + 45 cm = 113 cm	49 cm + 27 cm = 76 cm	37 cm + 46 cm = 83 cm
38 m + 44 m = 82 m	55 m + 37 m = 92 m	29 m + 34 m = 63 m	56 m + 35 m = 91 m	47 m + 45 m = 92 m
36 kg + 17 kg = 53 kg	47 kg + 27 kg = 74 kg	43 kg + 18 kg = 61 kg	52 kg + 17 kg = 69 kg	65 kg + 27 kg = 92 kg
43 L + 29 L = 72 L	66 L + 27 L = 93 L	44 L + 18 L = 62 L	48 L + 24 L = 72 L	57 L + 42 L = 99 L

Write the sum between the lines.

$33.00 + $19.00 = $52.00	$46.00 + $13.00 = $59.00	$75.00 + $26.00 = $101.00	$37.00 + $15.00 = $52.00

This page is similar to the previous page, but includes units of measure. Make sure that children include the units in their answers.

Adding

Write the sum between the lines.

23 + 17 + 16 = 56	29 + 38 + 17 = 84	56 + 19 + 24 = 99

THIS ADDS UP TO BIG TROUBLE!

Write the sum between the lines.

19 + 10 + 11 = 40	12 + 14 + 12 = 38	17 + 10 + 12 = 39		
19 + 32 + 12 = 63	12 + 25 + 33 = 70	17 + 26 + 13 = 56	19 + 13 + 14 = 46	16 + 21 + 32 = 69
32 + 20 + 26 = 78	45 + 26 + 25 = 96	60 + 14 + 8 = 82	50 + 21 + 31 = 102	30 + 42 + 25 = 97
65 + 15 + 5 = 85	55 + 35 + 5 = 95	45 + 5 + 5 = 55	35 + 25 + 10 = 70	25 + 15 + 5 = 45
62 + 12 + 5 = 79	56 + 16 + 7 = 79	45 + 32 + 13 = 90	34 + 16 + 9 = 59	23 + 45 + 32 = 100

Children should add the ones column first, regrouping when necessary.

Subtracting

Write the difference between the lines.

68 − 15 = 53	32 − 26 = 6	68 − 29 = 39

USE YOUR BRAIN!

Write the difference between the lines.

90 − 27 = 63	50 − 18 = 32	70 − 23 = 47	40 − 19 = 21	
71 − 36 = 35	64 − 45 = 19	85 − 37 = 48	62 − 15 = 47	
85 − 48 = 37	97 − 49 = 48	75 − 65 = 10	65 − 34 = 31	45 − 17 = 28
70 − 26 = 44	63 − 7 = 56	73 − 56 = 17	53 − 26 = 27	47 − 43 = 4
73 − 44 = 29	53 − 23 = 30	61 − 19 = 42	53 − 16 = 37	61 − 14 = 47
64 − 47 = 17	81 − 39 = 42	74 − 47 = 27	82 − 38 = 44	73 − 27 = 46

Most of the subtraction problems on this page require regrouping.

Subtracting

Write the answer between the lines.

55 cm − 16 cm = 39 cm	32 cm − 28 cm = 4 cm	74 cm − 39 cm = 35 cm

KEEP ON TAKING AWAY

85 cm − 47 cm = 38 cm	74 cm − 39 cm = 35 cm	73 cm − 48 cm = 25 cm	60 cm − 47 cm = 13 cm	45 cm − 26 cm = 19 cm
40 cm − 17 cm = 23 cm	74 cm − 38 cm = 36 cm	82 cm − 29 cm = 53 cm	63 cm − 44 cm = 19 cm	45 cm − 23 cm = 22 cm
43 cm − 17 cm = 26 cm	83 cm − 36 cm = 47 cm	62 cm − 27 cm = 35 cm	81 cm − 36 cm = 45 cm	61 cm − 27 cm = 34 cm

Write the answer between the lines.

90 m − 37 m = 53 m	84 m − 29 m = 55 m	75 m − 39 m = 36 m	37 m − 18 m = 19 m	50 m − 28 m = 22 m

Write the answer between the lines.

56 kg − 45 kg = 11 kg	79 kg − 27 kg = 52 kg	64 kg − 27 kg = 37 kg	47 kg − 38 kg = 9 kg	68 kg − 39 kg = 29 kg

This page is similar to the previous page, but includes units of measure. Make sure that children include the units in their answers.

Real-life problems

Superman has to fly 81 km. He's traveled 49 km. How many more kilometres has he left to go?

$$\begin{array}{r} 7\ 11 \\ 8\cancel{1} \\ -\ 49 \\ \hline 32 \end{array}$$

32 km

Solve the problem and then write the answer in the box.

Steel has 47 hammers. He makes another 24 before one battle but then loses 18 in a second battle. How many hammers does Steel have now?

$$\begin{array}{r} 1 \\ 47 \\ +\ 24 \\ \hline 71 \end{array} \qquad \begin{array}{r} 6\ 11 \\ 7\cancel{1} \\ -\ 18 \\ \hline 53 \end{array}$$

53 hammers

Lois has 70 pens and gives 26 of them to Clark. She buys 12 new pens to replace the ones she has given away. How many pens does Lois have now?

$$\begin{array}{r} 6\ 10 \\ 7\cancel{0} \\ -\ 26 \\ \hline 44 \end{array} \qquad \begin{array}{r} 44 \\ +\ 12 \\ \hline 56 \end{array}$$

56 pens

Clark Kent empties his trouser pockets and finds 26¢ in one pocket, 13¢ in another pocket, and 37¢ in another one. How much money has Clark found altogether?

$$\begin{array}{r} 1 \\ 26 \\ 13 \\ +\ 37 \\ \hline 76 \end{array}$$

76¢

Supergirl has 64 french fries with her burger. She eats 16 fries and gives 6 to Superboy. How many fries does Supergirl have left?

$$\begin{array}{r} 5\ 14 \\ 6\cancel{4} \\ -\ 16 \\ \hline 48 \end{array} \qquad \begin{array}{r} 48 \\ -\ 6 \\ \hline 42 \end{array}$$

42 fries

These problems require children to do multiple operations. If they have difficulty, discuss the problems and "walk" them through the steps.

Multiplying

Write the answers between the lines.

29	51	36
x 5	x 4	x 3
145	204	108

GET TO WORK, OR I WILL CRUSH YOU!

Write the answers between the lines.

78	57	94	85	64
x 2	x 2	x 2	x 2	x 2
156	114	188	170	128

94	32	58	41	19
x 3	x 3	x 3	x 3	x 3
282	96	174	123	57

74	18	67	43	26
x 4	x 4	x 4	x 4	x 4
296	72	268	172	104

33	49	67	28	63
x 5	x 5	x 5	x 5	x 5
165	245	335	140	315

15	53	64	85	72
x 6	x 6	x 6	x 6	x 6
90	318	384	510	432

47	84	51	85	37
x 8	x 8	x 8	x 8	x 8
376	672	408	680	296

Most of the multiplications require children to regroup. Go through any incorrect answers with children to find out whether the problem results from incorrect regrouping or poor knowledge of times tables.

Multiplying

Write the answers between the lines.

23	66	38	97
x 5	x 4	x 5	x 3
115	264	190	291

Write the answers between the lines.

37	47	87	17	97
x 4	x 5	x 6	x 7	x 8
148	235	522	119	776

43	50	37	29	16
x 7	x 7	x 7	x 7	x 7
301	350	259	203	112

61	14	36	58	27
x 9	x 9	x 9	x 9	x 9
549	126	324	522	243

45	67	12	31	98
x 10	x 10	x 10	x 10	x 10
450	670	120	310	980

58	38	78	28	18
x 6	x 7	x 8	x 9	x 10
348	266	624	252	180

69	89	59	29	49
x 9	x 8	x 7	x 6	x 5
621	712	413	174	245

See the comments for the previous page.

Dividing

Write the answer in the box.

30 ÷ 7 = [4 r 2]   [5 r 3]   [4 r 2]

$$\begin{array}{r} 4 \\ 7\overline{)30} \\ 28 \\ \hline 2 \end{array} \qquad \begin{array}{r} 5 \\ 5\overline{)28} \\ 25 \\ \hline 3 \end{array} \qquad \begin{array}{r} 4 \\ 8\overline{)34} \\ 32 \\ \hline 2 \end{array}$$

I'LL SOON DIVIDE THESE UP!

Write the answer in the box.

25 ÷ 3 = 8 r 1	20 ÷ 3 = 6 r 2	32 ÷ 3 = 10 r 2
13 ÷ 3 = 4 r 1	35 ÷ 4 = 8 r 3	13 ÷ 4 = 3 r 1
47 ÷ 4 = 11 r 3	4 ÷ 4 = 1	37 ÷ 5 = 7 r 2
12 ÷ 5 = 2 r 2	15 ÷ 5 = 3	24 ÷ 5 = 4 r 4
43 ÷ 6 = 7 r 1	6 ÷ 5 = 1 r 1	49 ÷ 5 = 9 r 4

Write the answer in the box.

$$\begin{array}{r} 4 \\ 8\overline{)32} \\ -32 \\ \hline 0 \end{array} \quad \begin{array}{r} 6\,r\,2 \\ 8\overline{)50} \\ -48 \\ \hline 2 \end{array} \quad \begin{array}{r} 1\,r\,2 \\ 8\overline{)10} \\ -8 \\ \hline 2 \end{array} \quad \begin{array}{r} 7\,r\,7 \\ 8\overline{)63} \\ -56 \\ \hline 7 \end{array} \quad \begin{array}{r} 3\,r\,3 \\ 8\overline{)27} \\ -24 \\ \hline 3 \end{array}$$

$$\begin{array}{r} 10 \\ 3\overline{)30} \\ -30 \\ \hline 0 \end{array} \quad \begin{array}{r} 4\,r\,2 \\ 3\overline{)14} \\ -12 \\ \hline 3 \end{array} \quad \begin{array}{r} 8\,r\,1 \\ 3\overline{)25} \\ -24 \\ \hline 1 \end{array} \quad \begin{array}{r} 2\,r\,1 \\ 2\overline{)5} \\ -4 \\ \hline 1 \end{array} \quad \begin{array}{r} 9 \\ 2\overline{)18} \\ -18 \\ \hline 0 \end{array}$$

Write the answer in the box.

45 ÷ 8 = 5 r 5	73 ÷ 8 = 9 r 1	56 ÷ 8 = 7
73 ÷ 9 = 8 r 1	41 ÷ 9 = 4 r 5	50 ÷ 9 = 5 r 5
54 ÷ 10 = 5 r 4	89 ÷ 10 = 8 r 9	42 ÷ 10 = 4 r 2

These division problems test children's knowledge of times tables. Children should be able to calculate the remainders easily.

Dividing

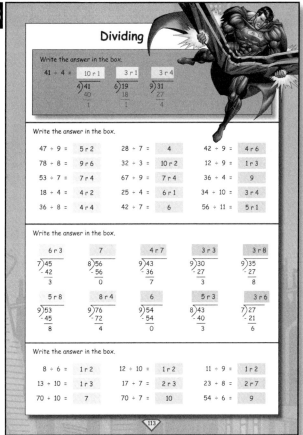

Write the answer in the box.

41 ÷ 4 = 10 r 1

4)41 → 3 r 1   6)19   3 r 4   9)31
  40   18   27
   1   1   4

Write the answer in the box.

47 ÷ 9 = 5 r 2	28 ÷ 7 = 4	42 ÷ 9 = 4 r 6
78 ÷ 8 = 9 r 6	32 ÷ 3 = 10 r 2	12 ÷ 9 = 1 r 3
53 ÷ 7 = 7 r 4	67 ÷ 9 = 7 r 4	36 ÷ 4 = 9
18 ÷ 4 = 4 r 2	25 ÷ 4 = 6 r 1	34 ÷ 10 = 3 r 4
36 ÷ 8 = 4 r 4	42 ÷ 7 = 6	56 ÷ 11 = 5 r 1

Write the answer in the box.

6 r 3	7	4 r 7	3 r 3	3 r 8
7)45	8)56	9)43	9)30	9)35
- 42	- 56	- 36	- 27	- 27
3	0	7	3	8

5 r 8	8 r 4	6	5 r 3	3 r 6
9)53	9)76	9)54	8)43	7)27
- 45	- 72	- 54	- 40	- 21
8	4	0	3	6

Write the answer in the box.

8 ÷ 6 = 1 r 2	12 ÷ 10 = 1 r 2	11 ÷ 9 = 1 r 2
13 ÷ 10 = 1 r 3	17 ÷ 7 = 2 r 3	23 ÷ 8 = 2 r 7
70 ÷ 10 = 7	70 ÷ 7 = 10	54 ÷ 6 = 9

See the comments for the previous page.

Choosing the operation

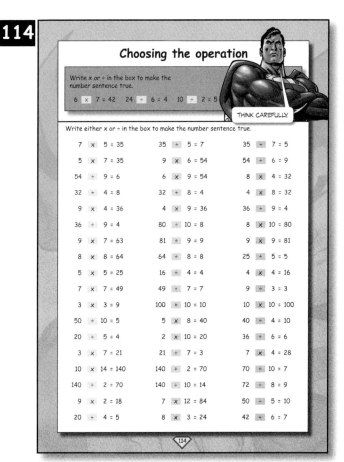

Write x or ÷ in the box to make the
number sentence true.

6 x 7 = 42   24 ÷ 6 = 4   10 ÷ 2 = 5

THINK CAREFULLY

Write either x or ÷ in the box to make the number sentence true.

7 x 5 = 35	35 ÷ 5 = 7	35 ÷ 7 = 5
5 x 7 = 35	9 x 6 = 54	54 ÷ 6 = 9
54 ÷ 9 = 6	6 x 9 = 54	8 x 4 = 32
32 ÷ 4 = 8	32 ÷ 8 = 4	4 x 8 = 32
9 x 4 = 36	4 x 9 = 36	36 ÷ 9 = 4
36 ÷ 9 = 4	80 ÷ 10 = 8	8 x 10 = 80
9 x 7 = 63	81 ÷ 9 = 9	9 x 9 = 81
8 x 8 = 64	64 ÷ 8 = 8	25 ÷ 5 = 5
5 x 5 = 25	16 ÷ 4 = 4	4 x 4 = 16
7 x 7 = 49	49 ÷ 7 = 7	9 ÷ 3 = 3
3 x 3 = 9	100 ÷ 10 = 10	10 x 10 = 100
50 ÷ 10 = 5	5 x 8 = 40	40 ÷ 4 = 10
20 ÷ 5 = 4	2 x 10 = 20	36 ÷ 6 = 6
3 x 7 = 21	21 ÷ 7 = 3	7 x 4 = 28
10 x 14 = 140	140 ÷ 2 = 70	70 ÷ 10 = 7
140 ÷ 2 = 70	140 ÷ 10 = 14	72 ÷ 8 = 9
9 x 2 = 18	7 x 12 = 84	50 ÷ 5 = 10
20 ÷ 4 = 5	8 x 3 = 24	42 ÷ 6 = 7

Children will probably realize that if the answer is larger than the first number, they should multiply, and if the answer is smaller than the first number they should divide. They can check some of their answers to make sure that they are correct.

Real-life problems

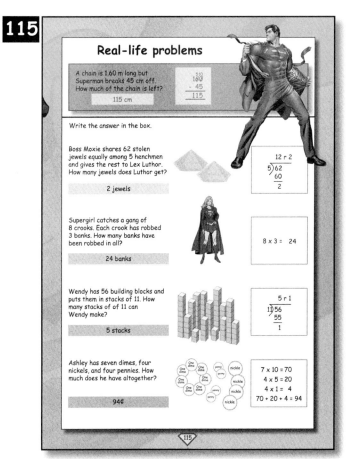

A chain is 1.60 m long but
Superman breaks 45 cm off.
How much of the chain is left?

115 cm

   5 10
   1.60
 - 45
   115

Write the answer in the box.

Boss Moxie shares 62 stolen
jewels equally among 5 henchmen
and gives the rest to Lex Luthor.
How many jewels does Luthor get?

2 jewels

12 r 2
5)62
  60
   2

Supergirl catches a gang of
8 crooks. Each crook has robbed
3 banks. How many banks have
been robbed in all?

24 banks

8 x 3 = 24

Wendy has 56 building blocks and
puts them in stacks of 11. How
many stacks of of 11 can
Wendy make?

5 stacks

5 r 1
11)56
  55
   1

Ashley has seven dimes, four
nickels, and four pennies. How
much does he have altogether?

94¢

7 x 10 = 70
4 x 5 = 20
4 x 1 = 4
70 + 20 + 4 = 94

Make sure that children understand which operation to perform for each problem.

Perimeter

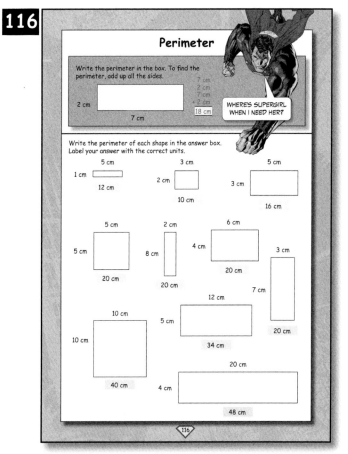

Write the perimeter in the box. To find the
perimeter, add up all the sides.

2 cm

7 cm

7 cm
2 cm
7 cm
+ 2 cm
18 cm

WHERE'S SUPERGIRL
WHEN I NEED HER?

Write the perimeter of each shape in the answer box.
Label your answer with the correct units.

5 cm 1 cm 12 cm
12 cm

3 cm 2 cm 10 cm
10 cm

5 cm 3 cm 16 cm
16 cm

5 cm 5 cm 20 cm
20 cm

2 cm 8 cm 20 cm
20 cm

6 cm 4 cm 20 cm
20 cm

3 cm 7 cm 20 cm
20 cm

10 cm 5 cm 12 cm
34 cm

10 cm 40 cm
40 cm

5 cm 4 cm 20 cm
48 cm

Some children may add all the four sides; others may double each different length and add the results; yet others may add the two different lengths and then double the sum. Each of these methods is acceptable.

Area

Write the area of the shape in the box. To find the area, multiply the length by the width.

METROPOLIS IS MY AREA!

$1 \times 7 = 7$

7 cm | 1 cm

7 cm²

Write the area of each shape in the answer box. Label your answer with the units.

12 cm²

10 cm²

6 cm²

16 cm²

20 cm²

12 cm²

4 cm²

9 cm²

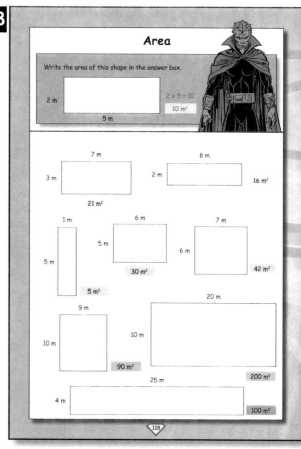

Area

Write the area of this shape in the answer box.

2 m

5 m

$2 \times 5 = 10$

10 m²

7 m | 3 m

21 m²

8 m | 2 m

16 m²

1 m | 5 m

5 m

5 m²

6 m | 5 m

30 m²

7 m | 6 m

42 m²

9 m | 10 m

10 m

90 m²

20 m | 10 m

25 m

200 m²

4 m

100 m²

Since the area of a shape is the amount of space inside it, the number of squares inside each shape gives the area. Children may realize that multiplying one side of a rectangle by the other will give the same result more quickly.

Following from the last page, this page requires children to find areas by multiplying the sides together. If they are unsure of the method, sketch in squares on the shapes to help.

Problems using time

Write the answer in the box.

How many minutes until 11 o'clock?

TIME TO GET GOING!

25 minutes

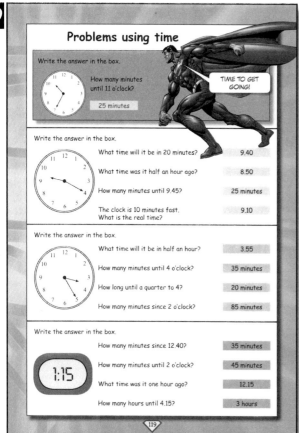

Write the answer in the box.

What time will it be in 20 minutes? | 9.40

What time was it half an hour ago? | 8.50

How many minutes until 9.45? | 25 minutes

The clock is 10 minutes fast. What is the real time? | 9.10

Write the answer in the box.

What time will it be in half an hour? | 3.55

How many minutes until 4 o'clock? | 35 minutes

How long until a quarter to 4? | 20 minutes

How many minutes since 2 o'clock? | 85 minutes

Write the answer in the box.

1:15

How many minutes since 12.40? | 35 minutes

How many minutes until 2 o'clock? | 45 minutes

What time was it one hour ago? | 12.15

How many hours until 4.15? | 3 hours

Children may use any method that gives the correct answer.

Reading timetables

	Metropolis	Smallville	Coast City	Krypton
Superman	8:00	8:02	8:06	8:25
Kryptonian skyship	8:10	8:23	No stop	8:53
Warsuit	8:30	9:05	10:20	No stop
Phantom zone portal	8:00	No stop	No stop	8:03

The timetable shows the time it takes different things to travel between Metropolis and Krypton.

Write the answer in the box.

How long does Superman take between Metropolis and Krypton? | 25 minutes

When does the Warsuit arrive at Smallville? | 9:05

Where does the Kryptonian skyship not stop? | Coast City

Where is Superman at 8:02? | Smallville

Does the Warsuit stop at Krypton? | No

How long does it take to travel to Krypton using the Phantom Zone portal? | 3 minutes

How long does it take the skyship to travel from Smallville to Krypton? | 30 minutes

How long does the Warsuit take between Metropolis and Coast City? | 1 hour, 50 minutes

Which vehicle arrives at Krypton at 8:53? | Kryptonian skyship

Where is Superman at 8:25? | Krypton

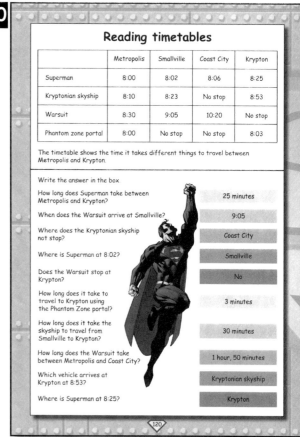

Children should find this exercise fairly straightforward. If they have difficulty, help them read accross the rows and down the columns to find the information they need.

Averages

Write the average of this row in the box.
To find the average, add the numbers together.
Then, divide the sum by the number of numbers
you added together (7, in this example).

4	2	2	2	3	6	2

The average is **3**

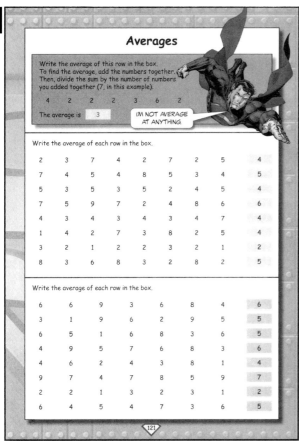

I'M NOT AVERAGE AT ANYTHING.

Write the average of each row in the box.

2	3	7	4	2	7	2	5	**4**
7	4	5	4	8	5	3	4	**5**
5	3	5	3	5	2	4	5	**4**
7	5	9	7	2	4	8	6	**6**
4	3	4	3	4	3	4	7	**4**
1	4	2	7	3	8	2	5	**4**
3	2	1	2	2	3	2	1	**2**
8	3	6	8	3	2	8	2	**5**

Write the average of each row in the box.

6	6	9	3	6	8	4	**6**
3	1	9	6	2	9	5	**5**
6	5	1	6	8	3	6	**5**
4	9	5	7	6	8	3	**6**
4	6	2	4	3	8	1	**4**
9	7	4	7	8	5	9	**7**
2	2	1	3	2	3	1	**2**
6	4	5	4	7	3	6	**5**

Estimating

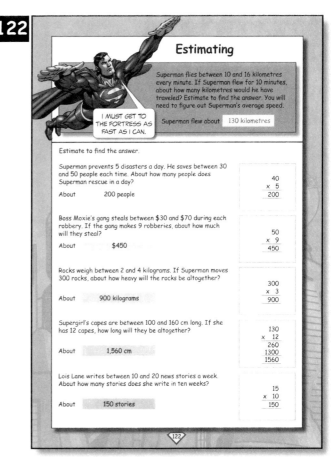

I MUST GET TO THE FORTRESS AS FAST AS I CAN.

Superman flies between 10 and 16 kilometres every minute. If Superman flew for 10 minutes, about how many kilometres would he have traveled? Estimate to find the answer. You will need to figure out Superman's average speed.

Superman flew about **130 kilometres**

Estimate to find the answer.

Superman prevents 5 disasters a day. He saves between 30 and 50 people each time. About how many people does Superman rescue in a day?

About **200 people**

$$\begin{array}{r} 40 \\ \times\ 5 \\ \hline 200 \end{array}$$

Boss Moxie's gang steals between $30 and $70 during each robbery. If the gang makes 9 robberies, about how much will they steal?

About **$450**

$$\begin{array}{r} 50 \\ \times\ 9 \\ \hline 450 \end{array}$$

Rocks weigh between 2 and 4 kilograms. If Superman moves 300 rocks, about how heavy will the rocks be altogether?

About **900 kilograms**

$$\begin{array}{r} 300 \\ \times\ 3 \\ \hline 900 \end{array}$$

Supergirl's capes are between 100 and 160 cm long. If she has 12 capes, how long will they be altogether?

About **1,560 cm**

$$\begin{array}{r} 130 \\ \times\ 12 \\ \hline 260 \\ 1300 \\ \hline 1560 \end{array}$$

Lois Lane writes between 10 and 20 news stories a week. About how many stories does she write in ten weeks?

About **150 stories**

$$\begin{array}{r} 15 \\ \times\ 10 \\ \hline 150 \end{array}$$

Children should use a compatible number—one that is easy to manipulate in the problem—while they estimate.

Calculating change

Circle the correct change.
Supergirl bought a ball costing 45 cents. She paid **one dollar**
How much change did she get?

quarter quarter one dime five cents — (quarter quarter five cents) — quarter quarter quarter — quarter one dime

I'M USED TO QUICK CHANGES. HOW ABOUT YOU?

Circle the correct change.

Menu
Banana 25¢
Pear 75¢
Apple 60¢

Superman bought an apple. He paid **one dollar**

How much change did he get?

one dime one dime one dime — (one dime one dime one dime one dime) — quarter quarter one dime one dime

Supergirl bought a banana. She paid **one dollar**

How much change did she get?

quarter quarter quarter one dime — (quarter quarter five cents one dime one dime) —

Lois Lane bought a pear. She paid **one dollar**

How much change did she get?

quarter quarter quarter five cents — quarter quarter quarter — (quarter)

Allow children to set up subtraction problems if they cannot complete the calculations mentally.

Counting money

Count the coins. Write the total amount.

quarter quarter quarter five cents five cents one dime

25¢ + 25¢ + 25¢ + 5¢ + 5¢ + 10¢ = **95¢**

BUT DON'T TAKE ANY CASH! I'M WATCHING YOU!

Count the coins. Write the total amount.

quarter one cent one cent one dime
one dime five cents
52¢

five cents one cent
one dime one dime one dime
36¢

quarter quarter one cent
one cent one cent one cent one dime
64¢

quarter five cents five cents
one cent one cent one dime one dime
57¢

quarter quarter quarter
quarter quarter one cent one dime
$1.36

five cents five cents five cents one cent
one cent one cent one cent one dime
one dime
49¢

As on the previous page, allow children to set up addition problems if they need to.

Number pairs

Look at the grid and then answer the questions below.

Give the coordinates of each letter.

A =	5, 2	E =	1, 1	I =	2, 10	M =	6, 7
B =	9, 5	F =	3, 9	J =	7, 6	N =	6, 1
C =	9, 1	G =	5, 5	K =	1, 4	O =	4, 0
D =	6, 8	H =	4, 7	L =	7, 3	P =	5, 6

Make sure that children understand that the order of the numbers within ordered pairs is important. The first number is from the horizontal or x axis, and the second number is from the vertical or y axis. Ordered pairs are written in parentheses, like this A = (1,2).

Multiply or divide?

Write x or ÷ in the box.

6 [x] 5 = 30   16 [÷] 4 = 4   6 [x] 10 = 60

Write x or ÷ in the box.

8 [x] 5 = 40	5 [x] 2 = 10	10 [÷] 5 = 2
25 [÷] 5 = 5	35 [÷] 5 = 7	3 [x] 8 = 24
18 [÷] 2 = 9	10 [x] 10 = 100	6 [x] 10 = 60
40 [÷] 10 = 4	36 [÷] 6 = 6	5 [x] 12 = 60
6 [x] 7 = 42	3 [x] 12 = 36	90 [÷] 9 = 10
80 [÷] 8 = 10	14 [÷] 7 = 2	18 [÷] 6 = 3

Write the answer in the box.

A number divided by 3 is 10. What is the number?	30
I multiply a number by 6 and the answer is 30. What is the number?	5
A number multiplied by 10 gives the answer 200. What is the number?	20
I divide a number by 8 and the answer is 5. What is the number?	40
A number divided by 7 is 5. What is the number?	35
I multiply a number by 2 and the answer is 18. What is the number?	9
A number multiplied by 5 is 45. What is the number?	9
I divide a number by 2 and the answer is 1. What is the number?	2

Write x or ÷ in the box.

7 [x] 10 = 70	7 [x] 7 = 49	10 [÷] 10 = 1
5 [÷] 5 = 1	9 [x] 3 = 27	50 [÷] 5 = 10
15 [÷] 5 = 3	20 [x] 5 = 100	3 [x] 3 = 9
20 [÷] 5 = 4	4 [x] 2 = 8	50 [÷] 5 = 10

The second section requires children to perform the inverse operation to reach the answer. For the other sections, children should realize that if the answer is larger than the first number, they must multiply, and if it is smaller, they must divide.

Lines of symmetry

Draw the line of symmetry on each shape.

Draw the line of symmetry on each shape.

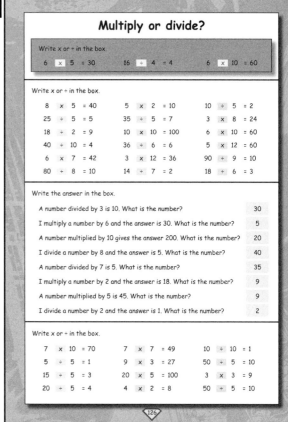

YOU'VE GOT TO DRAW THE LINE SOMEWHERE!

A   B   C
D   E   I
K   M   T

Half of each shape is drawn along with the line of symmetry. Draw the other half.

U   W   V
Y   3   8

If children pick an incorrect line of symmetry, you can use a small mirror to show them their mistake.

Counting by 3s, 4s, and 5s

Find the pattern. Continue each row.

Count by 3s.	9	12	15	18	21	24	27
Count by 4s.	8	12	16	20	24	28	32
Count by 5s.	55	50	45	40	35	30	25

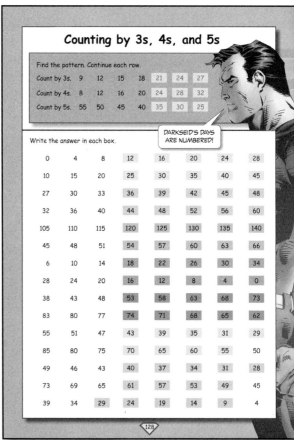

DARKSEID'S DAYS ARE NUMBERED!

Write the answer in each box.

0	4	8	12	16	20	24	28
10	15	20	25	30	35	40	45
27	30	33	36	39	42	45	48
32	36	40	44	48	52	56	60
105	110	115	120	125	130	135	140
45	48	51	54	57	60	63	66
6	10	14	18	22	26	30	34
28	24	20	16	12	8	4	0
38	43	48	53	58	63	68	73
83	80	77	74	71	68	65	62
55	51	47	43	39	35	31	29
85	80	75	70	65	60	55	50
49	46	43	40	37	34	31	28
73	69	65	61	57	53	49	45
39	34	29	24	19	14	9	4

Some of the patterns show an increase, while others show a decrease. Children should be able to complete these questions using mental math.

Multiples

Circle the numbers that are in the 2 times table.

3   5
(8)   9   (4)   (2)

Circle the numbers that are in the 2 times table.

19   (16)   27   13   (12)
(22)   21   (20)

Circle the numbers that are in the 2 times table.

(36)   (70)   25
57   (44)   73   57   (18)

Circle the numbers that are in the 5 times table.

(45)   (25)   51
(20)   34   54   (10)   11

Circle the numbers that are in the 5 times table.

7   (80)   56
53   (5)   (65)   (50)   81

Circle the numbers that are in the 10 times table.

(20)   24   1
(40)   15   58   (60)   44

Circle the numbers that are in the 10 times table.

327   605   275
485   (110)   99   (70)   (260)

These questions test children's familiarity with the 2, 5, and 10 times tables.

Comparing and ordering

Write these numbers in order, starting with the smallest.

482   597   632   382 | 382 | 482 | 597 | 632 |

KEEP THEM IN ORDER!

Write these numbers in order, starting with the smallest.

291	103	775	453	103	291	453	775
536	237	439	333	237	333	439	536
638	950	475	969	475	638	950	969
195	483	520	681	195	483	520	681
473	374	937	793	374	473	793	937
406	560	460	650	406	460	560	650
738	837	378	783	378	738	783	837
473	374	734	347	347	374	473	734
206	620	602	260	206	260	602	620
634	364	436	463	364	436	463	634
47	740	74	704	47	74	704	740
401	140	41	104	41	104	140	401
290	92	209	29	29	92	209	290
803	380	83	38	38	83	380	803
504	450	54	45	45	54	450	504

Make sure that children do not simply order the numbers according to the first digits.

Rounding

What is 428 rounded to the nearest 100?

400   420   440   460   480   500

| 400 |
↑
428

LET'S TIDY UP!

What is each number rounded to the nearest 100?

569	600	342	300	142	100	439	400
371	400	873	900	934	900	555	600
812	800	240	200	854	900	444	400
548	500	639	600	299	300	146	100
161	200	427	400	307	300	732	700

What is 250 rounded to the nearest 100?

200   210   220   230   240   250   260   270   280   290   300   310

| 300 |
↑
250

What is each number rounded to the nearest 100?

350	400	850	900	45	0	827	800
71	100	405	400	87	100	450	500
655	700	540	500	280	300	208	200
750	800	250	300	90	100	59	100
550	600	105	100	855	900	120	100

Children should recognize that amounts of 50 and above are rounded up, and amounts below 50 are rounded down. Make sure that children increase the hundreds digit by 1 when they round up.

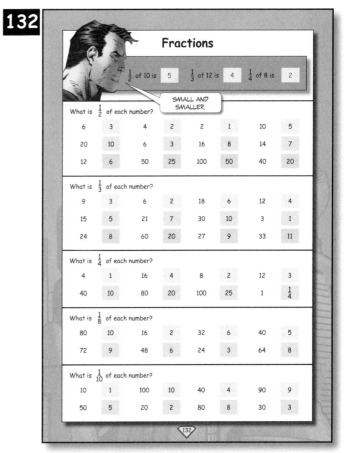

Fractions

$\frac{1}{2}$ of 10 is | 5 | $\frac{1}{3}$ of 12 is | 4 | $\frac{1}{4}$ of 8 is | 2 |

SMALL AND SMALLER.

What is $\frac{1}{2}$ of each number?

6	3	4	2	2	1	10	5
20	10	6	3	16	8	14	7
12	6	50	25	100	50	40	20

What is $\frac{1}{3}$ of each number?

9	3	6	2	18	6	12	4
15	5	21	7	30	10	3	1
24	8	60	20	27	9	33	11

What is $\frac{1}{4}$ of each number?

| 4 | 1 | 16 | 4 | 8 | 2 | 12 | 3 |
| 40 | 10 | 80 | 20 | 100 | 25 | 1 | $\frac{1}{4}$ |

What is $\frac{1}{8}$ of each number?

| 80 | 10 | 16 | 2 | 32 | 6 | 40 | 5 |
| 72 | 9 | 48 | 6 | 24 | 3 | 64 | 8 |

What is $\frac{1}{10}$ of each number?

| 10 | 1 | 100 | 10 | 40 | 4 | 90 | 9 |
| 50 | 5 | 20 | 2 | 80 | 8 | 30 | 3 |

Each of the fractions on this page is a unit fraction —it has a numerator of 1. Children should realize that multiplying by these fractions is the same as dividing by the denominator.

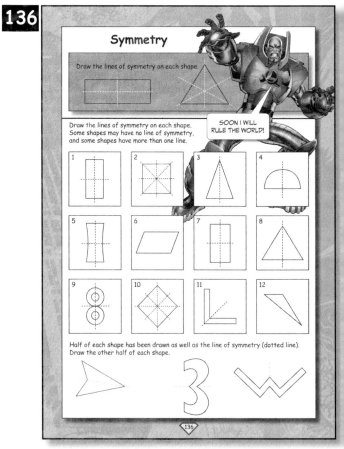

133

Multiplying

Write the answer in the box.

6 × 3 = 18   8 × 5 = 40   7 × 10 = 70

I'M GONNA TURN THE TABLES ON MY ENEMIES!

Write the answer in the box.

6 × 6 = 36	2 × 3 = 6	6 × 4 = 24	4 × 3 = 12
5 × 8 = 40	7 × 3 = 21	6 × 9 = 54	10 × 4 = 40
3 × 2 = 6	9 × 4 = 36	7 × 5 = 35	5 × 4 = 20
0 × 8 = 0	5 × 3 = 15	4 × 4 = 16	0 × 7 = 0
9 × 3 = 27	10 × 7 = 70	3 × 3 = 9	9 × 5 = 45

Write the answer in the box.

Four times a number is 12. What is the number?   3

A child draws 8 squares. How many sides have been drawn?   32

Lois Lane works for 5 days every week. How many days does she work in 9 weeks?   45

A girl is given 3 stickers for every point she gains in a spelling test. How many stickers will she receive if she gets 10 points?   30

A box contains 4 pieces of kryptonite. Lex Luthor has 7 of these boxes. How many pieces of kryptonite does Luthor have?   28

Mari is given eight 5¢ coins. How much money is she given?   40¢

Five times a number is 30. What is the number?   6

The *Daily Planet* has 20 pages. Each page has 3 stories on it. How many stories does the *Daily Planet* have in all?   60

Six times a number is 42. What is the number?   7

Children should be able to answer all the questions on this page using mental math.

134

Dividing

Work out each division problem. Some will have remainders, some will not.

18 ÷ 3 = 6   8 r 1   3 r 1
12 ÷ 5 = 2 r 2   2)17   3)10
                   16   9
                    1   1

Work out each division problem.

18 ÷ 3 = 6	36 ÷ 4 = 9	16 ÷ 4 = 4	24 ÷ 6 = 4
20 ÷ 5 = 4	36 ÷ 9 = 4	30 ÷ 10 = 3	27 ÷ 3 = 9
8 ÷ 2 = 4	24 ÷ 4 = 6	35 ÷ 7 = 5	100 ÷ 10 = 10
4 ÷ 1 = 4	33 ÷ 11 = 3	48 ÷ 6 = 8	36 ÷ 6 = 6

Work out each division problem. Some will have remainders, some will not.

5	10 r 2	2 r 2	1
4)20	3)32	5)12	10)10
20	30	10	10
0	2	2	0

4 r 1	8	5	3 r 3
4)17	3)24	5)25	10)33
16	24	25	30
1	0	0	3

Work out the answer to each problem.

Superman has 23 kryptonite crystals to share equally between four of his friends. How many crystals does each person get, and how many are left over for Superman?   5 kryptonite crystals, 3 are left over

5 r 3
4)23
20
3

Superman divides 36 coins between five sacks. How many coins go in each sack, and how many are left over?   7 coins, 1 is left over

7 r 1
5)36
35
1

Children should be able to answer all the questions on this page using mental math.

135

Bar graphs

LOIS'S PENS

How many pens does Lois Lane have?   8

CHECK THE DATA!

Look at this bar graph. Then answer the questions.

FAVORITE SUPER HERO

This graph shows the favorite super hero of some children.

How many children were asked which super hero they liked best?   22

How many children liked Steel best?   4

Which super hero did 8 children like?   Supergirl

Who was the favorite super hero?   Superman

Look at this bar graph. Then answer the questions.

This graph shows the most useful superpower of a group of super heroes.

MOST USEFUL SUPERPOWER

How many super heroes were asked which of their powers was most useful?   18

Which superpower did 5 super heroes think is most useful?   Flight

How many more super heroes thought X-ray vision was more useful than superstrength?   6

If children need help reading bar graphs, show them how to read across and up from the axis labels. To answer some of the questions, children will need to add and compare data.

136

Symmetry

Draw the lines of symmetry on each shape.

Draw the lines of symmetry on each shape. Some shapes may have no line of symmetry, and some shapes have more than one line.

SOON I WILL RULE THE WORLD!

1   2   3   4

5   6   7   8

9   10   11   12

Half of each shape has been drawn as well as the line of symmetry (dotted line). Draw the other half of each shape.

If children pick an incorrect line of symmetry, you can use a small mirror to show them their mistake.

Ordering

Write these numbers in order starting with the smallest.

560	506	650	605
506	560	605	650

LETS GET SOME ORDER INTO PROCEEDINGS!

Write these numbers in order starting with the smallest.

340	403	304	430
304	340	403	430

702	270	720	207
207	270	702	720

901	910	190	109
109	190	901	910

560	650	605	506
506	560	605	650

489	849	984	948
489	849	948	984

726	672	762	267
267	672	726	762

890	980	809	908
809	890	908	980

486	684	864	648
486	648	684	864

405	450	540	504
405	450	504	540

76	104	200	92
76	92	104	200

440	66	177	781
66	177	440	781

632	236	77	407
77	236	407	632

74	12	101	800
12	74	101	800

842	587	99	88
88	99	587	842

842	99	587	72
72	99	587	842

600	304	403	89
89	304	403	600

500	486	395	288
288	395	486	500

78	9	302	470
9	78	302	470

2	1	201	38
1	2	38	201

186	168	158	184
158	168	184	186

Make sure that children do not simply order the numbers according to the first digits.

Fractions of shapes

Shade half of each shape.

MAKE 'EM PRETTY.

Shade half of each shape.

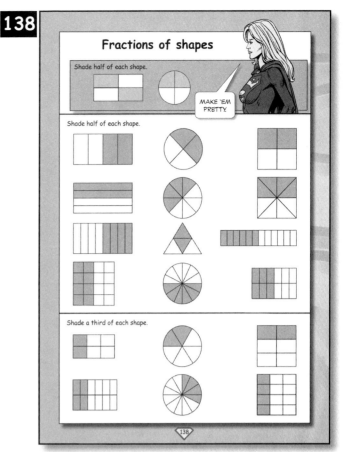

Shade a third of each shape.

Children may shade in any combination of the sections as long as the shaded area represents the fraction.

Choosing the operation

Write the answer in the box.

I add 30 to a number and the sum is 45. What number did I start with? 15

I subtract 17 and have 28 left. What number did I start with? 45

Write the answer in the box.

31 is added to a number and the sum is 56. What number did I begin with? 25

I take 12 piles of paper from the desk and end up with 19 piles. How many piles of paper did I start with? 31

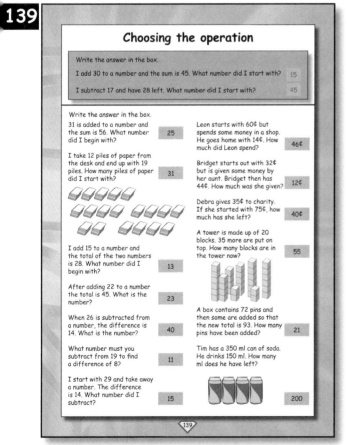

I add 15 to a number and the total of the two numbers is 28. What number did I begin with? 13

After adding 22 to a number the total is 45. What is the number? 23

When 26 is subtracted from a number, the difference is 14. What is the number? 40

What number must you subtract from 19 to find a difference of 8? 11

I start with 29 and take away a number. The difference is 14. What number did I subtract? 15

Leon starts with 60¢ but spends some money in a shop. He goes home with 14¢. How much did Leon spend? 46¢

Bridget starts out with 32¢ but is given some money by her aunt. Bridget then has 44¢. How much was she given? 12¢

Debra gives 35¢ to charity. If she started with 75¢, how much has she left? 40¢

A tower is made up of 20 blocks. 35 more are put on top. How many blocks are in the tower now? 55

A box contains 72 pins and then some are added so that the new total is 93. How many pins have been added? 21

Tim has a 350 ml can of soda. He drinks 150 ml. How many ml does he have left? 200

Children must choose between addition and subtraction to solve each problem. If they make an error, have them substitute their answer in the problem to help them understand why it is incorrect.

Choosing the operation

Write the answer in the box.

I divide a number by 5 and the answer is 6. What number did I begin with? 30

A number is multiplied by 7 and the result is 28. What is the number? 4

Write the answer in the box.

A number is multiplied by 7 and the result is 35. What is the number? 5

When a number is divided by 4 the result is 4. What is the number? 16

I multiply a number by 10, and the final number is 90. What number did I multiply? 9

After dividing a number by 9, I am left with 4. What number did I divide? 36

When 40 is multiplied by a number the result is 80. What number is used to multiply? 2

I divide a number by 3 and the result is 8. What is the number? 24

After multiplying a number by 2, I have 36. What was the number I started with? 18

I multiply a number by 9 and the result is 54. What number was multiplied? 6

After dividing a number by 4, I am left with 15. What number was divided? 60

$55 is shared equally by some super heroes. Each super hero receives $11. How many super heroes are there? 5

Each box contains 12 pens. I have 36 pens altogether. How many boxes do I have? 3

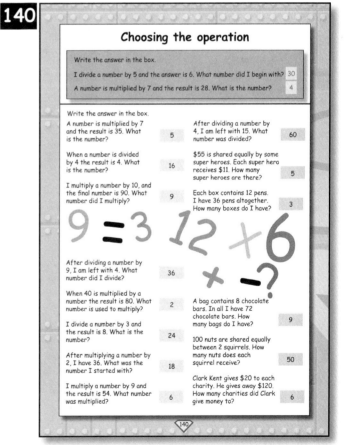

A bag contains 8 chocolate bars. In all I have 72 chocolate bars. How many bags do I have? 9

100 nuts are shared equally between 2 squirrels. How many nuts does each squirrel receive? 50

Clark Kent gives $20 to each charity. He gives away $120. How many charities did Clark give money to? 6

Children must choose between multiplication and division to solve each problem. If they make an error, have them substitute their answer in the problem to help them understand why it is incorrect.

Bar graphs and pictographs

BRAVERY AWARDS

Look at the bar graph and answer the question.

Which super hero has 3 bravery awards?

Supergirl

Look at the bar graph and answer the questions.

SUPER HERO RESCUES

Which super hero rescued three people? **Supergirl**

Which super hero rescued the most people? **Superman**

How many people did Steel rescue? **6**

Look at the pictograph and answer the questions.

CHILDREN'S WORST SUPER VILLAINS

Each shield stands for 2 children.

Which super villain is disliked by 3 children? **Parasite**

Which is the most disliked super villain? **Doomsday**

How many more children dislike Darkseid than dislike Parasite? **1**

If children need help reading bar graphs, show them how to read across and up from the axis labels. To answer some of the questions, children will have to compare and add data.

Adding two numbers

Find each sum.

```
  211      482
+ 214    + 573
-----    -----
  425    1,055
```

Remember to regroup if you have to.

JUST FIGURE IT OUT. I KNOW YOU CAN DO IT!

Find each sum.

```
  224      452      612      843
+ 365    + 227    + 345    + 291
-----    -----    -----    -----
  589      679      957    1,134

  485      563      535      481
+ 606    + 147    + 187    + 377
-----    -----    -----    -----
1,091      710      722      858
```

Write the answer in the box.

313 + 237 = **550**   635 + 267 = **902**

Write the missing number in the box.

```
  362      266      701      739
+ 419    + 581    + 264    + 240
-----    -----    -----    -----
  781      847      965      979
```

Find each sum.

Doomsday has 207 bony spikes on one arm and 143 spikes on the other. How many bony spikes does he have on his arms altogether? **350**

Doomsday has 164 bony spikes on his left leg and 341 spikes on his right leg. How many spikes does he have on both legs? **505**

The questions on this page involve straightforward addition work. If children have difficulty with the horizontal sums, suggest that they rewrite them in vertical form. Some errors may result from neglecting to regroup.

Adding two numbers

Find each sum.

```
  1,234      3,794
+ 5,642    + 5,125
-------    -------
  6,876      8,919
```

Remember to regroup if you need to.

GET THESE RIGHT BEFORE I FLY.

Find each sum.

```
  2,552      5,325      2,471
+ 3,214    + 2,653    + 4,238
-------    -------    -------
  5,766      7,978      6,709

  3,749      4,675      8,482
+ 2,471    + 3,916    + 1,349
-------    -------    -------
  6,220      8,591      9,831
```

Write the answer in the box.

2,431 + 4,621 = **7,052**   1,342 + 3,264 = **4,606**

1,738 + 4,261 = **5,999**   2,013 + 3,642 = **5,655**

Write the missing number in the box.

```
  3,741      1,652      3,642
+ 2,943    + 3,274    + 4,831
-------    -------    -------
  6,684      4,926      8,473
```

Find each sum.

On Monday, Superman saved 2,521 people from death, and Supergirl saved 2,443 people. How many people did they save on Monday? **4,964**

On Saturday, Supergirl rescued 4,476 people, and Steel rescued 3,478 people on Sunday. How many people did they rescue that weekend? **7,954**

This page is similar to the previous page, with larger numbers. If children have difficulty with the section on finding missing numbers, have them try various digits until they find the correct one.

Subtracting three-digit numbers

Write the difference between the lines.

```
  644      471 cm
- 223    - 252 cm
-----    -------
  421      219 cm
```

DO YOU KNOW THE DIFFERENCE?

Write the difference between the lines.

```
  363      578      745      693
- 151    - 334    - 524    - 481
-----    -----    -----    -----
  212      244      221      212

  480 m    559 m    750 m    472 m
- 130 m  - 218 m  - 640 m  - 362 m
-----    -----    -----    -----
  350 m    341 m    110 m    110 m
```

Write the difference in the box.

364 - 122 = **242**   799 - 354 = **445**

$776 - $515 = **$261** $840 - $730 = **$110**

$684 - $574 = **$110** $220 - $120 = **$100**

Write the difference between the lines.

```
  463      584      661      494
- 145    - 237    - 342    - 185
-----    -----    -----    -----
  318      347      319      309

  325      837      468      852
- 116    - 719    - 209    - 329
-----    -----    -----    -----
  209      118      259      523
```

Find the answer to each problem.

Metallo shoots 234 missiles, but 127 are destroyed. How many missiles are left? **107**

The city of Kandor has 860 palaces. 420 are knocked down. How many palaces remain? **440**

In some of these sums, children may incorrectly subtract the smaller digit from the larger one, when they should be subtracting the larger digit from the smaller one. In such cases, point out that they should regroup.

Subtracting three-digit numbers

Write the difference between the lines.

```
 6 10 15           6 10 11
  715 m            711 m
- 152            - 292 m
  563              419 m
```

I MUST GET CHANGED DOUBLE-QUICK!

Write the difference between the lines.

```
  624 m       419 m       747 m       815 m
- 263 m     - 137 m     - 456 m     - 193 m
  361 m       282 m       291 m       622 m
```

```
  614         826         521         915
- 407       - 727       - 355       - 786
  207          99         166         129
```

Write the difference in the box.

516 - 308 = [208]   748 - 339 = [409]

631 - 542 = [89]   477 - 198 = [279]

Write the difference between the lines.

```
  535         715         312         924
- 247       - 518       - 113       - 528
  288         197         199         396
```

Write the missing numbers in the box.

```
  7 2 3       6 6 2       4 1 6       5 3 2
- 1 2 8     - 3 1 7     - 3 1 7     - 1 8 5
  5 9 5       3 4 5         9 9       3 4 7
```

Find the answer to each problem.

A theater holds 745 people. 357 people buy tickets. How many seats are empty? [388]

There are 664 people in a park. 276 are boating on a lake. How many are taking part in other activities? [388]

145

If children have difficulty with the section on missing numbers, have them use trial and error until they find the correct number. Encourage them to use addition and subtraction fact families to find the number.

Multiplying by one digit numbers

Find each product.

```
   22      26      44
 x  2    x  3    x  4
   44      78     176
```

I'VE GOT A FAVOR TO ASK! HELP ME FIND EACH ANSWER.

Find each product.

```
   37      19      16      32
 x  2    x  2    x  4    x  3
   74      38      64      96
```

```
   21      25      16      33
 x  3    x  4    x  6    x  5
   63     100      96     165
```

```
   39      24      41      36
 x  2    x  2    x  2    x  3
   78      48      82     108
```

```
   29      35      28      26
 x  3    x  2    x  3    x  6
   87      70      78     156
```

```
   10      30      20      50
 x  6    x  2    x  4    x  3
   60      60      80     150
```

Find the answer to each problem.

Brainiac blasts 26 cities, but Doomsday destroys twice as many. How many cities does Doomsday destroy? [52]

A gas canister is 30 cm long. How long will 4 canisters be? [120 cm]

146

Errors made on this page generally highlight gaps in children's knowledge of the 2, 3, 4, 5, and 6 times tables. Other errors can also result from neglecting to regroup.

Multiplying by one-digit numbers

Find each product.

```
   43      76      35
 x  3    x  6    x  7
  129     456     245
```

GET ME THE PRODUCTS NOW!

Find each product.

```
   46      48      40      32      36
 x  8    x  5    x  7    x  6    x  9
  368     240     280     192     324
```

```
   54      55      58      96      42
 x  4    x  6    x  7    x  3    x  9
  216     330     406     288     378
```

```
   82      24      81      64      52
 x  3    x  9    x  7    x  4    x  6
  246     216     567     256     312
```

```
   37      40      50      30      20
 x  7    x  8    x  3    x  7    x  9
  259     320     150     210     180
```

```
   27      36      21      42      57
 x  5    x  4    x  6    x  9    x  2
  135     144     126     378     114
```

Find the answer to the problem.

Superman flies 48 kilometres in an hour. How many kilometres does he fly in 6 hours? [288 kilometres]

A canister belt can hold 7 gas canisters. How many canisters can 28 belts hold? [196]

147

Errors made on this page generally highlight gaps in children's knowledge of the 6, 7, 8, and 9 times tables. As on the previous page, other errors can also result from neglecting to regroup.

Division with remainders

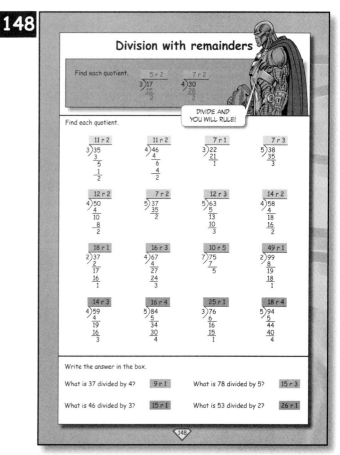

Find each quotient.

```
    5 r 2        7 r 2
3 ) 17       4 ) 30
    15           28
     2            2
```

DIVIDE AND YOU WILL RULE!

Find each quotient.

```
   11 r 2       11 r 2        7 r 1        7 r 3
3 ) 35       4 ) 46       3 ) 22       5 ) 38
    3            4            21           35
    5            6             1            3
    1            4
    2            2
```

```
   12 r 2        7 r 2       12 r 3       14 r 2
4 ) 50       5 ) 37       5 ) 63       4 ) 58
    4            35           5            4
   10            2           13           18
    8                        10           16
    2                         3            2
```

```
   18 r 1       16 r 3       10 r 5       49 r 1
2 ) 37       4 ) 67       7 ) 75       2 ) 99
    2            4            7            8
   17           27            5           19
   16           24                        18
    1            3                         1
```

```
   14 r 3       16 r 4       25 r 1       18 r 4
4 ) 59       5 ) 84       3 ) 76       5 ) 94
    4            5            6            5
   19           34           16           44
   16           30           15           40
    3            4            1            4
```

Write the answer in the box.

What is 37 divided by 4? [9 r 1]   What is 78 divided by 5? [15 r 3]

What is 46 divided by 3? [15 r 1]   What is 53 divided by 2? [26 r 1]

148

Children may have difficulty finding quotients with remainders. Have them perform long division until the remaining value to be divided is less than the divisor. That value is the remainder.

Division with remainders

Find each quotient.

$$6\overline{)33} \quad \frac{5\ r\ 3}{} \qquad 7\overline{)51} \quad \frac{7\ r\ 2}{}$$
$$\underline{30} \qquad\qquad \underline{49}$$
$$3 \qquad\qquad\quad 2$$

I'M ON THE CASE.

Find each quotient.

$\frac{7\ r\ 1}{6\overline{)43}}$	$\frac{4\ r\ 4}{9\overline{)40}}$	$\frac{9\ r\ 3}{8\overline{)75}}$	$\frac{16\ r\ 2}{6\overline{)98}}$
$\underline{42}$	$\underline{36}$	$\underline{72}$	$\underline{6}$
1	4	3	38
			$\underline{36}$
			2

$\frac{7\ r\ 4}{7\overline{)53}}$	$\frac{11\ r\ 5}{7\overline{)82}}$	$\frac{5\ r\ 8}{9\overline{)53}}$	$\frac{15\ r\ 4}{6\overline{)94}}$
$\underline{49}$	$\underline{7}$	$\underline{45}$	$\underline{6}$
4	12	8	34
	$\underline{7}$		$\underline{30}$
	5		4

$\frac{9\ r\ 2}{7\overline{)65}}$	$\frac{7\ r\ 7}{8\overline{)63}}$	$\frac{4\ r\ 2}{6\overline{)26}}$	$\frac{5\ r\ 5}{8\overline{)45}}$
$\underline{63}$	$\underline{56}$	$\underline{24}$	$\underline{40}$
2	7	2	5

$\frac{10\ r\ 2}{9\overline{)92}}$	$\frac{12\ r\ 1}{7\overline{)85}}$	$\frac{8\ r\ 2}{8\overline{)66}}$	$\frac{3\ r\ 6}{7\overline{)27}}$
$\underline{9}$	$\underline{7}$	$\underline{64}$	$\underline{21}$
2	15	2	6
	$\underline{14}$		
	1		

Write the answer in the box.

What is 97 divided by 7? **13 r 6** What is 84 divided by 8? **10 r 4**

What is 75 divided by 6? **12 r 3** What is 64 divided by 9? **7 r 1**

This page is similar to the previous page, but the divisors are numbers greater than 5. Children will need to know their 6, 7, 8, and 9 times tables to solve the problems.

Appropriate units of measure

Choose the best units to measure the length of each item.

millimetres	centimetres	metres
pen nib	notebook	swimming pool
millimetres	centimetres	metres

TO THE RESCUE!

Choose the best units to measure the length of each item.

millimetres	centimetres	metres
TV set	flea	toothbrush	football field
centimetres	millimetres	centimetres	metres
shoe	backyard	kayak	cat's claw
centimetres	metres	metres	millimetres

The height of a door is about 2 **metres**

The length of a pencil is about 18 **centimetres**

The height of a flagpole is about 7 **metres**

Choose the best units to measure the weight of each item.

grams	kilograms	tonnes
dog	ship	apple	pants
grams or kilograms	tonnes	grams	grams
hamburger	elephant	refrigerator	
grams	tonnes	kilograms	

The weight of a tennis ball is about 60 **grams**

The weight of a bag of potatoes is about 2 **kilograms**

The weight of a truck is about 4 **tonnes**

Children might come up with their own examples of items that measure about 1 centimetre, 1 metre, and 1 kilometre, as well as items that weigh about 1 gram, 1 kilogram, and 1 tonne. They can use these as benchmarks to find the appropriate unit.

Real-life problems

Perry White spent $4.68 at the store and had $4.77 left. How much did he start with? **$9.45**

$$\begin{array}{r} \overset{1\ 1}{4.77} \\ -\ 4.68 \\ \hline 9.45 \end{array}$$

Talia Head saves $30.00 a week. How much will she have if she saves all of it for 8 weeks? **$240**

$$\begin{array}{r} 30.00 \\ \times\ \ \ 8 \\ \hline 240.00 \end{array}$$

Smallville theater charges $4 for each matinee ticket. If it sells 560 tickets for a matinee performance, how much money does it take in? **$2,240**

$10

$$\begin{array}{r} \overset{2}{560} \\ \times\ \ \ 4 \\ \hline 2,240 \end{array}$$

Steel has saved $9.69. His niece has saved $3.24 less. How much does his niece have? **$6.45**

25¢ 5¢ 25¢ 25¢

$$\begin{array}{r} 9.69 \\ -\ 3.24 \\ \hline 6.45 \end{array}$$

The cost for 9 children to see a Superman film is $54. How much does each child pay? If only 6 children go, what will the total cost be? **$6 per child** **$36 for 6 children**

$$\frac{6}{9\overline{)54}}$$

$$6 \times 6 = 36$$

Steel has $12.95. Supergirl gives him another $3.64, and he goes out and buys a hammer for $3.25. How much does he have left? **$13.34**

$$\begin{array}{r} \overset{1}{12.95} \\ +\ 3.64 \\ \hline 16.59 \end{array}$$
$$\begin{array}{r} 16.59 \\ -\ 3.25 \\ \hline 13.34 \end{array}$$

Lex Luthor has $60 in savings. He decides to spend $\frac{1}{4}$ of it. How much will he have left? **$45**

$$60 \div 4 = 15$$
$$60 - 15 = 45$$

LET'S SOLVE THESE PROBLEMS.

This page provides children an opportunity to apply the skills they have practiced. To select the appropriate operation, discuss if they expect the answer to be larger or smaller. This can help them decide whether to add, multiply, subtract, or divide.

Perimeters of squares and rectangles

Find the perimeter of the white rectangle. To find the perimeter, add the lengths of the four sides:
8 cm + 8 cm + 5 cm + 5 cm = 26 cm

You can also do this with multiplication:
(2 × 8) cm + (2 × 5) cm
= 16 cm + 10 cm
= 26 cm

8 cm

5 cm

26 cm

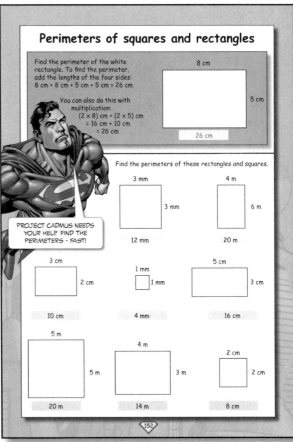

PROJECT CADMUS NEEDS YOUR HELP FIND THE PERIMETERS - FAST!

Find the perimeters of these rectangles and squares.

3 mm

3 mm

12 mm

10 cm

4 m

6 m

20 m

14 m

3 cm

2 cm

10 cm

1 mm

1 mm

4 mm

5 cm

3 cm

16 cm

5 m

5 m

20 m

4 m

3 m

14 m

2 cm

2 cm

8 cm

Make sure that children do not simply add the lengths of two sides of a figure rather than all four sides. Help children realize that the perimeter of a square can be found by multiplying the length of one side by 4.

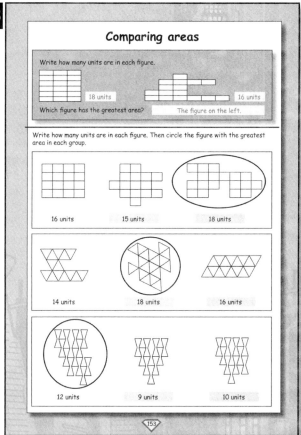

153 — Comparing areas

Write how many units are in each figure.

18 units | 16 units

Which figure has the greatest area? The figure on the left.

Write how many units are in each figure. Then circle the figure with the greatest area in each group.

16 units | 15 units | 18 units

14 units | 18 units | 16 units

12 units | 9 units | 10 units

Children may not realize that they can compare the areas of irregular figures. Make sure that they take care to count the units in each figure, rather than incorrectly assuming that the longest or tallest figure has the greater area.

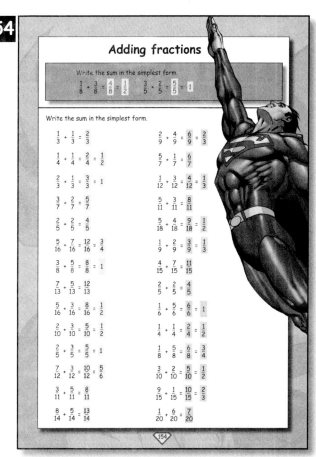

154 — Adding fractions

Write the sum in the simplest form.

$\frac{1}{8} + \frac{3}{8} = \frac{4}{8} = \frac{1}{2}$ $\frac{3}{5} + \frac{2}{5} = \frac{5}{5} = 1$

Write the sum in the simplest form.

$\frac{1}{3} + \frac{1}{3} = \frac{2}{3}$

$\frac{1}{4} + \frac{1}{4} = \frac{2}{4} = \frac{1}{2}$

$\frac{2}{3} + \frac{1}{3} = \frac{3}{3} = 1$

$\frac{3}{7} + \frac{2}{7} = \frac{5}{7}$

$\frac{2}{5} + \frac{2}{5} = \frac{4}{5}$

$\frac{5}{16} + \frac{7}{16} = \frac{12}{16} = \frac{3}{4}$

$\frac{3}{8} + \frac{5}{8} = \frac{8}{8} = 1$

$\frac{7}{13} + \frac{5}{13} = \frac{12}{13}$

$\frac{5}{16} + \frac{3}{16} = \frac{8}{16} = \frac{1}{2}$

$\frac{2}{10} + \frac{3}{10} = \frac{5}{10} = \frac{1}{2}$

$\frac{2}{5} + \frac{3}{5} = \frac{5}{5} = 1$

$\frac{7}{12} + \frac{3}{12} = \frac{10}{12} = \frac{5}{6}$

$\frac{3}{11} + \frac{5}{11} = \frac{8}{11}$

$\frac{8}{14} + \frac{5}{14} = \frac{13}{14}$

$\frac{2}{9} + \frac{4}{9} = \frac{6}{9} = \frac{2}{3}$

$\frac{5}{7} + \frac{1}{7} = \frac{6}{7}$

$\frac{1}{12} + \frac{3}{12} = \frac{4}{12} = \frac{1}{3}$

$\frac{5}{11} + \frac{3}{11} = \frac{8}{11}$

$\frac{5}{18} + \frac{4}{18} = \frac{9}{18} = \frac{1}{2}$

$\frac{1}{9} + \frac{2}{9} = \frac{3}{9} = \frac{1}{3}$

$\frac{4}{15} + \frac{7}{15} = \frac{11}{15}$

$\frac{2}{5} + \frac{2}{5} = \frac{4}{5}$

$\frac{1}{6} + \frac{5}{6} = \frac{6}{6} = 1$

$\frac{1}{4} + \frac{1}{4} = \frac{2}{4} = \frac{1}{2}$

$\frac{1}{8} + \frac{5}{8} = \frac{6}{8} = \frac{3}{4}$

$\frac{3}{10} + \frac{2}{10} = \frac{5}{10} = \frac{1}{2}$

$\frac{9}{15} + \frac{1}{15} = \frac{10}{15} = \frac{2}{3}$

$\frac{1}{20} + \frac{6}{20} = \frac{7}{20}$

Some children may incorrectly add both the numerators. Demonstrate that only the numerators should be added when the fractions have the same denominators: $\frac{1}{2} + \frac{1}{2}$ equals $\frac{2}{2}$ or 1, not $\frac{2}{4}$.

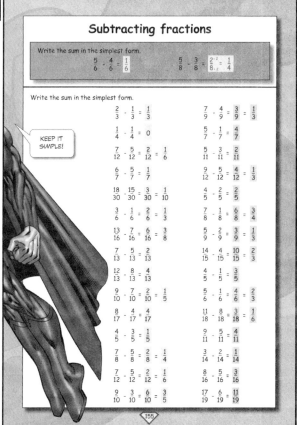

155 — Subtracting fractions

Write the sum in the simplest form.

$\frac{5}{6} - \frac{4}{6} = \frac{1}{6}$ $\frac{5}{8} - \frac{3}{8} = \frac{2}{8} = \frac{1}{4}$

Write the sum in the simplest form.

KEEP IT SIMPLE!

$\frac{2}{3} - \frac{1}{3} = \frac{1}{3}$

$\frac{1}{4} - \frac{1}{4} = 0$

$\frac{7}{12} - \frac{5}{12} = \frac{2}{12} = \frac{1}{6}$

$\frac{6}{7} - \frac{5}{7} = \frac{1}{7}$

$\frac{18}{30} - \frac{15}{30} = \frac{3}{30} = \frac{1}{10}$

$\frac{3}{6} - \frac{1}{6} = \frac{2}{6} = \frac{1}{3}$

$\frac{13}{16} - \frac{7}{16} = \frac{6}{16} = \frac{3}{8}$

$\frac{7}{13} - \frac{5}{13} = \frac{2}{13}$

$\frac{12}{13} - \frac{8}{13} = \frac{4}{13}$

$\frac{9}{10} - \frac{7}{10} = \frac{2}{10} = \frac{1}{5}$

$\frac{8}{17} - \frac{4}{17} = \frac{4}{17}$

$\frac{4}{5} - \frac{3}{5} = \frac{1}{5}$

$\frac{7}{8} - \frac{5}{8} = \frac{2}{8} = \frac{1}{4}$

$\frac{7}{12} - \frac{5}{12} = \frac{2}{12} = \frac{1}{6}$

$\frac{9}{10} - \frac{3}{10} = \frac{6}{10} = \frac{3}{5}$

$\frac{7}{9} - \frac{4}{9} = \frac{3}{9} = \frac{1}{3}$

$\frac{5}{7} - \frac{1}{7} = \frac{4}{7}$

$\frac{5}{11} - \frac{3}{11} = \frac{2}{11}$

$\frac{9}{12} - \frac{5}{12} = \frac{4}{12} = \frac{1}{3}$

$\frac{4}{5} - \frac{2}{5} = \frac{2}{5}$

$\frac{7}{8} - \frac{1}{8} = \frac{6}{8} = \frac{3}{4}$

$\frac{5}{9} - \frac{2}{9} = \frac{3}{9} = \frac{1}{3}$

$\frac{14}{15} - \frac{4}{15} = \frac{10}{15} = \frac{2}{3}$

$\frac{4}{5} - \frac{1}{5} = \frac{3}{5}$

$\frac{5}{6} - \frac{1}{6} = \frac{4}{6} = \frac{2}{3}$

$\frac{9}{11} - \frac{5}{11} = \frac{4}{11}$

$\frac{3}{14} - \frac{2}{14} = \frac{1}{14}$

$\frac{8}{16} - \frac{5}{16} = \frac{3}{16}$

$\frac{17}{19} - \frac{6}{19} = \frac{11}{19}$

On this page, children subtract fractions that have the same denominators. Some children may neglect to simplify their answers. Help them do so by finding common factors in the numerator and the denominator.

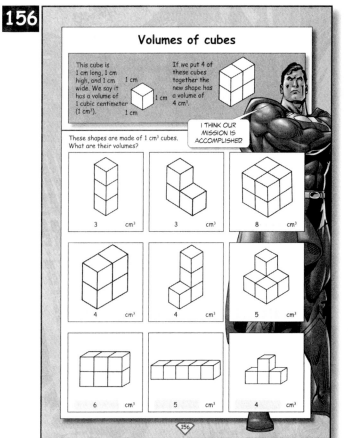

156 — Volumes of cubes

This cube is 1 cm long, 1 cm high, and 1 cm wide. We say it has a volume of 1 cubic centimeter (1 cm³). 1 cm

If we put 4 of these cubes together the new shape has a volume of 4 cm³.

I THINK OUR MISSION IS ACCOMPLISHED

These shapes are made of 1 cm³ cubes. What are their volumes?

3 cm³ | 3 cm³ | 8 cm³

4 cm³ | 4 cm³ | 5 cm³

6 cm³ | 5 cm³ | 4 cm³

To find the volume of some of the shapes on this page, children will need to visualize how many blocks cannot be seen in the illustrations. For example, in the third and sixth shapes, there is one block that is not shown.

Produced by The Brown Reference Group plc. for Dorling Kindersley Limited

Canadian Edition
Editors: Julia Roles, Julia March
Metrication: Colleen Evans
Production: Amy Bennett

Superman created by Jerry Siegel and Joe Shuster

First Canadian Edition, 2007

Dorling Kindersley is represented in Canada by
Tourmaline Editions Inc., 662 King Street West, Suite 304, Toronto, Ontario M5V 1M7

ISBN: 978-1-55363-733-2

Reproduced by Icon Reproduction Ltd., UK
Printed and bound by Donnelley's, US

07 08 09 10 11 10 9 8 7 6 5 4 3 2 1

Discover more at
www.dk.com